## Praise for *Difficult Conversations*

"A user-friendly guide to mastering the talks we dread . . . a keeper."
—*Fast Company* magazine

"Emotional intelligence applied to life's toughest moments."
— Daniel Goleman, bestselling author of *Working with Emotional Intelligence*

"The only people who shouldn't read *Difficult Conversations* are those who never work with people, anywhere."
— Peter M. Senge, bestselling author of *The Fifth Discipline*

"How do you confront your ex-spouse who's late picking up the kids? How do you tell a client their project took longer than expected and the bill is twice as high? How do you say 'I'm sorry'? Start by picking up *Difficult Conversations*."
—*Citizen*

"[*Difficult Conversations*] will be appreciated by readers who wish to improve oral communication in all aspects of their daily lives."
—*Library Journal*

"Stone, Patton, and Heen illustrate their points with anecdotes, scripted conversations and familiar examples in a clear, easy-to-browse format."
—*Publishers Weekly*

"The central insights of *Difficult Conversations* so resonate with common sense that it is easy to overlook just how remarkable of a book it is . . . a must-read."
—*Harvard Negotiation Law Review*

"Examples more clear-headed and advice more precise than we've seen before."
—*Dallas Morning News*

"Stone, Patton, and Heen have written an extremely clear and unpretentious exposition of how to develop effective communication skills and a guide to achieving openness and constructive outcomes in dialogue . . . this book is, and probably for some time to come will be definitive."
—*Southern Communication Journal*

PENGUIN BOOKS

# DIFFICULT CONVERSATIONS

**Douglas Stone** is a lecturer on Law at Harvard Law School and a founder of Triad Consulting Group (www.diffcon.com). In addition to corporate clients like Citigroup, Honda, HP, Johnson & Johnson, Microsoft, Shell, and Turner Broadcasting, Stone has worked with journalists, educators, doctors, diplomats, and political leaders in South Africa, Kashmir, and the Middle East, and in Geneva with the WHO and UN-AIDS. He has trained senior political appointees at the White House and was a keynote speaker at the 2006 World Negotiation Conference in São Paulo. His articles have appeared in publications ranging from the *New York Times* to *Real Simple*. He is a graduate of Harvard Law School, where for ten years he served as Associate and then Associate Director of the Harvard Negotiation Project. He is currently researching the relationships among productivity, feedback, and fulfillment in the workplace. He can be reached at dstone@post.harvard.edu.

**Bruce Patton** is cofounder and distinguished fellow of the Harvard Negotiation Project and a founder and partner of Vantage Partners, LLC (www.vantage partners.com), where his clients include some of the largest corporations in the world. Working with Roger Fisher, Patton pioneered the teaching of negotiation at Harvard Law School, where he has taught since 1981. In the public arena he helped to structure the resolution of the 1980 U.S.-Iranian hostage conflict (working at the behest of both governments); worked with Nobel Prize winner Oscar Arias to make his Central American Peace Plan self-implementing; worked with all parties in South Africa to structure and train mediators for the constitutional process that ended apartheid; and continues to work toward better conflict management in the Middle East and elsewhere. A graduate of Harvard College and Harvard Law School, Patton is coauthor with Roger Fisher and William Ury of the bestselling *Getting to YES: Negotiating Agreement Without Giving In*. He can be reached at bpatton@post.harvard.edu.

**Sheila Heen** is a lecturer on Law at Harvard Law School and a founder of Triad Consulting Group (www.diffcon.com). Her clients span five continents and include TimeWarner, the Federal Reserve Bank, Merck, PwC, Standard Chartered, Tatweer of Dubai, Cemex of Mexico, and Unilever. Heen often works with executive teams to engage conflict productively, repair working relationships, and make sound decisions. In the public sector she has consulted to the New England Organ Bank, the Singapore Supreme Court, Greek and Turkish Cypriots, and the Arctic Slope Regional Corporation in Barrow, Alaska. Heen has worked with theologians struggling with disagreement over the nature of truth and God and with senior political appointees for the White House. She has appeared on shows as diverse as *Oprah*, *Fox News*, CNBC's *Power Lunch*, and on National Public Radio. A graduate of Harvard Law School, she is schooled in negotiation daily by her three children. She can be reached at heen@post.harvard.edu.

DOUGLAS STONE, BRUCE PATTON, SHEILA HEEN

# Difficult Conversations

• • • • • • • • •

## How
## to Discuss
## What Matters
## Most

PENGUIN BOOKS

PENGUIN BOOKS

Published by the Penguin Group
Penguin Group (USA) Inc., 375 Hudson Street, New York, New York 10014, U.S.A.
Penguin Group (Canada), 90 Eglinton Avenue East, Suite 700, Toronto,
Ontario, Canada M4P 2Y3 (a division of Pearson Penguin Canada Inc.)
Penguin Books Ltd, 80 Strand, London WC2R 0RL, England
Penguin Ireland, 25 St Stephen's Green, Dublin 2, Ireland (a division of Penguin Books Ltd)
Penguin Group (Australia), 250 Camberwell Road, Camberwell,
Victoria 3124, Australia (a division of Pearson Australia Group Pty Ltd)
Penguin Books India Pvt Ltd, 11 Community Centre,
Panchsheel Park, New Delhi – 110 017, India
Penguin Group (NZ), 67 Apollo Drive, Rosedale, North Shore 0632,
New Zealand (a division of Pearson New Zealand Ltd)
Penguin Books (South Africa) (Pty) Ltd, 24 Sturdee Avenue,
Rosebank, Johannesburg 2196, South Africa

Penguin Books Ltd, Registered Offices:
80 Strand, London WC2R 0RL, England

First published in the United States of America by Viking Penguin,
a member of Penguin Putnam Inc. 1999
Published in Penguin Books 2000
This edition with a new preface and chapter published 2010

11  13  15  17  19  20  18  16  14  12

AUTHORS' NOTE

Research at Harvard University is undertaken with the expectation of publication. In such
publication the authors alone are responsible for statements of fact, opinions, recommendations,
and conclusions expressed. Publication in no way implies approval or endorsement by Harvard
University, any of its faculties, or by the President and Fellows of Harvard College.

THE LIBRARY OF CONGRESS HAS CATALOGED THE HARDCOVER EDITION AS FOLLOWS:
Stone, Douglas.
Difficult conversations: how to discuss what matters most/
Douglas Stone, Bruce Patton, Sheila Heen.
p.  cm.
ISBN 0-670-88339-5 (hc.)
ISBN 0 14 02.8852 X (previous pbk.)
ISBN 978-0-14-311844-2 (this pbk.)
1. Interpersonal communication.   2. Interpersonal communication–Case studies.
I. Patton, Bruce.   II. Heen, Sheila.   III. Title.
BF637.C45S78      1999
158.2—dc21        98-33346

Printed in the United States of America
Set in Electra    Designed by Francesca Belanger

To our families
with love and gratitude

and to our friend and mentor, Roger Fisher,
for his vision and commitment

# Preface to the Second Edition

When we completed *Difficult Conversations* ten years ago, we hoped it would catch on with businesses and help people in personal relationships. Happily, it's done both.

We regularly receive e-mail sharing stories of life-changing conversations, as well as e-mail of the "my wife gave me this book and it wasn't terrible" variety. We hear stories of rocky marriages righted and sibling relationships recovered, of conversations with a child about night terrors and with a dying friend about death, love, and those left behind. Parents use the book to work through differences in parenting strategies and to reach out to their teenagers, while neighbors use it to figure out what is or isn't "too loud." We're enormously grateful to those who have taken the time to tell us their stories.

The reception in the business community has been overwhelming. Our little book on talking has been embraced as a guide to taking on the hardest challenges — from how stakeholders with divergent interests can make tough but smart decisions, to giving difficult performance feedback, to making dysfunctional functions function, and good teams great. From new hires to CEOs, the book has helped people to break down silos and build up morale, showing the way past a culture of nice to a culture of efficiency, openness, and respect.

Most surprising has been *Difficult Conversations*'s reach. A dance instructor uses it to teach Argentinean tango. Palestinian educators built communication programs around the Arabic edition; Israeli mediators used the Hebrew edition to help with external and internal conflicts. Postwar Hutu and Tutsi leaders in Burundi have come together to develop a conflict resolution program for their youth using the French edition. Global organizations are using it to manage the challenges of working within and across cultures. At twenty-five languages and counting, it has even been downloaded, we're told, onto the International Space Station (where tight quarters can breed conflict).

The book has been used to train oil-rig operators in the North Sea, Iñupiat negotiators in the oil-rich Northern Slope of Alaska, and business leaders at Saudi Aramco. It's been used at the Boston Area Rape Crisis Center and the headquarters and field offices of UN-AIDS. Doctors, nurses, and administrators in hospitals across the United States have used it to deliver better patient care and develop more humane workplaces. Within the U.S. government, it's distributed at the Department of Justice, the IRS, the Federal Reserve, and the Postal Service. During one administration, the White House made it required reading for its top sixteen hundred political appointees. Law schools, business schools, and colleges assign it, as do high school teachers, life coaches, therapists, and ministers.

How to explain it all? Just this: people are people.

We have perceptions and thoughts and feelings, and we work and play with other human beings who have their own perceptions, thoughts, and feelings:

- Your organization is flat, aligned, and right-sized, but you still can't stand your boss.

- You fly three thousand miles and drive two hours to visit your elderly widowed father, and the first words out of his mouth are "You're late!"

- You've got four e-mail addresses, two voice-mail accounts, and sit only feet away from your five closest colleagues, but not one of them has found a way to talk to you about what they apparently call your "confrontational style."

- No matter how hard you try, you can't seem to get your sales, manufacturing, and product development teams to see themselves as members of the same organization.

People are people. It is true today, it was true ten years ago, and it was probably not much different ten thousand years before that: "After all I did to put this hunt together and make it a success, this is my share of the kill? *You call that fair?!*"

We don't outgrow difficult conversations or get promoted past them. The best workplaces and most effective organizations have them. The family down the street that everyone thinks is perfect has them. Loving couples and lifelong friends have them. In fact, we can make a reasonable argument that engaging (well) in difficult conversations is a sign of health in a relationship. Relationships that deal productively with the inevitable stresses of life are more durable; people who are willing and able to "stick through the hard parts" emerge with a stronger sense of trust in each other *and* the relationship, because now they have a track record of having worked through something hard and seen that the relationship survived.

So one explanation for the interest in this book is simply the delight of *individuals* happy to find a way through difficult relationship dilemmas, whether at home or at work. But we think there may be a broader organizational need driving interest in the business community: a recognition that the long-term success and even survival of many organizations may depend on their ability to master difficult conversations.

Why? Because the ability to handle difficult conversations well is a prerequisite to organizational change and adaptation. And because the combination of globalized competition and technological development have made rapid change and adaptation a necessity for organizational survival.

Of course, people in the business world have a certain cynicism when it comes to the "next big change initiative." We hear about a new commitment to learning organizations, total quality management, reengineering, or some other novel idea, and our eyes start to roll. Consultants show up with studies showing the huge potential value to be gained with the innovative approach, and enormous effort is expended, but at the end of the day the endeavor fades away with only a small fraction of its promised value achieved.

In our view, this is not because the studies were wrong or overhyped; the value *is* there to be captured. Nor is it because the individuals involved are lazy or don't care. A lot of us care passionately and put loads of effort into these projects.

We believe a major reason change efforts so often fail is that successful implementation eventually *requires* people to have difficult conversations — and they are not prepared to manage them skillfully. People inevitably have different views on priorities, levels of investment, measures of success, and exactly what correct implementation should entail.

With everyone taking for granted that their own view is right, and readily assuming that others' opposition is self-interested, progress quickly grinds to a halt. Decisions are delayed, and when finally made they are often imposed without buy-in from those who have to implement them. Relationships sour. Eventually people give up in frustration, and those driving the effort get distracted by new challenges or the *next* next big thing.

The ability to manage difficult conversations effectively is foundational, then, to achieving almost any significant change.

And in addition to supporting major change initiatives, these skills are increasingly needed simply to sustain business as usual. The relentless press of competition has forced most businesses to grow in scale to achieve efficiencies and competitive clout. Many industries are now global in reach. At the same time, the need to be responsive to the market — nimble, flexible, adaptive — has driven many organizations to be less hierarchical and to operate in a matrix that introduces more complexity to decision making and the ability to get things done.

This is a recipe for more conflict — and for more difficult conversations.

Think about it: Do the people in your organization deal with conflicts directly, routinely, and well? Or does the e-mail and watercooler chat continue to focus on all the ways the organization is dys-functional, even as important conversations are avoided? Having worked with countless businesses, we are tempted to say that the only reason some of them survive is because their competition is equally lousy at confronting the things that matter most.

And the pressures to work more effectively and efficiently are only going to increase. Businesses have spent the last twenty years focusing on process and technology improvements, and on cost cutting, and by now there's not much left to cut. For the next ten (or fifty) years, breakthrough performance is going to depend in-stead on people learning to deal with conflict more effectively and, indeed, leveraging it for competitive advantage. Ideally, conflict and differing perspectives, handled well and efficiently, should be-come a competitive asset — an engine for rapid learning and inno-vation.

And that's the upside: companies that nurture these communica-tion skills as a core competence for leaders will leave their competition in the dust.

.   .   .

In this second edition we have chosen to leave the main text of the original intact. We have, however, drawn from what we've learned from those who are using the book, and from our own ex-periences in coaching and consulting, and included some addi-tional commentary on a variety of critical topics. We present these in the form of answers to "Ten Questions People Ask about *Difficult Conversations.*" We hope this new material helps deepen and broaden your understanding and ability to manage poten-tially difficult conversations, and we look forward to the new ques-tions it stimulates.

Special thanks to Penguin's Rick Kot, editor to the stars, who fa-vored us throughout with his intelligence, humor, and baked goods. Had an unclear thought or misplaced word managed to find its way into our manuscript, Rick no doubt would have caught it.

We close this preface to the second edition with the story of one of the many correspondences with readers that have touched us over the last few years. We try to respond to every letter we receive, and in some cases get engaged in quite a conversation, as you'll see in the account below.[*]

In early 2002 Sheila received an e-mail from Ali, who wondered how to handle a challenging situation with his eleven-year-old son. His son, he believed, was taking money from him, and when confronted, the boy denied it. What to do? "I understand from your book," he wrote, "that the blame game is not the correct approach. I agree, but there are times when father and son need to understand the truth."

Sheila was at first tempted to respond with the simple reassurance that yes, at times a parent must confront and/or discipline a child, particularly if a child is stealing and lying about it. And she did offer this, but added a couple further suggestions: that Ali continue to inquire about his son's feelings and perceptions, and that he remain open to the possibility that he, Ali, doesn't yet know the whole story.

Several days later, Sheila received this e-mail:

Hi Sheila,

I greatly appreciate the time you had taken for the response. . . .

With great difficulty I initiated a conversation with my son and was able to find the cause of what happened. It appears that after the terrible incident on September 11, he was being bullied in school and to keep from being beaten up he was made to pay.

He felt fearful to tell us, for two reasons: first, since my wife and I have maintained regular contacts and friendship with our American friends, my son felt that we wouldn't understand. Second, he was just terrified by the bullies and felt they would take severe actions against him if he reported them.

---

[*]We have received permission from Ali to share his story; his correspondence has been edited slightly for concision.

After September 11th, we had really tried to explain the situation to him and get his feelings but he always brushed it aside by saying everything was fine. Unfortunately I took him at his word and didn't try to dig deeper. . . .

The initial hesitation on my part was because I know he has always been a very affectionate, caring and honest kid, and even after a few incidents it just didn't seem right that he would be the culprit. We have had a long conversation and are trying to instill in him the confidence that he can approach us no matter how difficult the situation.

We thank you sincerely for your help.

　　With best regards,

　　Ali

Thank you, Ali, for sharing with us this beautiful conversation with your son. We dedicate this second edition to you and to all those who shared their courage and stories with us.

　　　　　　　　　　　　　　　　　　　Douglas Stone
　　　　　　　　　　　　　　　　　　　Bruce Patton
　　　　　　　　　　　　　　　　　　　Sheila Heen

# Foreword

The Harvard Negotiation Project is best known for a book on negotiation and problem-solving called *Getting to YES* that has sold more than three million copies. Since its publication in 1981, readers all over the world have been persuaded that negotiators are more effective when they move away from adversarial posturing and instead work jointly to satisfy the interests of both sides.

The "Harvard Method," as it is sometimes called, emphasizes the importance of easy two-way communication. Yet in both negotiations and daily life, for good reasons or bad, we often *don't* talk to each other, and don't *want* to. And sometimes when we *do* talk, things only get worse. Feelings — anger, guilt, hurt — escalate. We become more and more sure that we are right, and so do those with whom we disagree.

This is the realm of *Difficult Conversations*, and why it is such a powerful and urgently needed book. It explores what it is that makes conversations difficult, why we avoid them, and why we often handle them badly. Although the inquiry grew initially from a desire to help negotiators, the subject has far deeper implications. *Difficult Conversations* addresses a critical aspect of human interaction. It applies to how we deal with children, parents, landlords, tenants, suppliers, customers, bankers, brokers, neighbors, team members, patients, employees, and colleagues of any kind.

In this book my colleagues Doug, Bruce, and Sheila take us by the hand and show us how to open the door to greater fulfillment in any relationship. They provide the stance of mind and heart and the skills of expression needed to achieve effective communication across the gulf of real differences in experiences, beliefs, and feelings, whether in personal relations, business dealings, or international affairs.

These are the skills needed to take a serious disagreement within a business organization and transform it from a drag on competitiveness into an engine for innovation. These are the skills we all can use to make a marriage more enjoyable and durable and to make relations between parents and teenagers something far better than a war zone. These skills can heal the wounds that keep so many of us apart. They offer each of us a better future.

Returning from several years in the U.S. Army Air Force during World War II, I discovered that my roommate, two of my closest friends, and dozens of classmates had been killed in that war. Ever since, I have worked to improve the skills with which we deal with our differences; to improve the prospects for our children's future; and to enlist others in that cause. This brilliant and compelling book by my younger colleagues at the Harvard Negotiation Project leaves me feeling optimistic that progress is being made on all three counts.

— Roger Fisher
Cambridge, Massachusetts

# Acknowledgments

This book draws from many wells.

The stories and conversations we share throughout the book come from our own lives and from our work with a diverse group of students, colleagues, and clients. For variety and to protect confidentiality, many of these stories are amalgams of different people's experiences that shared common and important dynamics, and as a rule all identifying facts have been changed. We are deeply grateful to those we've worked with for sharing with us so generously the conversations with which they were struggling. It is from their openness and their courage to try something new that we have learned the most.

In addition to our own research and reflection, this work incorporates and builds on ideas from many other disciplines. Our training was originally in negotiation, mediation, and law, but this book draws at least as much from the fields of organizational behavior; cognitive, client-centered, and family therapies; social psychology; communication theory; and the growing body of work around the idea of "dialogue."

This work began in a teaching collaboration with faculty from the Family Institute of Cambridge, who have contributed to it in countless ways. Dr. Richard Chasin and Dr. Richard Lee worked with Bruce Patton and Roger Fisher to develop what we call the Interpersonal Skills Exercise (itself inspired by a demonstration offered by psychodrama specialists Dr. Carl and Sharon Hollander) in which participants are coached on their toughest conversations. This exercise has been at the heart of Harvard Law School's Negotiation

Workshop, and of our learning, for more than a decade. In teaching this exercise with us, Dick, Rick, Sallyann Roth, Jody Scheier, and their associates from the Family Institute have taught us about family dynamics, influence, common reasons people get "stuck," and how to care for people in pain.

We are also grateful to Chris Argyris and to the partners of Action Design: Diana McLain Smith, Bob Putnam, and Phil McArthur. Their insights into the dilemmas of organizational life and interpersonal structures have proven invaluable to our understanding of conversations — how they go awry and how to put them back on course. A great many concepts in this book, including joint contribution, impact versus intent, and interpersonal intersections, are derived from their work. They are also the source of the two-column tool, the ladder and footprint metaphors, and methods of mapping. The two rules for expressing feelings come from Bob Putnam. Our understanding of how to tell your story and get off to a good start reflects the work of Don Schön and Diana Smith on framing, and input from John Richardson on roles. Diana and our colleagues at Vantage Partners have offered many useful illustrations of how these ideas explain and help with the challenges of organizational life.

From the field of cognitive therapy, we have benefited from the research and writings of Aaron Beck and David Burns. We are particularly indebted to them for their research on how cognitive distortions affect our self-image and emotions. David Kantor, a founder of family therapy and of the Family Institute, has helped us in understanding the landscape of what we call the Identity Conversation and how it plays out in group dynamics.

Insights from social psychology and communication theory are too pervasive to cite. It is perhaps a testament to the power of these insights that many of them are no longer the province of specialists. However, we owe a great debt to the late Jeff Rubin for bringing many ideas to our attention, as well as for his unceasing support and encouragement. Our work on listening and the power of authenticity was influenced by Carl Rogers, Sheila Reindl, and Suzanne Repetto. John Grinder gave us the concept of three viewpoints, or "positions," that correspond to your perspective, the other person's perspective, and an observer's perspective.

In the field of dialogue, we owe a debt of gratitude to Laura Chasin and her collaborators at the Public Conversations Project, to our friends at Conflict Management Group, and to Erica Fox. From them we have learned about the transformative power of telling one's story and speaking to the heart of the matter, a subject on which Bill Isaacs, Louise Diamond, Richard Moon, and others are also doing important work.

For providing early encouragement and opportunities to teach what we were learning we wish to thank Roger Fisher, Bob Mnookin, Frank Sander, and David Herwitz of Harvard Law School; Rob Ricigliano, Joe Stanford, and Don Thompson of Conflict Management Group; Eric Kornhauser of Conflict Management Australasia; Shirley Knight of CIBC Bank in Canada; Archie Epps, Harvard College Dean of Students; Colonels Denny Carpenter and Joe Trez of The Citadel in South Carolina; and Gary Jusela and Nancy Ann Stebbins of the Boeing Company (and Carolyn Gellerman, who introduced us); Deborah Kolb of the Program on Negotiation; and our colleagues at Conflict Management, Inc. Our friend and associate Stephen Smith helped us develop our work with family businesses and foundations and introduced us to our agent, Esther Newberg, who, along with her team at ICM, has been terrific. We are grateful for their confidence in us and their support over the years.

We are also blessed with a talented and caring group of friends and co-workers, who put aside their busy schedules to read drafts, make suggestions, and cheer us on along the way. Roger Fisher, Erica Fox, Michael Moffitt, Scott Peppet, John Richardson, Rob Ricigliano, and Diana Smith have lived with us and the work for perhaps longer than they would have chosen. By critiquing, rewriting, or outlining alternative sections or whole chapters, each has had a significant and lasting impact on the product. For stories, feedback, and support, we are grateful to Denis Achacoso, Lisle Baker, Bob Bordone, Bill Breslin, Scott Brown, Stevenson Carlbach, Toni Chayes, Diana Chigas, Amy Edmondson and George Daley, Elizabeth England, Danny Ertel, Keith Fitzgerald, Ron Fortgang, Brian Ganson, Lori Goldenthal,

Mark Gordon, Sherlock Graham-Haynes, Eric Hall, Terry Hill, Ed
Hillis, Ted Johnson, Helen Kim, Stu Kliman, Linda Kluz, Diane
Koskinas, Jim Lawrence, Susan McCafferty, Charlotte McCormick,
Patrick McWhinney, Jamie Moffitt, Linda Netsch, Monica Parker,
Robert and Susan Richardson, Don Rubenstein and Sylvie Carr,
Carol Rubin, Jeff Seul, Drew Tulumello, Robin Weatherill, Jeff
Weiss, Jim Young, Louisa Hackett, and many others.

Our families have spent years wondering if any such book as this
would ever actually come to be. They have read and critiqued drafts,
offered unconditional and greatly appreciated advice and moral support, and politely gone along with our versions of family stories, for
which we love them all the more and are deeply grateful: Robbie
and David Blackett, Jack and Joyce Heen, Jill and Jason Grennan,
Stacy Heen, Bill and Carol Patton, Bryan Patton and Devra Sisitsky,
John and Benjamin Richardson, Diana Smith, Don and Anne Stone,
Julie Stone and Dennis Doherty, and Randy Stone.

We could not have asked for a better editor and team at Viking
Penguin. Our editor, Jane von Mehren, is not only intelligent and in-
sightful but also fun and easy to work with. Jane, Susan Petersen,
Barbara Grossman, Ivan Held, Alisa Wyatt, and the team saw immediately what we were working toward, and we very much appreciate
their commitment to put it in the hands of as many people as possible.
Our line editor, Beena Kamlani, and copy editor, Janet Renard, had
the courage to take on the three of us, and the manuscript is the better
for it, even if we have insisted on using the plural "they," "them," etc.
to refer to indefinite singular antecedents as a way to maintain gender
neutrality. (As this usage has recently grown more common in speech,
younger readers may think it quite natural. However, we apologize in
advance to those who find it unusual or jarring.) Finally, Maggie
Payette and Francesca Belanger, our designers, have done a great job
of making the cover and text distinctive, accessible, and beautiful.

As usual, the good things about this book owe a great deal to
others while errors and omissions are solely our responsibility.

— Doug, Bruce & Sheila
Cambridge, Massachusetts

# Contents

# Introduction

Asking for a raise. Ending a relationship. Giving a critical performance review. Saying no to someone in need. Confronting disre-
spectful or hurtful behavior. Disagreeing with the majority in a
group. Apologizing.

At work, at home, and across the backyard fence, difficult conversations are attempted or avoided every day.

## A Difficult Conversation Is Anything
## You Find It Hard to Talk About

Sexuality, race, gender, politics, and religion come quickly to mind
as difficult topics to discuss, and for many of us they are. But discomfort and awkwardness are not limited to topics on the editorial page.
Anytime we feel vulnerable or our self-esteem is implicated, when
the issues at stake are important and the outcome uncertain, when
we care deeply about what is being discussed or about the people
with whom we are discussing it, there is potential for us to experience
the conversation as difficult.

We all have conversations that we dread and find unpleasant,
that we avoid or face up to like bad medicine:

One of the senior engineers at your company, an old friend, has
become a liability. Management has picked you to fire him.

You overheard your mother-in-law telling a neighbor that your sons are spoiled and undisciplined. As you prepare to spend the holidays at her house, you're not sure the two of you can get through the week without a confrontation.

The project you are working on took twice as long as you told the client it would. You can't afford not to bill for the extra time, but you dread informing the client.

You want to tell your father how much you love him, but fear that the intimacy might make both of you feel awkward.

You recently learned that several black colleagues on the police force refer to you as an Uncle Tom. You're infuriated, but you aren't sure whether talking about it would accomplish anything.

And, of course, there's the stuff of everyday life, conversations that feel more ordinary but cause anxiety nonetheless: returning merchandise without a receipt, asking your secretary to do some photocopying, telling the painters not to smoke in the house. These are the interactions we put off when we can and stumble through when we must. The ones we practice over and over in our head, trying to figure out in advance what to say and wondering afterward what we should have said.

What makes these situations so hard to face? It's our fear of the consequences — whether we raise the issue or try to avoid it.

## The Dilemma: Avoid or Confront, It Seems There Is No Good Path

We all know this dilemma. We go round and round on the same questions — Should I raise this? Or should I keep it to myself?

Perhaps the neighbors' dog keeps you up at night. "Should I talk to them?" you wonder. At first, you decide not to: "Maybe the barking will stop. Maybe I'll get used to it." But then the dog barks again, and you resolve that tomorrow you are going to talk to the neighbors once and for all.

Now you lie awake for a different reason. The thought of getting into a fight with the neighbors about their dog makes you nervous. You want the neighbors to like you; maybe you're overreacting. Eventually, you come back to thinking it's better to say nothing, and this calms your nerves. But just as you drop off to sleep, that darn dog howls again, and your cycle of indecision starts anew.

There doesn't seem to be any choice that will allow you to sleep.

Why is it so difficult to decide whether to avoid or to confront? Because at some level we know the truth: If we try to avoid the problem, we'll feel taken advantage of, our feelings will fester, we'll wonder why we don't stick up for ourselves, and we'll rob the other person of the opportunity to improve things. But if we confront the problem, things might get even worse. We may be rejected or attacked; we might hurt the other person in ways we didn't intend; and the relationship might suffer.

## There Is No Such Thing as a Diplomatic Hand Grenade

Desperate for a way out of the dilemma, we wonder if it is possible to be so tactful, so overwhelmingly pleasant that everything ends up fine.

Tact is good, but it's not the answer to difficult conversations. Tact won't make conversations with your father more intimate or take away your client's anger over the increased bill. Nor is there a simple diplomatic way to fire your friend, to let your mother-in-law know that she drives you crazy, or to confront your colleagues' hurtful prejudices.

*Delivering a difficult message is like throwing a hand grenade.* Coated with sugar, thrown hard or soft, a hand grenade is still going to do damage. Try as you may, there's no way to throw a hand grenade with tact or to outrun the consequences. And keeping it to yourself is no better. Choosing not to deliver a difficult message is like hanging on to a hand grenade once you've pulled the pin.

So we feel stuck. We need advice that is more powerful than "Be diplomatic" or "Try to stay positive." The problems run deeper than that; so must the answers.

## This Book Can Help

There is hope. Working at the Harvard Negotiation Project with thousands of people on all kinds of difficult conversations, we have found a way to make these conversations less stressful and more productive. A way to deal creatively with tough problems while treating people with decency and integrity. An approach that is helpful to *your* peace of mind, whether or not others join in.

We are going to help you get out of the hand grenade business altogether, by getting you out of the business of delivering (and receiving) messages. We will show you how to turn the damaging battle of warring messages into the more constructive approach we call a *learning conversation.*

### The Rewards Are Worth the Effort

Of course, changing how you deal with difficult conversations takes work. Like changing your golf swing, adapting to drive on the other side of the road, or learning a new language, the change can feel awkward at first. And it can feel threatening: breaking out of your comfort zone is rarely easy and is never risk-free. It requires you to look hard at yourself, and sometimes to change and grow. But better the ache of muscles growing from an unaccustomed workout than the sting of wounds from an unnecessary fight.

And the potential rewards are rich. If you follow the steps presented in this book, you will find difficult conversations becoming easier and causing less anxiety. You will be more effective and happier with the results. And as your anxiety goes down and your satisfaction goes up, you will find that you are choosing to engage more often in conversations that you should have been having all along.

In fact, the people we've worked with, who have learned new approaches to dealing with their most challenging conversations, report less anxiety and greater effectiveness in *all* of their conversations. They find they are less afraid of what others might say. They have a heightened sense of freedom of action in tough situations, more self-confidence, and a stronger sense of integrity and self-respect. They also learn that, more often than not, dealing constructively with tough topics and awkward situations strengthens a relationship. And that's an opportunity too good to pass up.

## Skeptical? A Few Thoughts

If you're skeptical, that's understandable. You may have been struggling with these issues for weeks, months, or years. The problems are complex, and the people involved are not easy to deal with. How can reading a book make a difference?

There *are* limits to how much you can learn about human interactions from a book. We don't know the specifics of your situation, what is at stake for you, or where your particular weaknesses and strengths lie. But we have discovered that, regardless of context, the things that make difficult conversations difficult, and the errors in thinking and acting that compound those difficulties, are the same. We all share the same fears and fall into the same few traps. No matter what you are facing, or whom, there is something in this book that can help.

It is true that some situations are unlikely to improve regardless of how skilled you become. The people involved may be so emotionally troubled, the stakes so high, or the conflict so intense that a book — or even professional intervention — is unlikely to help. However, for every case that is truly hopeless, there are a thousand that appear hopeless but are not. People often come to us saying, "I want some advice, but I have to warn you, this situation is beyond fixing."

And they are wrong. Together we are able to find some avenue of change that ends up having a *significant* positive impact on the conversation.

Of course, you may not be ready or able to engage or reengage fully in a difficult situation or relationship. You may be grieving, licking your wounds, or just needing time away. You may be lost in anger or confused about what you want. But even if you are not yet ready to take on an actual conversation, this book can help you sort through your feelings and assist you as you find your way to a healthier place.

## We Need to Look in New Places

What can we suggest that you haven't already thought of? Probably quite a bit. Because the question isn't whether you've been looking hard enough for the "answer" to difficult conversations, it's whether you've been looking in the right places. At heart, the problem isn't in your actions, it's in your thinking. So long as you focus only on what to *do* differently in difficult conversations, you will fail to break new ground.

This book offers plenty of advice on how to conduct a difficult conversation. But first and more important, it will help you understand better what you're up against and why it makes sense to shift from a "message delivery stance" to a "learning stance." Only then will you be able to understand and implement the steps of a learning conversation.

## Difficult Conversations Are a Normal Part of Life

No matter how good you get, difficult conversations will always challenge you. The authors know this from experiences in our own lives. We know what it feels like to be deeply afraid of hurting someone or of getting hurt. We know what it means to be consumed by guilt for how our actions have affected others, or for how we have let ourselves down. We know that even with the best of intentions, human relationships can corrode or become tangled, and, if we are honest, we also know that we don't always have the best of intentions. We know just how fragile are the heart and the soul.

So it is best to keep your goals realistic. Eliminating fear and anxiety is an unrealistic goal. *Reducing* fear and anxiety and learning how to manage that which remains are more obtainable. Achieving perfect results with no risk will not happen. Getting *better* results in the face of tolerable odds might.

And that, for most of us, is good enough. For if we are fragile, we are also remarkably resilient.

# The Problem

• • • • •

# 1

# Sort Out the
# Three Conversations

Jack is about to have a difficult conversation.

He explains: "Late one afternoon I got a call from Michael, a good friend and occasional client. 'I'm in a tight spot,' he told me. 'I need a financial brochure laid out and printed by tomorrow afternoon.' He said his regular designer was out and that he was under a lot of pressure.

"I was in the middle of another project, but Michael was a friend, so I dropped everything and worked late into the night on his brochure.

"Early the next morning Michael reviewed the mock-up and gave the go-ahead to have it printed. I had the copies on his desk by noon. I was exhausted, but I was glad I'd been able to help him out.

"Then I got back to my office and discovered this voice-mail message from Michael:

Well, you really screwed this one up! Look, Jack, I know you were under time pressure on this, but . . . . [sigh]. The earnings chart isn't presented clearly enough, and it's slightly off. It's just a disaster. This is an important client. I assume you'll fix it right away. Give me a call as soon as you get in.

"Well, you can imagine how I felt about *that* message. The chart was off, but microscopically. I called Michael right away."

Their conversation went like this:

JACK: Hi, Michael, I got your message —
MICHAEL: Yeah, look Jack, this thing has to be done over.
JACK: Well, wait a second. I agree it's not perfect, but the chart is clearly labeled. Nobody's going to misunderstand —
MICHAEL: C'mon, Jack. You know as well as I do that we can't send this thing out like this.
JACK: Well, I think that —
MICHAEL: There's really nothing to argue about here. Look, we all screw up. Just fix it and let's move on.
JACK: Why didn't you say something about this when you looked at it this morning?
MICHAEL: I'm not the one who's supposed to be proofreading. Jack, I'm under tremendous pressure to get this done and to get it done *right*. Either you're on the team or you're not. I need a yes or a no. Are you going to redo it?
JACK: [pause] Alright, alright. I'll do it.

This exchange has all the hallmarks of a difficult conversation going off the rails. Months later, Jack still feels lousy about this conversation and his relationship with Michael remains strained. He wonders what he could have done differently, and what he should do about it now.

But before we get to that, let's look at what Jack and Michael's conversation can teach us about how difficult conversations work.

## Decoding the Structure of Difficult Conversations

Surprisingly, despite what appear to be infinite variations, all difficult conversations share a common structure. When you're caught up in the details and anxiety of a particular difficult conversation, this structure is hard to see. But understanding that structure is essential to improving how you handle your most challenging conversations.

## There's More Here Than Meets the Ear

In the conversation between Jack and Michael recounted above, the words reveal only the surface of what is really going on. To make the structure of a difficult conversation visible, we need to understand not only what is said, but also what is *not* said. We need to understand what the people involved are thinking and feeling but not saying to each other. In a difficult conversation, this is usually where the real action is.

Look at what Jack is thinking and feeling, but not saying, as this conversation proceeds:

| What Jack Thought and Felt But Didn't Say | What Jack and Michael Actually Said |
|---|---|
| How could he leave a message like that?! After I drop everything, break a dinner date with my wife, and stay up all night, that's the thanks I get?! | JACK: Hi, Michael, I got your message — <br> MICHAEL: Yeah, look Jack, this thing has to be done over. |
| A total overreaction. Not even a CPA would be able to tell that the graph is off. At the same time, I'm angry with myself for making such a stupid mistake. | JACK: Well, wait a second. I agree it's not perfect, but the chart is clearly labeled. Nobody's going to misunderstand — <br> MICHAEL: C'mon, Jack, you know as well as I do that we can't send this thing out like this. |

| What Jack Thought and Felt But Didn't Say | What Jack and Michael Actually Said |
|---|---|
| Michael tries to intimidate colleagues into getting his way. But he shouldn't treat *me* that way. I'm a friend! I want to stand up for myself, but I don't want to get into a big fight about this. I can't afford to lose Michael as a client or as a friend. I feel stuck. | JACK: Well, I think that — <br> MICHAEL: There's really nothing to argue about here. Look, we all screw up. Just fix it and let's move on. |
| Screw up!? This isn't *my* fault. *You* approved it, remember? | JACK: Why didn't you say something about this when you looked at it this morning? |
| Is that how you see me? As a proofreader? | MICHAEL: I'm not the one who's supposed to be proofreading. I'm under tremendous pressure to get this done and to get it done *right*. Either you're on the team or you're not. I need a yes or a no. Are you going to redo it? |
| I'm sick of this whole thing. I'm going to be bigger than whatever pettiness is driving him. The best way out is for me just to be generous and redo it. | JACK: [pause] Alright, alright. I'll do it. |

Meanwhile, there's plenty that Michael is thinking and feeling but not saying. Michael is wondering whether he should have hired Jack in the first place. He hasn't been all that happy with Jack's work in the past, but he decided to go out on a limb with his partners to give his friend another chance. Michael is now frustrated with Jack and confused about whether hiring Jack was a good decision — personally or professionally.

The first insight, then, is a simple one: there's an awful lot going on between Jack and Michael that is not being spoken.

That's typical. In fact, the gap between what you're really think-ing and what you're saying is part of what makes a conversation diffi-cult. You're distracted by all that's going on inside. You're uncertain about what's okay to share, and what's better left unsaid. And you know that just saying what you're thinking would probably *not* make the conversation any easier.

## Each Difficult Conversation Is Really Three Conversations

In studying hundreds of conversations of every kind we have discov-ered that there is an underlying structure to what's going on, and understanding this structure, in itself, is a powerful first step in im-proving how we deal with these conversations. It turns out that no matter what the subject, our thoughts and feelings fall into the same three categories, or "conversations." And in each of these conversa-tions we make predictable errors that distort our thoughts and feel-ings, and get us into trouble.

Everything problematic that Michael and Jack say, think, and feel falls into one of these three "conversations." And everything in your difficult conversations does too.

1. The "What Happened?" Conversation. Most difficult con-versations involve disagreement about what has happened or what should happen. Who said what and who did what? Who's right, who meant what, and who's to blame? Jack and Michael tussle over these issues, both out loud and internally. *Does* the chart need to be re-done? *Is* Michael trying to intimidate Jack? Who *should* have caught the error?

2. The Feelings Conversation. Every difficult conversation also asks and answers questions about feelings. Are my feelings valid? Ap-propriate? Should I acknowledge or deny them, put them on the ta-ble or check them at the door? What do I do about the other person's feelings? What if they are angry or hurt? Jack's and Michael's thoughts are littered with feelings. For example, "This is the thanks I

get?!" signals hurt and anger, and "I'm under tremendous pressure" reveals anxiety. These feelings are not addressed directly in the conversation, but they leak in anyway.

**3. The Identity Conversation.** This is the conversation we each have with ourselves about what this situation means to us. We conduct an internal debate over whether this means we are competent or incompetent, a good person or bad, worthy of love or unlovable. What impact might it have on our self-image and self-esteem, our future and our well-being? Our answers to these questions determine in large part whether we feel "balanced" during the conversation, or whether we feel off-center and anxious. In the conversation between Jack and Michael, Jack is struggling with the sense that he has been incompetent, which makes him feel less balanced. And Michael is wondering whether he acted foolishly in hiring Jack.

Every difficult conversation involves grappling with these Three Conversations, so engaging successfully requires learning to operate effectively in each of the three realms. Managing all three simultaneously may seem hard, but it's easier than facing the consequences of engaging in difficult conversations blindly.

## What We Can't Change, and What We Can

No matter how skilled we become, there are certain challenges in each of the Three Conversations that we can't change. We will still run into situations where untangling "what happened" is more complicated than we initially suspect. We will each have information the other person is unaware of, and raising each other's awareness is not easy. And we will still face emotionally charged situations that feel threatening because they put important aspects of our identity at risk.

What we *can* change is the way we respond to each of these challenges. Typically, instead of exploring what information the other person might have that we don't, we assume we know all we need to know to understand and explain things. Instead of working to manage our feelings constructively, we either try to hide them or let loose in ways that we later regret. Instead of exploring the identity issues that may be deeply at stake for us (or them), we proceed with the conversation as if it says nothing about us — and never come to grips with what is at the heart of our anxiety.

By understanding these errors and the havoc they wreak, we can begin to craft better approaches. Let's explore each conversation in more depth.

# The "What Happened?" Conversation: What's the Story Here?

The "What Happened?" Conversation is where we spend much of our time in difficult conversations as we struggle with our different stories about who's right, who meant what, and who's to blame. On each of these three fronts — truth, intentions, and blame — we make a common but crippling assumption. Straightening out each of these assumptions is essential to improving our ability to handle difficult conversations well.

## The Truth Assumption

As we argue vociferously for our view, we often fail to question one crucial assumption upon which our whole stance in the conversation is built: I am right, you are wrong. This simple assumption causes endless grief.

What am I right about? I am right that you drive too fast. I am right that you are unable to mentor younger colleagues. I am right that your comments at Thanksgiving were inappropriate. I am right that the patient should have received more medication after such a painful operation. I am right that the contractor overcharged me. I am right that I deserve a raise. I am right that the brochure is fine as it is. The number of things I am right about would fill a book.

There's only one hitch: I am not right.

How could this be so? It seems impossible. Surely I must be right *sometimes!*

Well, no. The point is this: difficult conversations are almost never about getting the facts right. They are about conflicting perceptions, interpretations, and values. They are not about what a contract states, they are about what a contract *means*. They are not about which child-rearing book is most popular, they are about which child-rearing book *we* should follow.

They are not about what is true, they are about what is important.

Let's come back to Jack and Michael. There is no dispute about whether the graph is accurate or not. They both agree it is not. The dispute is over whether the error is worth worrying about and, if so, how to handle it. These are not questions of right and wrong, but questions of interpretation and judgment. Interpretations and judgments are important to explore. In contrast, the quest to determine who is right and who is wrong is a dead end.

In the "What Happened?" Conversation, moving away from the truth assumption frees us to shift our purpose from proving we are right to understanding the perceptions, interpretations, and values of both sides. It allows us to move away from delivering messages and toward asking questions, exploring how each person is making sense of the world. And to offer our views as perceptions, interpretations, and values — not as "the truth."

## The Intention Invention

The second argument in the "What Happened?" Conversation is over intentions — yours and mine. Did you yell at me to hurt my feelings or merely to emphasize your point? Did you throw my cigarettes out because you're trying to control my behavior or because you want to help me live up to my commitment to quit? What I think about your intentions will affect how I think about you and, ultimately, how our conversation goes.

The error we make in the realm of intentions is simple but profound: we assume we know the intentions of others when we don't. Worse still, when we are unsure about someone's intentions, we too often decide they are bad.

The truth is, intentions are invisible. We assume them from other people's behavior. In other words, we make them up, we invent them. But our invented stories about other people's intentions are accurate much less often than we think. Why? Because people's intentions, like so much else in difficult conversations, are complex. Sometimes people act with mixed intentions. Sometimes they act with no intention, or at least none related to us. And sometimes they act on good intentions that nonetheless hurt us.

Because our view of others' intentions (and their views of ours) are so important in difficult conversations, leaping to unfounded assumptions can be a disaster.

## The Blame Frame

The third error we make in the "What Happened?" Conversation has to do with blame. Most difficult conversations focus significant attention on who's to blame for the mess we're in. When the company loses its biggest client, for example, we know that there will shortly ensue a ruthless game of blame roulette. We don't care where the ball lands, as long as it doesn't land on us. Personal relationships are no different. Your relationship with your stepmother is strained? She's to blame. She should stop bugging you about your messy room and the kids you hang out with.

In the conflict between Jack and Michael, Jack believes the problem is Michael's fault: the time to declare your hypersensitivity to formatting is before the brochure goes to print, not after. And, of course, Michael believes the problem is Jack's fault: Jack did the layout, mistakes are his responsibility.

But talking about fault is similar to talking about truth — it produces disagreement, denial, and little learning. It evokes fears

of punishment and insists on an either/or answer. Nobody wants
to be blamed, especially unfairly, so our energy goes into defending
ourselves.

Parents of small children know this well. When the twins act up
in the back seat of the car, we know that trying to affix blame will always yield an outcry: "But she hit me first!" or "I hit her because she
called me a baby." Each child denies blame not just to avoid losing
her dessert, but also from a sense of justice. Neither feels like the
problem is solely her fault, because it isn't.

From the front seat looking back, it is easy to see how each child
has contributed to the fight. It's much more difficult to see how we've
contributed to the problems in which we ourselves are involved. But
in situations that give rise to difficult conversations, it is almost always
true that what happened is the result of things *both* people did — or
failed to do. And punishment is rarely relevant or appropriate. When
competent, sensible people do something stupid, the smartest move
is to try to figure out, first, what kept them from seeing it coming and,
second, how to prevent the problem from happening again.

Talking about blame distracts us from exploring why things went
wrong and how we might correct them going forward. Focusing instead on understanding the contribution system allows us to learn
about the real causes of the problem, and to work on correcting
them. The distinction between blame and contribution may seem
subtle. But it is a distinction worth working to understand, because it
will make a significant difference in your ability to handle difficult
conversations.

## The Feelings Conversation:
## What Should We Do with Our Emotions?

Difficult conversations are not just about what happened; they also
involve emotion. The question is not whether strong feelings will
arise, but how to handle them when they do. Should you tell your
boss how you *really* feel about his management style, or about the

colleague who stole your idea? Should you share with your sister how hurt you feel that she stayed friends with your ex? And what should you do with the anger you are likely to experience if you decide to talk with that vendor about his sexist remarks?

In the presence of strong feelings, many of us work hard to stay rational. Getting too deep into feelings is messy, clouds good judgment, and in some contexts — for example, at work — can seem just plain inappropriate. Bringing up feelings can also be scary or uncomfortable, and can make us feel vulnerable. After all, what if the other person dismisses our feelings or responds without real understanding? Or takes our feelings to heart in a way that wounds them or irrevocably damages the relationship? And once we've gotten our feelings off our chest, it's their turn. Are we up to hearing all about their anger and pain?

This line of reasoning suggests that we stay out of the Feelings Conversation altogether — that Jack is better off not sharing his feelings of anger and hurt, or Michael his sense of disappointment. Better to stick to questions about the brochure. Better to stick to "business."

Or is it?

## An Opera Without Music

The problem with this reasoning is that it fails to take account of one simple fact: difficult conversations do not just *involve* feelings, they are at their very core *about* feelings. Feelings are not some noisy byproduct of engaging in difficult talk, they are an integral part of the conflict. Engaging in a difficult conversation without talking about feelings is like staging an opera without the music. You'll get the plot but miss the point. In the conversation between Jack and Michael, for example, Jack never explicitly says that he feels mistreated or underappreciated, yet months later Jack can still summon his anger and resentment toward Michael.

Consider some of your own difficult conversations. What feelings are involved? Hurt or anger? Disappointment, shame, confusion? Do you feel treated unfairly or without respect? For some of us, even saying "I love you" or "I'm proud of you" can feel risky.

In the short term, engaging in a difficult conversation without talking about feelings may save you time and reduce your anxiety. It may also seem like a way to avoid certain serious risks — to you, to others, and to the relationship. But the question remains: if feelings are the issue, what have you accomplished if you don't address them?

Understanding feelings, talking about feelings, managing feelings — these are among the greatest challenges of being human. There is nothing that will make dealing with feelings easy and risk-free. Most of us, however, can do a better job in the Feelings Conversation than we are now. It may not seem like it, but talking about feelings is a skill that can be learned.

Of course, it doesn't always make sense to discuss feelings. As the saying goes, sometimes you should let sleeping dogs lie. Unfortunately, a lack of skill in discussing feelings may cause you to avoid not only sleeping dogs, but all dogs — even those that won't let *you* sleep.

## The Identity Conversation: What Does This Say About Me?

Of the Three Conversations, the Identity Conversation may be the most subtle and the most challenging. But it offers us significant leverage in managing our anxiety and improving our skills in the other two conversations.

The Identity Conversation looks inward: it's all about who we are and how we see ourselves. How does what happened affect my self-esteem, my self-image, my sense of who I am in the world? What impact will it have on my future? What self-doubts do I harbor? In short: before, during, and after the difficult conversation, the Identity Conversation is about what I am saying to myself *about me*.

You might think, "I'm just trying to ask my boss for a raise. Why does my sense of who I am in the world matter here?" Or Jack might be thinking, "This is about the brochure, not about me." In fact, anytime a conversation feels difficult, it is in part precisely because it is about You, with a capital Y. Something beyond the apparent substance of the conversation is at stake for you.

It may be something simple. What does it say about you when you talk to your neighbors about their dog? It may be that growing up in a small town gave you a strong self-image as a friendly person and good neighbor, so you are uncomfortable with the possibility that your neighbors might see you as aggressive or as a troublemaker.

Asking for a raise? What if you get turned down? In fact, what if your boss gives you good reasons for turning you down? What will that do to your self-image as a competent and respected employee? Ostensibly the subject is money, but what's really making you sweat is that your self-image is on the line.

Even when you are the one delivering bad news, the Identity Conversation is in play. Imagine, for example, that you have to turn down an attractive new project proposal from Creative. The prospect of telling the people involved makes you anxious, even if you aren't responsible for the decision. In part, it's because you fear how the conversation will make you feel about yourself: "I'm not the kind of person who lets people down and crushes enthusiasm. I'm the person people respect for *finding* a way to do it, not for shutting the door." Your self-image as a person who helps others get things done butts up against the reality that you are going to be saying no. If you're no longer the hero, will people see you as the villain?

## Keeping Your Balance

As you begin to sense the implications of the conversation for your self-image, you may begin to lose your balance. The eager young head of Creative, who reminds you so much of yourself at that age, looks disbelieving and betrayed. You suddenly feel confused; your anxiety skyrockets. You wonder whether it really makes sense to drop the idea so early in the process. Before you know it, you stammer out something about the possibility that the rejection will be reconsidered, even though you have absolutely no reason to believe that's likely.

In its mildest form, losing our balance may cause us to lose confidence in ourselves, to lose concentration, or to forget what we were going to say. In more extreme cases, it can feel earth-shattering. We may feel paralyzed, overcome by panic, stricken with an urge to flee, or even have trouble breathing.

Just knowing that the Identity Conversation is a component of difficult conversations can help. And, as in the other two conversations, you can do much better than mere awareness. While losing your balance sometimes is inevitable, the Identity Conversation need not cause as much anxiety as it does. Like dealing with feelings, grappling with the Identity Conversation gets easier with the development of certain skills. Indeed, once you find your footing in the Identity Conversation, you can turn what is often a source of anxiety into a source of strength.

## Moving Toward a Learning Conversation

Despite what we sometimes pretend, our initial purpose for having a difficult conversation is often to prove a point, to give them a piece of our mind, or to get them to do or be what we want. In other words, to deliver a message.

Once you understand the challenges inherent in the Three Conversations and the mistakes we make in each, you are likely to find that your purpose for having a particular conversation begins to shift. You come to appreciate the complexity of the perceptions and intentions involved, the reality of joint contribution to the problem, the central role feelings have to play, and what the issues mean to each person's self-esteem and identity. And you find that a message delivery stance no longer makes sense. In fact, you may find that you no longer have a message to deliver, but rather some information to share and some questions to ask.

Instead of wanting to persuade and get your way, you want to understand what has happened from the other person's point of view, explain your point of view, share and understand feelings, and work together to figure out a way to manage the problem going forward. In so doing, you make it more likely that the other person will be open to being persuaded, and that you will learn something that significantly changes the way you understand the problem.

Changing our stance means inviting the other person into the conversation with us, to help us figure things out. If we're going to achieve our purposes, we have lots we need to learn from them and lots they need to learn from us. We need to have a learning conversation.

The differences between a typical battle of messages and a learning conversation are summarized in the chart on the following pages.

|  | A Battle of Messages | A Learning Conversation |
|---|---|---|
| **The "What Happened?" Conversation** **Challenge:** The situation is more complex than either person can see. | **Assumption:** I know all I need to know to understand what happened. **Goal:** Persuade them I'm right. | **Assumption:** Each of us is bringing different information and perceptions to the table; there are likely to be important things that each of us doesn't know. **Goal:** Explore each other's stories: how we understand the situation and why. |
|  | **Assumption:** I know what they intended. **Goal:** Let them know what they did was wrong. | **Assumption:** I know what I intended, and the impact their actions had on me. I don't and can't know what's in their head. **Goal:** Share the impact on me, and find out what they were thinking. Also find out what impact I'm having on them. |
|  | **Assumption:** It's all their fault. (Or it's all my fault.) **Goal:** Get them to admit blame and take responsibility for making amends. | **Assumption:** We have probably *both* contributed to this mess. **Goal:** Understand the contribution system: how our actions interact to produce this result. |

|  | **A Battle of Messages** | **A Learning Conversation** |
|---|---|---|
| **The Feelings Conversation**<br><br>Challenge: The situation is emotionally charged. | Assumption: Feelings are irrelevant and wouldn't be helpful to share. (Or, my feelings are their fault and they need to hear about them.)<br><br>Goal: Avoid talking about feelings. (Or, let 'em have it!) | Assumption: Feelings are the heart of the situation. Feelings are usually complex. I may have to dig a bit to understand my feelings.<br><br>Goal: Address feelings (mine and theirs) without judgments or attributions. Acknowledge feelings before problem-solving. |
| **The Identity Conversation**<br><br>Challenge: The situation threatens our identity. | Assumption: I'm competent or incompetent, good or bad, lovable or unlovable. There is no in-between.<br><br>Goal: Protect my all-or-nothing self-image. | Assumption: There may be a lot at stake psychologically for both of us. Each of us is complex, neither of us is perfect.<br><br>Goal: Understand the identity issues on the line for each of us. Build a more complex self-image to maintain my balance better. |

This book will help you turn difficult conversations into learning conversations by helping you handle each of the Three Conversations more productively and improving your ability to handle all three at once.

The next five chapters explore in depth the mistakes people commonly make in each of the Three Conversations. This will help you shift to a learning stance when it's your difficult conversation and you

aren't feeling very open. Chapters 2, 3, and 4 investigate the three assumptions in the "What Happened?" Conversation. Chapter 5 shifts
to the Feelings Conversation, and Chapter 6 takes up the Identity
Conversation. These chapters will help you sort out your thoughts
and feelings. This preparation is essential before you step into any
difficult conversation.

In the final six chapters we turn to the conversation itself, beginning with when to raise an issue and when to let go, and if you're
going to raise it, what you can hope to achieve and what you can't —
what purposes make sense. Then we turn to the mechanics of how to
talk productively about the issues that matter to you: finding the best
ways to begin, inquiring and listening to learn, expressing yourself
with power and clarity, and solving problems jointly, including how
to get the conversation back on track when the going gets rough. Finally, we return to how Jack might have a follow-up conversation
with Michael to illustrate how this all might look in practice.

# Shift to a
# Learning Stance

· · · · ·

# The "What Happened?" Conversation

· · · · ·

# 2

# Stop Arguing About Who's Right:
## *Explore Each Other's Stories*

Michael's version of the story is different from Jack's:

> In the past couple of years I've really gone out of my way to try to help Jack out, and it seems one thing or another has always gone wrong. And instead of assuming that the client is always right, he argues with me! I just don't know how I can keep using him.
>
> But what really made me angry was the way Jack was making excuses about the chart instead of just fixing it. He knew it wasn't up to professional standards. And the revenue graphs were the critical part of the financial presentation.

One of the hallmarks of the "What Happened?" Conversation is that people disagree. What's the best way to save for retirement? How much money should we put into advertising? Should the neighborhood boys let your daughter play stick ball? Is the brochure up to professional standards?

Disagreement is not a bad thing, nor does it necessarily lead to a difficult conversation. We disagree with people all the time, and often no one cares very much.

But other times, we care a lot. The disagreement seems at the heart of what is going wrong between us. They won't agree with what we want them to agree with and they won't do what we need them to do. Whether or not we end up getting our way, we are left feeling frustrated, hurt, or misunderstood. And often the disagreement continues into the future, wreaking havoc whenever it raises its head.

When disagreement occurs, arguing may seem natural, even reasonable. But it's not helpful.

## Why We Argue, and Why It Doesn't Help

Think about your own difficult conversations in which there are important disagreements over what is really going on or what should be done. What's your explanation for what's causing the problem?

### We Think *They* Are the Problem

In a charitable mood, you may think, "Well, everyone has their opinion," or, "There are two sides to every story." But most of us don't really buy that. Deep down, we believe that the problem, put simply, is *them*.

- **They're selfish.** "My girlfriend won't go to a couples' counselor with me. She says it's a waste of money. I say it's important to me, but she doesn't care."

- **They're naive.** "My daughter's got these big ideas about going to New York and 'making it' in the theater. She just doesn't understand what she's up against."

- **They're controlling.** "We always do everything my boss's way. It drives me crazy, because he acts like his ideas are better than anyone else's, even when he doesn't know what he's talking about."

- **They're irrational.** "My Great Aunt Bertha sleeps on this sagging old mattress. She's got terrible back problems, but no matter what I say, she refuses to let me buy her a new mattress. Everyone in the family tells me, 'Rory, Aunt Bertha is just crazy. You can't reason with her.' I guess it's true."

If this is what we're thinking, then it's not surprising that we end up arguing. Rory, for example, cares about her Aunt Bertha. She wants to help, and she has the capacity to help. So Rory does what we all do: If the other person is stubborn, we assert harder in an attempt to break through whatever is keeping them from seeing what is sensible. ("If you would just try a new mattress, you'd see how much more comfortable it is!")

If the other person is naive, we try to educate them about how life really is, and if they are being selfish or manipulative, we may try to be forthright and call them on it. We persist in the hope that what we say will eventually make a difference.

But instead, our persistence leads to arguments. And these arguments lead nowhere. Nothing gets settled. We each feel unheard or poorly treated. We're frustrated not only because the other person is being so unreasonable, but also because we feel powerless to do anything about it. And the constant arguing isn't doing the relationship any good.

Yet we're not sure what to do instead. We can't just pretend there is no disagreement, that it doesn't matter, or that it's all the same to us. It *does* matter, it's *not* all the same to us. That's why we feel so strongly about it in the first place. But if arguing leads us nowhere, what else can we do?

The first thing we should do is hear from Aunt Bertha.

## They Think *We* Are the Problem

Aunt Bertha would be the first to agree that her mattress is indeed old and battered. "It's the one I shared with my husband for forty years, and it makes me feel safe," she says. "There are so many other changes in my life, it's nice to have a little haven that stays the same." Keeping it also provides Bertha with a sense of control over her life. When she complains, it's not because she wants answers, it's because she likes the connection she feels when she keeps people current on her daily comings and goings.

About Rory, Aunt Bertha has this to say: "I love her, but Rory can be a difficult person. She doesn't listen or care much about what other people think, and when I tell her that, she gets very angry and unpleasant." Rory thinks the problem is Aunt Bertha. Aunt Bertha, it seems, thinks the problem is Rory.

This raises an interesting question: Why is it always the *other* person who is naive or selfish or irrational or controlling? Why is it that we never think we are the problem? If you are having a difficult conversation, and someone asks why you disagree, how come you never say, "Because what I'm saying makes absolutely no sense"?

## We Each Make Sense in Our Story of What Happened

We don't see ourselves as the problem because, in fact, we aren't. What we are saying *does* make sense. What's often hard to see is that what the other person is saying *also* makes sense. Like Rory and Aunt Bertha, we each have different stories about what is going on in the world. In Rory's story, Rory's thoughts and actions are perfectly sensible. In Aunt Bertha's story, Aunt Bertha's thoughts and actions are equally sensible. But Rory is not just a character in her own story, she is also a visiting character in Aunt Bertha's story. And in Aunt Bertha's story, what Rory says seems pushy and insensitive. In Rory's story, what Aunt Bertha says sounds irrational.

In the normal course of things, we don't notice the ways in which our story of the world is different from other people's. But difficult conversations arise at precisely those points where important parts of our story collide with another person's story. We assume the collision is because of how the other person is; they assume it's because of how we are. But really the collision is a result of our stories simply being different, with neither of us realizing it. It's as if Princess Leia were trying to talk to Huck Finn. No wonder we end up arguing.

## Arguing Blocks Us from Exploring Each Other's Stories

But arguing is not only a *result* of our failure to see that we and the other person are in different stories — it is also part of the *cause*. Arguing inhibits our ability to learn how the other person sees the world. When we argue, we tend to trade conclusions — the "bottom line" of what we think: "Get a new mattress" versus "Stop trying to control me." "I'm going to New York to make it big" versus "You're naive." "Couples counseling is helpful" versus "Couples counseling is a waste of time."

But neither conclusion makes sense in the other person's story. So we each dismiss the other's argument. Rather than helping us understand our different views, arguing results in a battle of messages. Rather than drawing us together, arguing pulls us apart.

## Arguing Without Understanding Is Unpersuasive

Arguing creates another problem in difficult conversations: it inhibits change. *Telling* someone to change makes it less rather than more likely that they will. This is because people almost never change without first feeling understood.

Consider Trevor's conversation with Karen. Trevor is the financial administrator for the state Department of Social Services. Karen is a social worker with the department. "I cannot get Karen to turn in her paperwork on time," explains Trevor. "I've told her over and over that she's missing the deadlines, but it doesn't help. And when I bring it up, she gets annoyed."

Of course we know there's another side to this story. Unfortunately, Trevor doesn't know what it is. Trevor is telling Karen what she is supposed to do, but has not yet engaged her in a two-way conversation about the issue. When Trevor shifts his purposes from trying to change Karen's behavior — arguing why being late is wrong — to trying first to *understand* Karen, and then to be understood *by* her, the situation improves dramatically:

Karen described how overwhelmed and overworked she is. She puts all of her energy into her clients, who are very needy. She was feeling like I didn't appreciate that, which actually, I really didn't. On my end, I explained to her how I have to go through all kinds of extra work when she submits her paperwork late, and I explained the extra work in detail to her. She felt badly about that, and it was clear that she just hadn't thought about it from my perspective. She promised to put a higher priority on getting her work in on time, and so far she has.

Finally, each has learned something, and the stage for meaningful change is set.

To get anywhere in a disagreement, we need to understand the other person's story well enough to see how their conclusions make sense within it. And we need to help them understand the story in which our conclusions make sense. Understanding each other's stories from the inside won't necessarily "solve" the problem, but as with Karen and Trevor, it's an essential first step.

## Different Stories: Why We Each See the World Differently

As we move away from arguing and toward trying to understand the other person's story, it helps to know why people have different stories in the first place. Our stories don't come out of nowhere. They aren't random. Our stories are built in often unconscious but systematic ways. First, we take in information. We experience the world — sights, sounds, and feelings. Second, we interpret what we see, hear, and feel; we give it all meaning. Then we draw

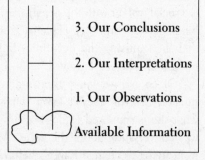

3. Our Conclusions

2. Our Interpretations

1. Our Observations

Available Information

**Where Our Stories Come From**

conclusions about what's happening. And at each step, there is an opportunity for different people's stories to diverge.

Put simply, we all have different stories about the world because we each take in different information and then interpret this information in our own unique ways.

In difficult conversations, too often we trade only conclusions back and forth, without stepping down to where most of the real action is: the information and interpretations that lead each of us to see the world as we do.

# 1. We Have Different Information

There are two reasons we all have different information about the world. First, as each of us proceeds through life — and through any difficult situation — the information available to us is overwhelming. We simply can't take in all of the sights, sounds, facts, and feelings involved in even a single encounter. Inevitably, we end up noticing some things and ignoring others. And what we each choose to notice and ignore will be different. Second, we each have access to different information.

**We Notice Different Things.** Doug took his four-year-old nephew, Andrew, to watch a homecoming parade. Sitting on his uncle's shoulders, Andrew shouted with delight as football players, cheerleaders, and the school band rolled by on lavish floats. Afterward Andrew exclaimed, "That was the best truck parade I've ever seen!"

Each float, it seems, was pulled by a truck. Andrew, truck obsessed as he was, saw nothing else. His Uncle Doug, truck indifferent, hadn't noticed a single truck. In a sense, Andrew and his uncle watched completely different parades.

Like Doug and Andrew, what we notice has to do with who we are and what we care about. Some of us pay more attention to feelings and relationships. Others to status and power, or to facts and logic. Some of us are artists, others are scientists, others pragmatists. Some of us want to prove we're right; others want to avoid conflict or smooth it over. Some of us tend to see ourselves as victims, others as heroes, observers, or survivors. The information we attend to varies accordingly.

Of course, neither Doug nor Andrew walked away from the parade thinking, "I enjoyed my particular perspective on the parade based on the information I paid attention to." Each walked away thinking, "I enjoyed *the* parade." Each assumes that what he paid attention to was what was significant about the experience. Each assumes he has "the facts."

In a more serious setting, Randy and Daniel, coworkers on an assembly line, experience the same dynamic. They've had a number of tense conversations about racial issues. Randy, who is white, believes that the company they work for has a generally good record on minority recruitment and promotion. He notices that of the seven people on his assembly team, two are African Americans and one is Latino, and that the head of the union is Latino. He has also learned that his supervisor is originally from the Philippines. Randy believes in the merits of a diverse workplace and has noticed approvingly that several people of color have recently been promoted.

Daniel, who is Korean American, has a different view. He has been on the receiving end of unusual questions about his qualifications. He has experienced several racial slurs from coworkers and one from a foreman. These experiences are prominent in his mind. He also knows of several minority coworkers who were overlooked for promotion, and notices that a disproportionate number of the top executives at the company are white. And Daniel has listened repeatedly to executives who talk as if the only two racial categories that mattered were white and African American.

While Randy and Daniel have some information that is shared, they have quite a bit of information that's not. Yet each assumes that the facts are plain, and his view is reality. In an important sense, it's as if Randy and Daniel work at different companies.

Often we go through an entire conversation — or indeed an entire relationship — without ever realizing that each of us is paying attention to different things, that our views are based on different information.

**We Each Know Ourselves Better Than Anyone Else Can.** In addition to *choosing* different information, we each have *access* to different information. For example, others have access to information about themselves that we don't. They know the constraints they are under; we don't. They know their hopes, dreams, and fears; we don't. We act as if we've got access to all the important information there is to know about them, but we don't. Their internal experience is far more complex than we imagine.

Let's return to the example of Jack and Michael. When Michael describes what happened, he doesn't mention anything about Jack's staying up all night. He might not know that Jack stayed up all night, and even if he does, his "knowledge" would be quite limited compared to what Jack knows about it. Jack was there. Jack knows what it felt like as he struggled to stay awake. He knows how uncomfortable it was when the heat was turned off at midnight. He knows how angry his wife was that he had to cancel their dinner together. He knows about the anxiety he felt putting aside other important work to do Michael's project. Jack also knows how happy he felt to be doing a favor for a friend.

And there is plenty that Jack is not aware of. Jack doesn't know that Michael's client blew up just that morning over the choice of photograph in another brochure Michael had prepared. Jack doesn't know that the revenue figures are a particularly hot topic because of questions about some of the client's recent business decisions. Jack doesn't know that Michael's graphic designer has taken an unscheduled personal leave in the midst of their busiest season, affecting not just this project but others as well. Jack doesn't know that Michael has been dissatisfied with some of Jack's work in the past. And Jack doesn't know how happy Michael felt to be doing a favor for a friend.

Of course, in advance, we don't know what we don't know. But rather than assuming we already know everything we need to, we should assume that there is important information we don't have access to. It's a good bet to be true.

## 2. We Have Different Interpretations

"We never have sex," Alvie Singer complains in the movie *Annie Hall*. "We're constantly having sex," says his girlfriend. "How often *do* you have sex?" asks their therapist. "Three times a week!" they reply in unison.

A second reason we tell different stories about the world is that, even when we have the same information, we interpret it differently — we give it different meaning. I see the cup as half empty; you see it as a metaphor for the fragility of humankind. I'm thirsty; you're a poet. Two especially important factors in how we interpret what we see are (1) our past experiences and (2) the implicit rules we've learned about how things should and should not be done.

**We Are Influenced by Past Experiences.** The past gives meaning to the present. Often, it is only in the context of someone's past experience that we can understand why what they are saying or doing makes any kind of sense.

To celebrate the end of a long project, Bonnie and her coworkers scraped together the money to treat their supervisor, Caroline, to dinner at a nice restaurant. Throughout the meal, Caroline did little but complain: "Everything is overpriced," "How can they get away with this?" and "You've got to be kidding. Five dollars for dessert!" Bonnie went home embarrassed and frustrated, thinking, "We knew she was cheap, but this is ridiculous. We paid so she wouldn't have to worry about the money, and still she complained about the cost. She ruined the evening."

Though the story in Bonnie's head was that Caroline was simply a cheapskate or wet blanket, Bonnie eventually decided to ask Caroline why she had such a strong reaction to the expense of eating out. Upon reflection, Caroline explained:

> I suppose it has to do with growing up during the Depression. I can still hear my mother's voice from when I was little, getting ready to

go off to school in the morning. "Carrie, there's a nickel on the counter for your lunch!" she'd call. She was so proud to be able to buy my lunch every day. Once I got to be eight or nine, a nickel wasn't enough to buy lunch anymore. But I never had the heart to tell her.

Years later, even a moderately priced meal can feel like an extravagance to Caroline when filtered through the images and feelings of this experience.

Every strong view you have is profoundly influenced by your past experiences. Where to vacation, whether to spank your kids, how much to budget for advertising — all are influenced by what you've observed in your own family and learned throughout your life. Often we aren't even aware of how these experiences affect our interpretation of the world. We simply believe that this is the way things are.

**We Apply Different Implicit Rules.** Our past experiences often develop into "rules" by which we live our lives. Whether we are aware of them or not, we all follow such rules. They tell us how the world works, how people should act, or how things are supposed to be. And they have a significant influence on the story we tell about what is happening between us in a difficult conversation.

We get into trouble when our rules collide.

Ollie and Thelma, for example, are stuck in a tangle of conflicting rules. As sales representatives, they spend a lot of time together on the road. One evening, they agreed to meet at 7:00 the next morning in the hotel lobby to finish preparing a presentation. Thelma, as usual, arrived at 7:00 sharp. Ollie showed up at 7:10. This was not the first time Ollie had arrived late, and Thelma was so frustrated that she had trouble focusing for the first twenty minutes of their meeting. Ollie was frustrated that Thelma was frustrated.

It helps to clarify the implicit rules that each is unconsciously applying. Thelma's rule is "It is unprofessional and inconsiderate to be late." Ollie's rule is "It is unprofessional to obsess about small things so much that you can't focus on what's important." Because

Thelma and Ollie both interpret the situation through the lens of their own implicit rule, they each see the other person as acting inappropriately.

Our implicit rules often take the form of things people "should" or "shouldn't" do: "You should spend money on education, but not on clothes." "You should never criticize a colleague in front of others." "You should never leave the toilet seat up, squeeze the toothpaste in the middle, or let the kids watch more than two hours of TV." The list is endless.

There's nothing wrong with having these rules. In fact, we need them to order our lives. But when you find yourself in conflict, it helps to make your rules explicit and to encourage the other person to do the same. This greatly reduces the chance that you will be caught in an accidental duel of conflicting rules.

## 3. Our Conclusions Reflect Self-Interest

Finally, when we think about why we each tell our own stories about the world, there is no getting around the fact that our conclusions are partisan, that they often reflect our self-interest. We look for information to support our view and give that information the most favorable interpretation. Then we feel even more certain that our view is right.

Professor Howard Raiffa of the Harvard Business School demonstrated this phenomenon when he gave teams of people a set of facts about a company. He told some of the teams they would be negotiating to buy the company, and others that they would be selling the company. He then asked each team to value the company as objectively as possible (not the price at which they would offer to buy or sell, but what they believed it was actually worth). Raiffa found that sellers, in their heart of hearts, believed the company to be worth on average 30 percent more than the independently assessed fair market value. Buyers, in turn, valued it at 30 percent less.

Each team developed a self-serving perception without realizing they were doing so. They focused more on things that were consistent with what they wanted to believe and tended to ignore, explain away, and soon forget those that weren't. Our colleague Roger Fisher captured this phenomenon in a wry reflection on his days as a litigator: "I sometimes failed to persuade the court that I was right, but I never failed to persuade myself!"

This tendency to develop unconsciously biased perceptions is very human, and can be dangerous. It calls for a dose of humility about the "rightness" of our story, especially when we have something important at stake.

## Move from Certainty to Curiosity

There's only one way to come to understand the other person's story, and that's by being curious. Instead of asking yourself, "How can they think that?!" ask yourself, "I wonder what information they have that I don't?" Instead of asking, "How can they be so irrational?" ask, "How might they see the world such that their view makes sense?" Certainty locks us out of their story; curiosity lets us in.

### Curiosity: The Way into Their Story

Consider the disagreement between Tony and his wife, Keiko. Tony's sister has just given birth to her first child. The next day Keiko is getting ready to visit the hospital. To her shock, Tony says he's not going with her to visit his sister, but instead is going to watch the football game on TV. When Keiko asks why, Tony mumbles something about this being a "big game," and adds, "I'll stop by the hospital tomorrow."

Keiko is deeply troubled by this. She thinks to herself, "What kind of person thinks football is more important than family? That's the most selfish, shallow, ridiculous thing I've ever heard!" But she catches herself in her own certainty, and instead of saying, "How could you do such a thing?" she negotiates herself to a place of curiosity. She wonders what Tony knows that she doesn't, how he's seeing the world such that his decision seems to make sense.

The story Tony tells is different from what Keiko had imagined. From the outside, Tony is watching a game on TV. But to Tony it's a matter of his mental health. Throughout the week, he works ten hours a day under extremely stressful conditions, then comes home and plays with his two boys, doing whatever they want. After the struggle of getting them to bed, he spends time with Keiko, talking mostly about her day. Finally, he collapses into bed. For Tony, watching the game is the one time during the week when he can truly relax. His stress level goes down, almost as if he's meditating, and this three hours to himself has a significant impact on his ability to take on the week ahead. Since Tony believes that his sister won't care whether he comes today or tomorrow, he chooses in favor of his mental health.

Of course, that's not the end of the issue. Keiko needs to share her story with Tony, and then, once everything is on the table, together they can figure out what to do. But that will never happen if Keiko simply assumes she knows Tony's story, no matter how certain she is at the outset that she does.

## What's *Your* Story?

One way to shift your stance from the easy certainty of feeling that you've thought about this from every possible angle is to get curious about what you don't know about *yourself*. This may sound like an odd thing to worry about. After all, you're with yourself all the time; wouldn't you be pretty familiar with your own perspective?

In a word, no. The process by which we construct our stories about the world often happens so fast, and so automatically, that we are not even aware of all that influences our views. For example, when we saw what Jack was really thinking and feeling during his conversation with Michael, there was nothing about the heat being turned off, or about his wife's anger at canceling their dinner plans. Even Jack wasn't fully aware of all the information behind his reactions.

And what implicit rules are important to him? Jack thinks to himself, "I can't believe the way Michael treated me," but he is unaware that this is based on an implicit rule of how people "should" treat each other. Jack's rule is something like "You should always show appreciation to others no matter what." Many of us agree with this rule, but it is not a truth, just a rule. Michael's rule might be "Good friends can get angry with each other and not take it personally." The point isn't whose rule is better; the point is that they are different. But Jack won't know they're different unless he first considers what rules underlie his own story about what happened.

Recall the story of Andrew and his Uncle Doug at the parade. We referred to Andrew as "truck obsessed." This description is from his uncle's point of view. Uncle Doug is aware of "how Andrew is," but he is less aware of how he himself "is." Andrew is truck obsessed if we use as the baseline his Uncle Doug's level of interest in trucks, which is zero. But from Andrew's point of view, Uncle Doug might be considered "cheerleader obsessed." Among the four-year-old crowd, Andrew's view is more likely the norm.

## Embrace Both Stories: Adopt the "And Stance"

It can be awfully hard to stay curious about another person's story when you have your own story to tell, especially if you're thinking that only one story can really be right. After all, your story is so different from theirs, and makes so much sense to you. Part of the stress of staying curious can be relieved by adopting what we call the "And Stance."

We usually assume that we must either accept or reject the other person's story, and that if we accept theirs, we must abandon our own. But who's right between Michael and Jack, Ollie and Thelma, or Bonnie and her boss, Caroline? Who's right between a person who likes to sleep with the window open and another who prefers the window closed?

The answer is that the question makes no sense. Don't choose between the stories; embrace both. That's the And Stance.

The suggestion to embrace both stories can sound like double-talk. It can be heard as "Pretend both of your stories are right." But in fact, it suggests something quite different. Don't pretend anything. Don't worry about accepting or rejecting the other person's story. First work to understand it. The mere act of understanding someone else's story doesn't require you to give up your own. The And Stance allows you to recognize that how you *each* see things matters, that how you each feel matters. Regardless of what you end up doing, regardless of whether your story influences theirs or theirs yours, both stories matter.

The And Stance is based on the assumption that the world is complex, that you can feel hurt, angry, and wronged, *and* they can feel just as hurt, angry, and wronged. They can be doing their best, *and* you can think that it's not good enough. You may have done something stupid, *and* they will have contributed in important ways to the problem as well. You can feel furious with them, *and* you can also feel love and appreciation for them.

The And Stance gives you a place from which to assert the full strength of your views and feelings without having to diminish the views and feelings of someone else. Likewise, you don't need to give up anything to hear how someone else feels or sees things differently. Because you may have different information or different interpretations, both stories can make sense at the same time.

It may be that as you share them, your stories change in response to new information or different perspectives. But they still may not end up the same, and that's all right. Sometimes people have honest disagreements, but even so, the most useful question is not "Who's right?" but "Now that we really understand each other, what's a good way to manage this problem?"

## Two Exceptions That Aren't

You may be thinking that the advice to shift from certainty and arguing to curiosity and the And Stance generally makes sense, but that there must be exceptions. Let's look at two important questions that may look like exceptions, but aren't: (1) What about times when I absolutely *know* I'm right? and (2) Does the suggestion to "understand the other person's story" always apply, even when, for example, I'm firing or breaking up with someone?

## I Really *Am* Right

There's an old story of two clerics arguing about how to do God's work. In the spirit of conciliation, one finally says to the other, "You and I see things differently, and that's okay. We don't need to agree. You can do God's work your way, and I'll do God's work His way."

The tendency to think this way can be overwhelming. Even if you understand another person's story with genuine insight and empathy, you may still stumble on the next step, thinking that however much their story makes sense to them, you are still "right" and they are still "wrong."

For example, what about the conversation you have with your daughter about her smoking? You know you are right that smoking is bad for her, that the sooner she stops the better.

Fair enough. About each of those things, you *are* right. But here's the rub: *that's not what the conversation is really about.* It's about how you each feel about your daughter's smoking, what she should do about it, and what role you should play. It's about the terrible fear and sadness you feel as you imagine her becoming sick, and your rage at feeling powerless to make her stop. It's about her need to feel independent, to break out of the "good girl" mold that feels so suffocating. It's about her own ambivalence doing something that makes her feel good and at the same time truly frightens her. The conversation is about many issues between the two of you that are complex and important to explore. It is not about the truth of whether smoking is bad for one's health. Both of you already agree on that.

Even when it seems the dispute is about what's true, you may find that being the one who's right doesn't get you very far. Your friend may deny that he is an alcoholic and that his drinking is affecting his marriage. But even if the whole world agrees with your assessment, asserting that you are right and trying to get him to admit it probably won't help you help your friend.

What *may* help is to tell him about the impact his drinking has on you, and, further, to try to understand his story. What is keeping him in denial? What would it mean to him to admit he has a problem? What gets in the way? Until you understand his story, and share yours with him, you can't help him find a way to rewrite the next chapter for the better. In this case, you may be right and your friend may be wrong, but merely being right doesn't do you much good.

## Giving Bad News

What if you have to fire someone, end a relationship, or let a supplier know you're cutting back on orders by 80 percent? In many difficult conversations, you don't have the power to impose an outcome unilaterally. When firing someone or breaking up or reducing orders, you do. In such situations, it's reasonable to wonder whether the other person's story is still relevant.

Most of the difficulty in firing someone or in breaking up takes place in the Feelings and Identity Conversations, which we'll explore later. But the question of differing perspectives is also important. Remember, understanding the other person's story doesn't mean you have to agree with it, nor does it require you to give up your own. And the fact that you are willing to try to understand their view doesn't diminish the power you have to implement your decision, and to be clear that your decision is final.

In fact, the And Stance is probably the most powerful place to stand when engaging in a difficult conversation that requires you to deliver or enforce bad news. If you are breaking up with someone, it allows you to say "I'm breaking up with you because it's the right thing for me [here's why], *and* I understand how hurt you are, and that you think we should try again, *and* I'm not changing my mind, *and* I understand that you think I should have been more clear about my confusion earlier, *and* I don't think that makes me a bad person, *and* I understand that I've done things that have hurt you, *and* I know you've done things that have hurt me, *and* I know I might regret this decision, *and* I'm still making it. . . . And, and, and."

"And" helps you to be curious *and* clear.

## To Move Forward, First Understand Where You Are

As you head down the path of improving how you deal with difficult conversations, you will notice that the question of how we each make sense of our worlds follows you like the moon in the night sky. It's a beacon you can return to no matter where you are or with what difficult problem you are grappling.

Coming to understand the other person, and yourself, more deeply doesn't mean that differences will disappear or that you won't have to solve real problems and make real choices. It doesn't mean that all views are equally valid or that it's wrong to have strongly held beliefs. It will, however, help you evaluate whether your strong views make sense in light of new information and different interpretations, and it will help you help others to appreciate the power of those views.

Wherever you want to go, understanding — imagining yourself into the other person's story — has got to be your first step. Before you can figure out how to move forward, you need to understand where you are.

The next two chapters delve more deeply into two problematic aspects of our story — our tendency to misunderstand their intentions, and our tendency to focus on blame.

# 3

# Don't Assume They Meant It:
## *Disentangle Intent from Impact*

The question of who intended what is central to our story about what's happening in a difficult situation. Intentions strongly influence our judgments of others: If someone intended to hurt us, we judge them more harshly than if they hurt us by mistake. We're willing to be inconvenienced by someone if they have a good reason; we're irritated if we think they just don't care about the impact of their actions on us. Though either blocks our way just as surely, we react differently to an ambulance double-parked on a narrow street than we do to a BMW.

## The Battle Over Intentions

Consider the story of Lori and Leo, who have been in a relationship for two years and have a recurring fight that is painful to both of them. The couple was at a party thrown by some friends, and Lori was about to reach for another scoop of ice cream, when Leo said, "Lori, why don't you lay off the ice cream?" Lori, who struggles with her weight, shot Leo a nasty look, and the two avoided each other for a while. Later that evening things went from bad to worse:

> LORI: I really resented it at the party, the way you treated me in front of our friends.

LEO: The way I treated you? What are you talking about?

LORI: About the ice cream. You act like you're my father or something. You have this need to control me or put me down.

LEO: Lori, I wasn't trying to hurt you. You said you were on a diet, and I'm just trying to help you stick to it. You're so defensive. You hear everything as an attack on you, even when I'm trying to help.

LORI: Help!? Humiliating me in front of my friends is your idea of helping?

LEO: You know, I just can't win with you. If I say something, you think I'm trying humiliate you, and if I don't, you ask me why I let you overeat. I am so sick of this. Sometimes I wonder whether you don't start these fights on purpose.

This conversation left both Lori and Leo feeling angry, hurt, and misunderstood. What's worse, it's a conversation they have over and over again. They are engaged in a classic battle over intentions: Lori accuses Leo of hurting her on purpose, and Leo denies it. They are caught in a cycle they don't understand and don't know how to break.

## Two Key Mistakes

There is a way out. Two crucial mistakes in this conversation make it infinitely more difficult than it needs to be — one by Lori and one by Leo. When Lori says "You have this need to control me or put me down," she is talking about Leo's intentions. Her mistake is to assume she knows what Leo's intentions are, when in fact she doesn't. It's an easy — and debilitating — mistake to make. And we do it all the time.

Leo's mistake is to assume that once he clarifies that his intentions were good, Lori is no longer justified in being upset. He explains that he "wasn't trying to hurt" Lori, that in fact he was trying to help. And having explained this, he thinks that should be the end of it. As a result, he doesn't take the time to learn what Lori is really feeling or why. This mistake, too, is as common as it is crippling.

Fortunately, with some awareness, both mistakes can be avoided.

## The First Mistake: Our Assumptions About Intentions Are Often Wrong

Exploring "Lori's mistake" requires us to understand how our minds work when devising stories about what others intend, and to learn to recognize the set of questionable assumptions upon which these stories are built. Here's the problem: While we care deeply about other people's intentions toward us, we don't actually know what their intentions are. We can't. Other people's intentions exist only in their hearts and minds. They are invisible to us. However real and right our assumptions about other people's intentions may seem to us, they are often incomplete or just plain wrong.

### We Assume Intentions from the Impact on Us

Much of the first mistake can be traced to one basic error: we make an attribution about another person's intentions based on the impact of their actions on us. We feel hurt; therefore they intended to hurt us. We feel slighted; therefore they intended to slight us. Our thinking is so automatic that we aren't even aware that our conclusion is only an assumption. We are so taken in by our story about what they intended that we can't imagine how they could have intended anything else.

**We Assume the Worst.** The conclusions we draw about intentions based on the impact of others' actions on us are rarely charitable. When a friend shows up late to the movie, we don't think, "Gee, I'll bet he ran into someone in need." More likely we think, "Jerk. He doesn't care about making me miss the beginning of the movie."

When we've been hurt by someone else's behavior, we assume the worst.

Margaret fell into this pattern. She had had her hip operated on by a prominent surgeon, a man she found gruff and hard to talk to. When Margaret hobbled in for her first appointment after surgery, the receptionist told her that the doctor had unexpectedly extended his vacation. Angry, Margaret imagined her wealthy doctor cavorting in the Caribbean with his wife or girlfriend, too self-important and inconsiderate to return on schedule. The picture compounded her anger.

When Margaret finally saw the doctor a week later, she asked curtly how his vacation had been. He responded that it had been wonderful. "I'll bet," she said, wondering whether to raise her concerns. But the doctor went on: "It was a working vacation. I was helping set up a hospital in Bosnia. The conditions there are just horrendous."

Learning what the doctor was really doing didn't erase the inconvenience Margaret had endured. Yet knowing that he was not acting out of selfishness, but from an unrelated and generous motivation, left Margaret feeling substantially better about having to wait the extra week.

We attribute intentions to others all the time. With business and even personal relationships increasingly conducted via e-mail, voice mail, faxes, and conference calls, we often have to read between the lines to figure out what people really mean. When a customer writes "I don't suppose you've gotten to my order yet . . . ," is he being sarcastic? Is he angry? Or is he trying to tell you that he knows you're busy? Without tone of voice to guide us, it is easy to assume the worst.

**We Treat Ourselves More Charitably.** What's ironic — and all too human — about our tendency to attribute bad intentions to others is how differently we treat ourselves. When your husband forgets to pick up the dry cleaning, he's irresponsible. When you forget to book the airline tickets, it's because you're overworked and stressed out. When a coworker criticizes your work in front of department colleagues, she is trying to put you down. When you offer suggestions to others in the same meeting, you are trying to be helpful.

When we're the ones acting, we know that much of the time we don't intend to annoy, offend, or upstage others. We're wrapped up in our own worries, and are often unaware that we're having any negative impact on others. When we're the ones acted upon, however, our story too easily slides into one about bad intentions and bad character.

**Are There Never Bad Intentions?** Of course, sometimes we get hurt because someone meant to hurt us. The person we are dealing with is nasty or inconsiderate, out to make us look bad or steal our best friend. But these situations are rarer than we imagine, and without hearing from the other person, we can't really know their intentions.

## Getting Their Intentions Wrong Is Costly

Intentions matter, and guessing wrong is hazardous to your relationships.

**We Assume Bad Intentions Mean Bad Character.** Perhaps the biggest danger of assuming the other person had bad intentions is that we easily jump from "they had bad intentions" to "they are a bad person." We settle into judgments about their character that color our view of them and, indeed, affect not only any conversation we might have, but the entire relationship. Once we think we have someone figured out, we see all of their actions through that lens, and the stakes rise. Even if we don't share our view with them, the impact remains. The worse our view of the other person's character, the easier it is to justify avoiding them or saying nasty things behind their back.

When you find yourself thinking "That traffic cop is a control freak" or "My boss is manipulative" or "My neighbor is impossible," ask yourself why this is your view. What is it based on? If it's based on feeling powerless, fearing manipulation, or being frustrated, notice that your conclusion is based solely on the impact of their behavior on you — which is not a sufficient basis to be sure of someone else's intentions or character.

**Accusing Them of Bad Intentions Creates Defensiveness.** Our assumptions about other people's intentions can also have a significant impact on our conversations. The easiest and most common way of expressing these assumptions is with an accusatory question: "How come you wanted to hurt me?" "Why do you ignore me like this?" "What have I done that makes you feel it's okay to step all over me?"

We think we are sharing our hurt, frustration, anger, or confusion. We are trying to begin a conversation that will end in greater understanding, perhaps some improved behavior, and maybe an apology. What *they* think we are doing is trying to provoke, accuse, or malign them. (In other words, they make the same mistaken leap in judging *our* intentions.) And given how frequently our assumptions are incomplete or wrong, the other person often feels not just accused, but falsely accused. Few things are more aggravating.

We should not be surprised, then, that they try to defend themselves, or attack back. From their point of view, they are defending themselves from false accusations. From our point of view, they are just being defensive — we're right, they just aren't big enough to admit it. The result is a mess. No one learns anything, no one apologizes, nothing changes.

Lori and Leo fall right into this. Leo is defensive throughout, and at the end, when he says that he sometimes wonders if Lori "starts these fights on purpose," he actually accuses Lori of bad intentions. And thus begins a cycle of accusation. If interviewed about their conversation afterward, *both* Lori and Leo would report that they were the victim of the other's bad intentions. Each would claim that their own statements were made in self-defense. Those are the two classic characteristics of the cycle: both parties think they are the victim, and both think they are acting only to defend themselves. This is how well-intentioned people get themselves into trouble.

**Attributions Can Become Self-Fulfilling.** Our assumptions about the other person's intentions often come true, even when they aren't true to begin with. You think your boss isn't giving you enough responsibility. You assume that this is because she doesn't trust you to do the work well. You feel demotivated by this state of affairs, figuring that nothing you do will change your boss's mind. Your work suffers, and your boss, who hadn't been concerned about your work before, is now quite worried. So she gives you even less responsibility than before.

When we think others have bad intentions toward us, it affects our behavior. And, in turn, how we behave affects how they treat us. Before we know it, our assumption that they have bad intentions toward us has come true.

# The Second Mistake: Good Intentions Don't Sanitize Bad Impact

As we've seen, the mistake Lori makes of assuming she knows Leo's intentions, though seemingly small, has big consequences. Now let's come back to Leo, who makes an equally costly error in the conversation. He assumes that because he had good intentions, Lori should not feel hurt. The thinking goes like this: "You said I meant to hurt you. I have now clarified that I didn't. So you should now feel fine, and if you don't, that's your problem."

## We Don't Hear What They Are Really Trying to Say

The problem with focusing only on clarifying our intentions is that we end up missing significant pieces of what the other person is trying to say. When they say, "Why were you trying to hurt me?" they are really communicating two separate messages: first, "I know what you intended," and, second, "I got hurt." When we are the person accused, we focus only on the first message and ignore the second. Why? Because we feel the need to defend ourselves. Because Leo is so busy defending himself, he fails to hear that Lori is hurt. He doesn't take in what this all means to her, how hurt she is, or why these issues are so painful.

Working to understand what the other person is really saying is particularly important because when someone says "You intended to hurt me" that isn't quite what they mean. A literal focus on intentions ends up clouding the conversation. Often we say "You intended to hurt me" when what we really mean is "You don't care enough about me." This is an important distinction.

The father who is too busy at work to attend his son's basketball game doesn't intend to hurt his son. He would prefer not to hurt his son. But his desire not to hurt his son is not as strong as his desire or need to work. Most of us on the receiving end make little distinction between "He wanted to hurt me" and "He didn't want to hurt me, but he didn't make me a priority." Either way, it hurts. If the father responds to his son's complaint by saying "I didn't intend to hurt you," he's not addressing his son's real concern: "You may not have intended to hurt me, but you knew you were hurting me, and you did it anyway."

It *is* useful to attempt to clarify your intentions. The question is when. If you do it at the beginning of the conversation, you are likely doing it without fully understanding what the other person really means to express.

## We Ignore the Complexity of Human Motivations

Another problem with assuming that good intentions sanitize a negative impact is that intentions are often more complex than just "good" or "bad." Are Leo's intentions purely angelic? *Is* he just trying to help Lori with her diet? Perhaps he himself is embarrassed by Lori's tendency to overeat and felt compelled to say something. Or maybe he wants her to lose weight not so much for herself, but for him. If he really cares about her, as he says he does, shouldn't he be more aware of how his words affect her?

As is so often the case, Leo's intentions are probably mixed. He may not even be fully aware of what is actually motivating him. But the answer to the question of what is truly motivating Leo is less important than his willingness to ask the question and look for an answer. If his first response to Lori is "No, I had good intentions," then he is putting up a barrier to any learning he might get from the conversation. And he is sending a message to Lori that says, "I'm more interested in defending myself than I am in investigating the complexities of what might be going on for me in our relationship."

Interestingly, when people take on the job of thinking hard about their own intentions, it sends a profoundly positive message to the other person about the importance of the relationship. After all, you'd only do that kind of hard work for somebody who matters to you.

## We Aggravate Hostility — Especially Between Groups

This dynamic of attributing intentions, defending ourselves, and ignoring the impact we've had on others is especially common in conflicts between groups, whether the groups are union members and management, neighborhood organizations and developers, administrative staff and the professionals they support, or my family and your family. The desire to sanitize impact is especially common in situations involving issues of "difference," like race, gender, or sexual orientation.

A few years ago a newspaper was experiencing racial strife among its workers. African American and Hispanic reporters complained about the absence of minority voices at the editorial level, and threatened to organize a boycott unless practices were changed. In response, the executive editors met behind closed doors to consider what to do. No minority staffers were invited to the meeting. When the minority reporters learned of the meeting, they were outraged. "They're telling us once again that they don't care what we have to say," said one reporter.

When one of the white editors heard this, she felt wrongly accused and sought to clarify the intention of the meeting: "I can see why you felt excluded. But that wasn't our intention. It was simply a meeting of editors trying to figure out a good next step for how to *include* minority voices." The white editor felt that now that her intentions were clarified, the issue of the "meaning of the meeting" was over. After all, everything was now clear. But it's never that simple. The intentions of the white editors are important. What's also important is that whether or not the intention was to exclude, people *felt* excluded. And such feelings may take time and thought on everyone's part to work through.

## Avoiding the Two Mistakes

The good news is that the two mistakes around intentions and impact are avoidable.

### Avoiding the First Mistake: Disentangle Impact and Intent

How can Lori avoid the mistake of attributing intentions to Leo that he may not have? Her first step is simply to recognize that there is a difference between the impact of Leo's behavior on her and what Leo intended. She can't get anywhere without disentangling the two.

Separating impact from intentions requires us to be aware of the automatic leap from "I was hurt" to "You intended to hurt me." You can make this distinction by asking yourself three questions:

1. **Actions:** "What did the other person actually say or do?"

2. **Impact:** "What was the impact of this on me?"

3. **Assumption:** "Based on this impact, what assumption am I making about what the other person intended?"

**Hold Your View as a Hypothesis.** Once you have clearly answered these three questions, the next step is to make absolutely

certain that you rec-
ognize that your as-
sumption about their
intentions is just an
assumption. It is a
guess, a hypothesis.

Your hypothesis
is not based on noth-
ing; you know what

**Disentangle Impact and Intent**

| Aware of | Unaware of |
|---|---|
| My intentions | Other person's intentions |
| Other person's impact on me | My impact on other person |

was said or done. But as we've seen, this is not a lot of evidence to go
on. Your guess might be right and it might be wrong. In fact, your reaction might even say as much about you as it does about what they
did. Perhaps you've had a past experience that gives their action special meaning to you. Many people find certain kinds of teasing hostile, for example, because of bad experiences with siblings, while
others think of teasing (in moderation) as a way to connect and show
affection. Given the stakes, however, you can't afford to level an accusation based on tenuous data.

**Share the Impact on You; Inquire About Their Intentions.** You
can use your answers to the three questions listed above to begin the
difficult conversation itself: say what the other person did, tell them
what its impact was on you, and explain your assumption about their
intentions, taking care to label it as a hypothesis that you are checking rather than asserting to be true.

Consider how this would change the beginning of the conversation between Lori and Leo. Instead of beginning with an accusation,
Lori can begin by identifying what Leo said, and what the impact
was on her:

LORI: You know when you said, "Why don't you lay off the ice
cream"? Well, I felt hurt by that.
LEO: You did?
LORI: Yeah.
LEO: I was just trying to help you stay on your diet. Why does
that make you upset?

LORI: I felt embarrassed that you said it in front of our friends.
Then what I wonder is whether you said it on purpose to em-
barrass or hurt me. I don't know why you'd want to do that,
but that's what I'm thinking when it happens.

LEO: Well, I'm certainly not doing it on purpose. I guess I didn't
realize it was so upsetting. I'm confused about what it is you
want me to say if I see you going off your diet . . . .

The conversation is only beginning, but it is off to a better start.

**Don't Pretend You Don't Have a Hypothesis.** Note that
we aren't suggesting you should get rid of your assumptions about
their intentions. That just isn't realistic. Nor do we suggest hiding your
view. Instead, recognize your assumptions for what they are — mere
guesses subject to modification or disproof. Lori doesn't say "I have no
thoughts on why you said what you said," or "I know you didn't mean
to hurt me." That would not be authentic. When you share your
assumptions about their intentions, simply be clear that you are sharing assumptions — guesses — and that you are sharing them for the
purpose of testing whether they make sense to the other person.

**Some Defensiveness Is Inevitable.** Of course, no matter how
skillfully you handle things, you are likely to encounter some defensiveness. The matter of intentions and impacts is complex, and sometimes the distinctions are fine. So it's best to anticipate a certain
amount of defensiveness, and to be prepared to clarify what you are
trying to communicate, and what you are not.

The more you can relieve the other person of the need to defend
themselves, the easier it becomes for them to take in what you are
saying and to reflect on the complexity of their motivations. For example, you might say, "I was surprised that you made that comment.
It seemed uncharacteristic of you. . . ." Assuming this is true (that it is
uncharacteristic), you are giving some balance to the information
you are bringing to their attention. If there was some malice mixed
in with what they said, this balance makes it easier for them to own
up to it.

## Avoiding the Second Mistake: Listen for Feelings, and Reflect on Your Intentions

When we find ourselves in Leo's position — being accused of bad intentions — we have a strong tendency to want to defend ourselves: "That is not what I intended." We are defending our intentions and our character. However, as we've seen, starting here leads to trouble.

**Listen Past the Accusation for the Feelings.** Remember that the accusation about our bad intentions is always made up of two separate ideas: (1) we had bad intentions and (2) the other person was frustrated, hurt, or embarrassed. Don't pretend they aren't saying the first. You'll want to respond to it. But neither should you ignore the second. And if you *start* by listening and acknowledging the feelings, and then return to the question of intentions, it will make your conversation significantly easier and more constructive.

**Be Open to Reflecting on the Complexity of Your Intentions.** When it comes time to consider your intentions, try to avoid the tendency to say "My intentions were pure." We usually think that about ourselves, and sometimes it's true. But often, as we've seen, intentions are more complex.

We can imagine how the initial conversation might have gone if Leo followed this advice with Lori:

LORI: I really resented it at the party, the way you treated me in front of our friends.

LEO: The way I treated you? What do you mean?

LORI: About the ice cream. You act like you're my father or something. You have this need to control me or put me down.

LEO: Wow. It sounds like what I said really hurt.

LORI: Of course it hurt. What did you expect?

LEO: Well, at the time I was thinking that you'd said you were on a diet, and that maybe I could help you stick to it. But I can see how saying something in front of everyone would be embarrassing. I wonder why I didn't see that?

LORI: Maybe you were embarrassed to have to say something.

LEO: Yeah, maybe. I could have seen you as out of control, which is a big issue for me.

LORI: That's true. And I probably was a little out of control.

LEO: Anyway, I'm sorry. I don't like hurting you. Let's think about what I *should* do or say, if anything, in situations like that.

LORI: Good idea. . . .

.   .   .

Understanding how we distort others' intentions, making difficult conversations even more difficult, is crucial to untangling what happened between us. However, there's still one more piece to the "What Happened?" Conversation that can get us into trouble — the question of who is to blame.

# 4

# Abandon Blame:
## *Map the Contribution System*

The ad agency you work for flies you to Boulder to pitch executives at *ExtremeSport*, a burgeoning sportswear company and a potentially important client. You turn to begin your presentation, only to discover that you've got the wrong storyboards. Right client, wrong campaign. Shaken, you stumble through an unfocused talk. With one slip, your assistant, who packs your briefcase, has undermined weeks of hard work.

## In Our Story, Blame Seems Clear

You blame your assistant, not just because she's a convenient target for your frustration or because letting others know it was she and not you who screwed up may help salvage your reputation, but because it is the simple truth: this was her fault.

When you and your assistant finally discuss what went wrong, you can take one of two approaches. You can blame her explicitly, saying something like "I don't know how you could have let this happen!" Or, if you tend to be less confrontational (or have been taught that blaming people isn't helpful), you can blame her implicitly, with something less threatening, like "Let's do better next time." Either way, she'll get the message: she's to blame.

# We're Caught in Blame's Web

Blame is a prominent issue in many difficult conversations. Whether on the surface or below, the conversation revolves around the question of who is to blame. Who is the bad person in this relationship? Who made the mistake? Who should apologize? Who gets to be righteously indignant?

Focusing on blame is a bad idea. Not because it's hard to talk about. Nor because it can injure relationships and cause pain and anxiety. Many subjects are hard to discuss and have potentially negative side effects and are nonetheless important to address.

Focusing on blame is a bad idea because *it inhibits our ability to learn what's really causing the problem and to do anything meaningful to correct it*. And because blame is often irrelevant and unfair. The urge to blame is based, quite literally, on a misunderstanding of what has given rise to the issues between you and the other person, and on the fear of *being* blamed. Too often, blaming also serves as a bad proxy for talking directly about hurt feelings.

But the advice "Don't blame others" is no answer. You can't move away from blame until you understand what blame is, what motivates us to want to blame each other, and how to move toward something else that will better serve your purposes in difficult conversations. That something else is the concept of *contribution*. The distinction between blame and contribution is not always easy to grasp, but it is essential to improving your ability to handle difficult conversations well.

# Distinguish Blame from Contribution

At heart, blame is about *judging* and contribution is about *understanding*.

## Blame Is About Judging, and Looks Backward

When we ask the question "Who is to blame?" we are really asking three questions in one. First, did this person cause the problem? Did your assistant's actions (or inaction) cause you to have the wrong storyboards? Second, if so, how should her actions be judged against some standard of conduct? Was she incompetent, unreasonable, unethical? And third, if the judgment is negative, how should she be punished? Will she be yelled at? Warned? Perhaps even fired?

When we say "This was your fault," it is shorthand for giving condemning answers to all three questions. We mean not only that you caused this, but that you did something bad and should be punished. It's no wonder that blame is such a loaded issue, and that we are quick to defend ourselves when we sense its approach.

When blame is in play, you can expect defensiveness, strong emotion, interruptions, and arguments about what "good assistants," "loving spouses," or "any reasonable person" should or shouldn't do. When we blame someone, we are offering them the role of "the accused," so they do what accused people do: they defend themselves any way they can. Given what's at stake, it's easy to see why the dance of mutual finger-pointing often turns nasty.

## Contribution Is About Understanding, and Looks Forward

Contribution asks a related but different set of questions. The first question is "How did we *each* contribute to bringing about the current situation?" Or put another way: "What did we each do or not do to get ourselves into this mess?" The second question is "Having identified the contribution system, how can we change it? What can we do about it as we go forward?" In short, contribution is useful when our goal is to understand what actually happened so that we can improve how we work together in the future. In the worlds of both business and personal relationships, too often we deal in blame when our real goals are understanding and change.

To illustrate, let's return to the *ExtremeSport* story and imagine two contrasting conversations between you and your assistant. The first conversation focuses on blame, the second on contribution.

YOU: I wanted to talk to you about my presentation at *Extreme-Sport*. You packed the wrong storyboards. The situation was unbelievably awkward, and made me look terrible. We simply can't work this way.

ASSISTANT: I heard. I'm so sorry. I just, well, you probably don't want to hear my excuses.

YOU: I just don't understand how you could let this happen.

ASSISTANT: I'm *really* sorry.

YOU: I know you didn't do it on purpose, and I know you feel bad, but I don't want this to happen again. You understand what I'm saying?

ASSISTANT: It won't. I promise you.

All three elements of blame are present: you caused this, I'm judging you negatively, and implicit in what I am saying is that one way or another you will be punished, especially if it happens again.

In contrast, a conversation about contribution might sound like this:

YOU: I wanted to talk to you about my presentation at *Extreme-Sport*. When I arrived I found the wrong storyboards in my briefcase.

ASSISTANT: I heard. I'm so sorry. I feel terrible.

YOU: I appreciate that. I'm feeling bad too. Let's retrace our steps and think about how this happened. I suspect we may each have contributed to the problem. From your point of view, did I do anything differently this time?

ASSISTANT: I'm not sure. We were working on three accounts at once, and on the one just before this one, when I asked about which boards you wanted packed, you got angry. I know it is my responsibility to know which boards you want, but sometimes when things get hectic, it can get confusing.

You: If you're unsure, you should always ask. But it sounds like you're saying I don't always make it easy to do that.

Assistant: Well, I do feel intimidated sometimes. When you get really busy, it's like you don't want to be bothered. The day you left you were in that kind of mood. I was trying to stay out of your way, because I didn't want to add to your frustration. I had planned to double-check which boards you wanted when you got off the phone, but then I had to run to the copy center. After you left I remembered, but I knew you usually double-checked your briefcase, so I figured it was okay.

You: Yeah, I do usually double-check, but this time I was so overwhelmed I forgot. I think we'd both better double-check every time. And I do get in those moods. I know it can be hard to interact with me when I'm like that. I need to work on being less impatient and abrupt. But if you're unsure, I need you to ask questions no matter what kind of mood I'm in.

Assistant: So you want me to ask questions even if I think it will annoy you?

You: Yes, although I'll try to be less irritable. Can you do that?

Assistant: Well, talking about it like this makes it easier. I realize it's important.

You: You can even refer to this conversation. You can say, "I know you're under pressure, but you made me promise I'd ask this . . . ." Or just say, "Hey, you promised not to be such a jerk!"

Assistant: [laughs] Okay, that works for me.

You: And we might also think about how you could track better which appointments are going to be for which campaigns. . . .

In the second conversation, you and your assistant have begun to identify the contributions that you each brought to the problem, and the ways in which each of your reactions are part of an overall pattern: You feel anxious and distracted about an upcoming presentation, and snap at your assistant. She assumes you want her out of your way, and withdraws. Something falls through the cracks, and then you are even more annoyed and worried the next time you are preparing, since you're no longer sure you can trust your assistant to help you. So you become more abrupt, increasingly unapproachable, and the communication between you continues to erode. Mistakes multiply.

As you get a handle on the interactive system the two of you have created, you can see what you each need to do to avoid or alter that system in the future. As a result, this second conversation is much more likely than the first to produce lasting change in the way you work together. Indeed, the first conversation runs the risk of reinforcing the problem. Since part of the system is that your assistant feels discouraged from talking to you because she fears provoking your anger, a conversation about blame is likely to make that tendency worse, not better. If you go that way, she'll eventually conclude that you're impossible to work with, and you'll report that she's incompetent.

## Contribution Is Joint and Interactive

Focusing on the contributions of both the boss and the assistant — seeking understanding rather than judgment — is critical. This is not just good practice, it accords more closely with reality. As a rule, when things go wrong in human relationships, everyone has contributed in some important way.

Of course, this is not how we usually *experience* contribution. A common distortion is to see contribution as singular — that what has gone wrong is either entirely our fault or (more often) entirely theirs.

Only in a B movie is it that simple. In real life causation is almost always more complex. A contribution *system* is present, and that system includes inputs from both people. Think about a baseball pitcher facing a batter. If the batter strikes out in a crucial situation, he might explain that he wasn't seeing well, that his wrist injury was still bothering him, or perhaps that he simply failed to come through in the clutch. The pitcher, however, might describe the strikeout by saying, "I knew he was thinking curve, so I came in with a high fastball," or, "I was in a zone. I knew I had him before he even got in the batter's box."

Who is right, the batter or the pitcher? Of course, the answer is both, at least in part. Whether the batter strikes out or hits a home run is a result of the interaction between the batter and the pitcher. Depending on your perspective, you might focus on the actions of one or the other, but the actions of both are required for the outcome.

It's the same in difficult conversations. Other than in extreme cases, such as child abuse, almost every situation that gives rise to a conversation is the result of a joint contribution system. Focusing on only one or the other of the contributors obscures rather than illuminates that system.

## The Costs of the Blame Frame

There *are* situations in which focusing on blame is not only important, but essential. Our legal system is set up to apportion blame, both in the criminal and civil courts. Assigning blame publicly, against clearly articulated legal or moral standards, tells people what is expected of them and allows society to exercise justice.

### When Blame Is the Goal, Understanding Is the Casualty

But even in situations that require a clear assignment of blame, there is a cost. Once the specter of punishment — legal or otherwise — is raised, learning the truth about what happened becomes more difficult. People are understandably less forthcoming, less open, less willing to apologize. After a car accident, for example, an automaker expecting to be sued may resist making safety improvements for fear it will seem an admission that the company should have done something *before* the accident.

"Truth commissions" often are created because of this trade-off between assigning blame and gaining an understanding of what really happened. A truth commission offers clemency in return for honesty. In South Africa, for example, it is unlikely that so much would now be known about past abuses under the apartheid system if criminal investigations and trials had been the only means of discovery.

## Focusing on Blame Hinders Problem-Solving

When the dog disappears, who's to blame? The person who opened the gate or the one who failed to grab her collar? Should we argue about that or look for the dog? When the tub overflows and ruins the living room ceiling below, should we blame the forgetful bather? The spouse who called the bather downstairs? The manufacturer who designed an overflow drain that is too small? The plumber who failed to mention it? The answer to who *contributed* to the problem is all of the above. When your real goal is finding the dog, fixing the ceiling, and preventing such incidents in the future, focusing on blame is a waste of time. It neither helps you understand the problem looking back, nor helps you fix it going forward.

## Blame Can Leave a Bad System Undiscovered

Even if punishment seems appropriate, using it as a substitute for really figuring out what went wrong and why is a disaster. The VP of Commodity Corp. championed the decision to build a new manufacturing plant as a way to increase profits. However, not only did the plant fail to increase profits, but the resulting increase in market supply actually brought profits down. At the time of the original decision to build the plant, several people privately predicted this, but didn't speak up.

To address the situation, the VP was fired and a new strategic planner was brought on board. By removing the person who made the bad decision and replacing him with someone "better," it was assumed that the management issue was now fixed. But while the company had changed one "part" in the contribution system, it had failed to look at the system as a whole. Why did those who predicted failure keep silent? Were there implicit incentives that encouraged this? What structures, policies, and processes continue to allow poor decisions, and what would it take to change them?

Removing one player in a system is sometimes warranted. But the cost of doing so as a substitute for the hard work of examining the larger contribution system is often surprisingly high.

## The Benefits of Understanding Contribution

Fundamentally, using the blame frame makes conversations more difficult, while understanding the contribution system makes a difficult conversation easier and more likely to be productive.

### Contribution Is Easier to Raise

Joseph runs an overseas office for a multinational corporation. His greatest frustration comes from headquarters' unwillingness or inability to communicate with him effectively. Joseph doesn't hear about policy changes until after they're made, and is often informed by clients (or in one case, the newspaper!) about work his own firm is doing in his region. Joseph decides to raise the matter with the home office.

Before he does, one of Joseph's managers points out Joseph's own role in the problem. Joseph installed a computer system incompatible with the one at headquarters. And he rarely takes the initiative to ask the kinds of questions he probably should. Unfortunately, instead of seeing his own contributions as part of the whole system, Joseph falls into the blame frame and begins to wonder whether the fault really lies with him rather than with headquarters. He doesn't raise the issue after all, and his frustration continues.

The blame frame creates a difficult burden. You have to feel confident that others are at fault, and that you aren't, to feel justified in raising an issue. And since, as we've described, there are always ways in which you've contributed, you're likely to end up failing to raise important issues. That would be a shame, because you'll lose the opportunity to understand why communication between you isn't working well, and how it might be improved.

## Contribution Encourages Learning and Change

Imagine a couple confronting the wife's infidelity. Accusations fly as questions of blame are raised. After much anguish, the husband chooses to stay in the marriage under the condition that such infidelity never happen again. There is an apparent resolution, but what has each person learned from the experience?

As one-sided as an affair may seem, it often involves some contribution from both partners. Unless these contributions are sorted out, the problems and patterns in the marriage that gave rise to the affair will continue to cause difficulty. Some questions need to be asked: Does the husband listen to his wife? Does he stay at work late? Was his wife feeling sad, lonely, undesirable? If so, why?

And to understand the *system*, the couple then needs to follow up with more questions: If the husband doesn't listen to his wife, what's she doing to contribute to that? What does she say or do that encourages him to shut down or withdraw? Does she work every weekend, or withdraw when she's feeling upset? How does their relationship work? If the factors that contributed to the infidelity are to be understood and addressed, these questions must be explored — the contribution system must be mapped.

# Three Misconceptions About Contribution

Three common misunderstandings can keep people from fully embracing or benefiting from the concept of contribution.

## Misconception #1: I Should Focus Only on My Contribution

Advice that you should search for joint contribution to a problem is sometimes heard as "You should overlook the other person's contribution and focus on your own." This is a mistake. *Finding your contribution doesn't in any way negate the other person's contribution.* It has taken both of you to get into this mess. It will probably take both of you to get out.

Recognizing that everyone involved in a situation has contributed to the problem doesn't mean that everyone has contributed equally. You can be 5 percent responsible or 95 percent responsible — there is still joint contribution. Of course, quantifying contribution is not easy, and in most cases not very helpful. Understanding is the goal, not assigning percentages.

## Misconception #2: Putting Aside Blame Means Putting Aside My Feelings

Seeking to understand the contribution system rather than focusing on blame doesn't mean putting aside strong emotions. Quite the contrary. As you and the other person look at how you have each contributed to the problem, sharing your feelings is essential.

Indeed, the very impulse to blame is often stimulated by strong emotions that lie unexpressed. When you learn of your wife's infidelity, you want to say, "You are responsible for ruining our marriage! How could you do something so stupid and hurtful?!" Here, you are focusing on blame as a proxy for your feelings. Speaking more directly about your strong feelings — "I feel devastated by what you did" or "My ability to trust you has been shattered" — actually reduces the impulse to blame. Over time, as you look ahead, it frees you to talk more comfortably and productively in terms of contribution.

If you find yourself mired in a continuing urge to blame, or with an unceasing desire for the other person to admit that they were wrong, you may find some relief by asking yourself: "What feelings am I failing to express?" and "Has the other person acknowledged my feelings?" As you explore this terrain, you may find yourself naturally shifting from a blame frame to a contribution frame. You may learn that what you really seek is understanding and acknowledgment. What you want the other person to say isn't "It was my fault," but rather "I understand that I hurt you and I'm sorry." The first statement is about judgment, the second about understanding.

## Misconception #3: Exploring Contribution Means "Blaming the Victim"

When someone blames the victim, they are suggesting that the victim "brought it on themselves," that they deserved or even wanted to be victimized. This is often terribly unfair and painful for both the victim and others.

Looking for joint contribution is not about blame of any kind. Imagine that you are mugged while walking alone down a dark street late at night. Blame asks: "Did you do something wrong? Did you break the law? Did you act immorally? Should you be punished?" The answer to all of these questions is no. You didn't do anything wrong; you didn't deserve to be mugged. Being mugged was not your fault.

Contribution asks a different set of questions. Contribution asks: "What did I do that helped cause the situation?" You can find contribution even in situations where you carry no blame; you did contribute to being mugged. How? By choosing to walk alone at night. If you'd been somewhere else, or in a group, getting mugged would have been less likely. If we are looking to punish someone for what happened, we would punish the mugger. If we are looking to help you feel empowered in the world, we would encourage you to find your contribution. You may not be able to change other people's contributions, but you can often change your own.

In his autobiography, *A Long Walk to Freedom*, Nelson Mandela provides an example of how people who have been overwhelmingly victimized can still seek to understand their own contribution to their problems. He describes how he learned this from an Afrikaner:

> Reverend Andre Scheffer was a minister of the Dutch Reformed Mission Church in Africa. . . . He had a dry sense of humor and liked to poke fun at us. "You know," he would say, "the white man has a more difficult task than the black man in this country. Whenever there is a problem, we [white men] have to find a solution. But whenever you blacks have a problem, you have an excuse. You can simply say, '*Ingabilungu*,' " . . . . a Xhosa expression that means, "It is the whites."
>
> He was saying that we could always blame all of our troubles on the white man. His message was that we must also look within ourselves and become responsible for our actions — sentiments with which I wholeheartedly agreed.

Mandela does not believe blacks are to blame for their situation. He does believe that blacks must look for and take responsibility for their contribution to the problems of South Africa, if the nation is to move forward successfully.

By identifying what you are doing to perpetuate a situation, you learn where you have leverage to affect the system. Simply by changing your own behavior, you gain at least some influence over the problem.

## Finding Your Fair Share: Four Hard-to-Spot Contributions

"The concept of contribution makes sense," you may be thinking. Even so, as you reflect on your own most pressing entanglement, you are baffled: "In this particular situation, I just don't see how I have any contribution." Spotting your own contribution becomes easier with practice. But it helps to be familiar with four common contributions that are often overlooked.

## 1. Avoiding Until Now

One of the most common contributions to a problem, and one of the easiest to overlook, is the simple act of avoiding. You have allowed the problem to continue unchecked by not having addressed it earlier. It may be that your ex-husband has been late every time he's picked up your kids for the last two years, but you've never mentioned to him that it was a problem. It may be that your boss has trampled thoughtlessly on your self-esteem since you began work four years ago, but you've chosen not to share with her the impact on you.

One of your store managers deserves a warning or even to be fired. But his file is full of "Satisfactory" performance reviews dating back years. Why? Partly because you wanted to avoid the effort of documenting the problem, but mostly because you and other supervisors haven't wanted the hassle of having an ongoing difficult conversation with an argumentative person. And because managers in your company tolerate and collude in a norm of avoiding such conversations.

A particularly problematic form of avoiding is complaining to a third party instead of to the person with whom you're upset. It makes you feel better, but puts the third party in the middle with no good way to help. They can't speak for you, and if they try, the other person may get the idea that the problem is so terrible that you can't discuss it directly. On the other hand, if they keep quiet, the third party is burdened with only your partisan and incomplete version of the story.

This isn't to say that it's not okay to get advice from a friend about how to conduct a difficult conversation. It does suggest that if you do so, then you should also report back to that friend about any change in your feelings as a result of having the difficult conversation, so that they aren't left with an unbalanced story.

## 2. Being Unapproachable

The flip side of not bringing something up is having an interpersonal style that keeps people at bay. You contribute by being uninterested, unpredictable, short-tempered, judgmental, punitive, hypersensitive, argumentative, or unfriendly. Of course, whether you are really any of these things or intend this impact is not the point. If someone experiences you this way, they are less likely to raise things with you, and this becomes part of the system of avoidance between you.

## 3. Intersections

Intersections result from a simple difference between two people in background, preferences, communication style, or assumptions about relationships. Consider Toby and Eng-An, who have been married for about four months. Their fights have begun falling into a predictable pattern. Toby is usually the one to initiate a discussion about an issue — who is doing more of the housework, why Eng-An didn't stick up for him with her mother, whether to save or spend her year-end bonus. When things become heated, Eng-An ends the discussion by saying, "Look, I just don't want to talk about this right now," and walking out.

When Eng-An shuts down or walks out, Toby is left feeling abandoned and responsible for coping with the problems in their relationship on his own. He complains to friends that "Eng-An is incapable of dealing with feelings, hers or mine. She goes into denial when the tiniest thing is wrong." Toby becomes increasingly frustrated with their inability to make tough decisions, or simply to have it out.

Meanwhile, Eng-An is confiding in her sister: "Toby is smothering me. Everything is an emergency, everything has to be discussed *right now*. He has no sensitivity for how I feel about it or whether it's a good time for me. He wanted to hunt down a three-dollar discrepancy in our checking account on the night before my big presentation to the board! He's constantly making these minuscule disagreements into huge problems that we've got to discuss for hours."

When Toby and Eng-An finally talk explicitly about what's happening, they realize that their past experiences have created an intersection of conflicting assumptions about communication and relationships. Toby's mother had alcohol problems that escalated over the course of his childhood. Toby was the only member of the family willing to speak up about what was happening. His father and sisters went into denial, acting as if nothing were wrong and ignoring his mother's erratic behavior, no doubt clinging unconsciously to the hope that it would somehow get better. But it didn't. Perhaps as a result, Toby has a deep sense that raising and addressing problems immediately is crucial to the ongoing health of his relationship with Eng-An.

Eng-An's home was quite different. Her brother is mentally handicapped, and life revolved around his schedule and needs. While Eng-An loved her brother very much, she sometimes needed a respite from the constant emotional turmoil of worry, crises, and caretaking that surrounded him. She learned not to react too quickly to a potential problem and worked hard to create the distance she needed in an emotionally intense family. Toby's reactions to their disagreements threaten this carefully nurtured space.

We see how combining the two worldviews produces a system of interaction in which Toby talks and Eng-An withdraws. Operating in a blame frame, Toby concluded that their difficulties were Eng-An's fault because she was "in denial" and "couldn't handle feelings." Eng-An decided that their difficulties were Toby's fault, because he "overreacts" and "smothers me." By shifting to a contribution frame, the couple was able to piece together the elements of the system that led to their fights and talk about how to handle it. Only then did communication improve.

Toby and Eng-An were fortunate that they came to understand their intersection in time to do something about it. The failure to do so can be disastrous. In fact, treating an intersection as a question of right versus wrong leads to the death of a great many relationships.

## Mapping a Contribution System

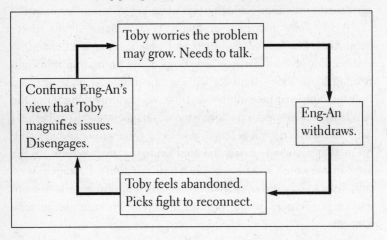

When a relationship begins, infatuation may keep each partner from noticing any flaws in the other. Later, as the relationship deepens, each notices some minor annoyances in how the other does things, but the tendency is not to worry. We assume that in time, watching us, the other will learn to show more affection, be more spontaneous, or demonstrate more concern for living within a budget.

The problem is that things *don't* change, because each is waiting for *the other* to change. We begin to wonder: "Don't they love me enough to do the right thing? Do they really love me at all?"

So long as we each continue to see this as a matter of right versus wrong, rather than as an intersection, there is no way to avoid a train wreck. In contrast, successful relationships, whether in our personal life or with our colleagues at work, are built on the knowledge that in intersections there is no one to blame. People are just different. If we hope to stay together over the long haul, we will sometimes have to compromise our preferences and meet in the middle.

## 4. Problematic Role Assumptions

A fourth hard-to-spot contribution involves assumptions, often unconscious, about your role in a situation. When your assumptions differ from those of others you can have an intersection such as Toby
and Eng-An's. But role assumptions can be problematic even when
they are shared.

The members of George's family, for example, all knew their
parts in a repetitive family dynamic. Seven-year-old George would
do something annoying, like bang a spoon against the dog dish.
Eventually George's mother would say to her husband, "Can't you
make him stop that?" whereupon George's dad would yell "Stop it!"
George would jump, and perhaps cry, and his mom would then turn
back to her husband and say, "Well you didn't have to yell at him."
Dad would sigh and return to reading the paper. And after a few minutes, George would find another irritating way to get attention, and
the pattern would repeat. While no member of the family particularly *enjoyed* this dynamic, it did help them connect emotionally.

Obviously, this form of connecting — fighting to show love — has
limitations. Yet it and many other less-than-ideal dynamics are surprisingly common, at home and in the workplace. Why? First, because despite its problems the familiar pattern is comfortable, and
the members of the group work to keep each person playing their
role. Second, because changing a contribution system requires more
than just spotting it and recognizing its limitations. The people involved also have to find another way to provide its benefits. George
and his parents need to find better ways to demonstrate affection and
maintain closeness. And this is likely to require some tough work in
their Feelings and Identity Conversations.

In an organization, this explains why people find it hard to
change how they work together even when they see the limitations of
common role assumptions, such as "Leaders set strategy; subordinates implement it." To change how people interact, they need both
an alternate model everyone thinks is better *and* the skills to make
that model work at least as well as the current approach.

## Two Tools for Spotting Contribution

If you are still unable to see your contribution, try one of the following two approaches.

### Role Reversal

Ask yourself, "What would they say I'm contributing?" Pretend you
are the other person and answer the question in the first person, using pronouns such as I, me, and my. Seeing yourself through someone else's eyes can help you understand what you're doing to feed the
system.

### The Observer's Insight

Step back and look at the problem from the perspective of a disinter-
ested observer. Imagine that you are a consultant called in to help
the people in this situation better understand why they are getting
stuck. How would you describe, in a neutral, nonjudgmental way,
what each person is contributing?

   If you have trouble getting out of your own shoes in this way, ask
a friend to try for you. If what your friend comes up with surprises
you, don't reject it immediately. Rather, imagine that it is true. Ask
how that could be, and what it would mean.

## Moving from Blame to Contribution —
## An Example

Shifting your stance away from assessing blame and toward exploring
contribution doesn't happen overnight. It takes hard work and persistence. You will repeatedly find yourself and others slipping back into

a blame frame, and will need to be vigilant in constantly correcting your course.

Sydney learned this while leading a team of engineers on a consulting assignment in Brazil. She was the only woman on the project, and the youngest on the team by fifteen years. One of the team members, Miguel, was particularly hostile to her leadership, and she set out to win him over by assigning him to work with her on a number of subcomponents of the project. The two executed several tasks together successfully, and each began to feel more comfortable with the other's style and competence.

Then one evening while working through dinner at the hotel restaurant, Miguel changed the currency of their relationship. "You are so beautiful," Miguel said to Sydney. "And we're so far away from home." He leaned across the table and stroked her hair. Uncomfortable, Sydney suggested they "get back to these figures." She avoided his eyes and wrapped things up quickly.

Miguel's provocative behavior continued over the next few days. He would stand close to Sydney, pay more attention to her than to other members of the team, seek her out at every opportunity. Although he never issued a direct invitation for physical involvement, Sydney wondered whether this was what he was after.

Initially, like many of us, Sydney fell into a blame frame. She judged Miguel's behavior as inappropriate and felt victimized by it. But along with blame came several doubts. Just as she would get up the courage to tell Miguel his behavior was wrong, Sydney worried that she was overreacting or misinterpreting his actions. Perhaps it was just a cultural difference.

Sydney also feared that accusing Miguel would take things from bad to worse. "The situation is uncomfortable but manageable," she thought. "If I tell Miguel his behavior is wrong, I run the risk that he will explode, disrupt the team, or do something to endanger the project. And the project is my first priority." By continuing to think in terms of blame, Sydney kept the stakes of raising the issue unmanageably high.

## Map the Contribution System

The first step in moving away from blame is to reorient your own thinking about the situation. You can begin to diagnose the system by looking for the contributions you've each made to create the problem. Some of us are prone to focus on the other person's contribution and have a harder time seeing our own. As "shifters" we tend to see ourselves as innocent victims — when something goes wrong, it's always because of what someone else did. Others of us have the opposite tendency: we are all too aware of the negative consequences of our own actions. In the face of this, others' contributions seem insignificant. An "absorber" tends to feel responsible for everything.

Knowing your predisposition can help you fight it, enabling you to get a balanced picture of what each person is contributing. To understand a contribution system, you have to understand all its components.

**What Are They Contributing?** Miguel's contributions are relatively easy to identify. He is expressing romantic affection, but failing to clarify his intentions or the extent of his interest. He chooses to stand close to Sydney, to spend more time and energy talking with her than with his other colleagues, to hint at feelings of longing for her. He chooses (consciously or unconsciously) to ignore the nonverbal signals Sydney is sending. She changes the subject. She changes the staffing assignments. She moves away. He follows. He has chosen not to inquire about how she feels about what is happening.

Miguel may or may not be aware of Sydney's discomfort. His actions may or may not be blameworthy. And it may or may not be appropriate to punish him. But these are separate inquiries from the question of contribution. What is important here is that these are the pieces of the puzzle that come from Miguel.

**What Am I Contributing?** Sydney's contributions begin to surface once we shift out of the blame frame. She was particularly attentive to Miguel's concerns about the team and went out of her way to work with him. He may have read this as interest on her part. Sydney has avoided telling Miguel — at least directly — that she's felt at all uncomfortable. Regardless of how justified or understandable Sydney's actions are, these actions and inactions on her part contributed to their current situation; they make it easier to understand why Miguel continues to act as he does.

### List Each Person's Contribution

| My Contributions | His Contributions |
|---|---|
| • Gave M. special attention at beginning<br>• Went out of my way to work with him 1-on-1<br>• Haven't told him I'm uncomfortable | • Telling me he's in love, wants to spend private time together, etc.<br>• Isn't clear about his intentions<br>• Isn't getting, or is ignoring, my indirect signals<br>• Doesn't ask me if I am comfortable with his suggestions |

**Who Else Is Involved?** Often there are other important contributors to the system. For example, with Toby and Eng-An, their families played an important role. In Sydney's case, other members of the team may have inadvertently encouraged Miguel or passed up opportunities to help Sydney. When exploring a contribution system, consider whether other players may be contributing something important.

## Take Responsibility for Your Contribution Early

Raising contribution during the conversation itself can be surprisingly easy. Getting the other person to shift from blame to contribution can be more difficult. One of the best ways to signal that you want to leave behind the question of who's to blame is to acknowledge your own contribution early in the conversation. For example, Sydney might say to Miguel:

> I apologize for not bringing this up earlier, before it became such a big deal for me. Also, I realize that arranging for us to work together at the beginning of the project may have sent a confusing signal, though all I intended was to improve our professional relationship. What was your reaction?

She might also ask, "Are there other things I've done that were ambiguous or that suggested I might be interested in something else?" Sydney would learn important information about her own impact, and also set the stage for discussion of Miguel's contribution.

You may fear that being the first to own up to some contribution puts you in a vulnerable position for the rest of the conversation. What if the other person remains focused on blame, is more than happy to acknowledge your contribution (saying, in effect, "I agree that this is your fault"), and then is adamant that they contributed nothing?

This is an important concern, especially if you tend to be a contribution absorber. Acknowledging your contribution is a risk. But not acknowledging your contribution also involves risks. If Sydney starts by pointing out Miguel's contributions, Miguel is likely to become defensive and feel that the conversation is unfairly one-sided. Rather than acknowledging his contribution, Miguel may be tempted to deflect attention from it, and the easiest way to do that is to point out Sydney's part in the problem. Taking responsibility for your contribution up front prevents the other person from using it as a shield to avoid a discussion of their own contribution.

If you feel the focus is somehow on you alone, you can say so: "It's not okay to look only at my contribution. That's not reality as I see it. I feel like I'm trying to look at both of us. Is there anything I'm doing to make it hard for you to look at yourself?"

## Help Them Understand Their Contribution

In addition to taking responsibility for what you contributed, there are things you can do to help them locate their contribution.

**Make Your Observations and Reasoning Explicit.** To make sure that you're working from the same information and understand each other's interpretations, share, as specifically as you can recall it what the other person did or said that triggered your reaction. Sydney might say, for example, "When you stroked my hair or asked if we could spend some private time at the beach, I was confused about what you wanted from our relationship. And I began to worry that if you wanted romance, then I would have a real problem on my hands."

Or Toby could tell Eng-An: "When you left the house last night in the middle of our fight, I felt abandoned and angry. I think that's why I picked a fight with you this morning over the orange juice. I needed to reconnect with you, even if it was just by yelling at you." By jotting down the things that triggered you to react, you are starting to get a handle on the actions and reactions that make up the contribution system.

**Clarify What You Would Have Them Do Differently.** In addition to explaining what triggered your reaction, you should be prepared to say what you would have them do differently in the future, and explain how this would help *you* behave differently as well. The husband trying to repair the relationship with his adulterous wife might say:

> I want to do a better job of listening to you and not withdrawing in the future. One thing that would help me to listen is if you could first ask me how my day was, and whether this is a good time to talk. Sometimes I'm preoccupied or anxious about work, and when you start telling me about the problems you're having with your boss, I

just get overloaded and shut down. And sometimes I feel angry, because it makes me think you don't care about what's going on with me. So if you just asked first, I think I'd be in a much better place to listen to you. Is there anything that would make that difficult?

Making a specific request for how the other person can change their contribution *in the service of helping you change yours* can be a powerful way of helping them understand what they are doing to create and perpetuate the problem. And it goes to the heart of the purpose of understanding the contribution system — to see what you each need to do differently to influence and improve the situation.

. . .

Whether you're talking about your contrasting stories, your intentions, or your contributions, the goal isn't to get an admission. The goal is to understand better what's happened between you, so that you can start to talk constructively about where to go next.

But in addition to clarifying the "What Happened?" Conversation, there are two other conversations that need untangling. The next two chapters examine the Feelings and Identity Conversations.

# The Feelings
# Conversation

# 5

# Have Your Feelings
# (Or They Will Have You)

A mother hears a crash in the living room and runs in to find her four-year-old son, baseball bat in hand, standing next to a shattered vase. "What happened?" she asks. Contrite, looking away, the boy answers, "Nothing."

When it comes to acknowledging difficult emotions, we often adopt the strategy of the young batter. If we deny that the emotions are there, then maybe we can avoid the consequences of feeling them. But we have about the same chance of hiding our emotions as the boy has of convincing his mother that all is well with the vase. Feelings are too powerful to remain peacefully bottled. They will be heard one way or another, whether in leaks or bursts. And if handled indirectly or without honesty, they contaminate communication.

## Feelings Matter: They Are Often at the Heart of Difficult Conversations

Feelings, of course, are part of what makes good relationships so rich and satisfying. Feelings like passion and pride, silliness and warmth, and even jealousy, disappointment, and anger let us know that we are fully alive.

At the same time, managing feelings can be enormously challenging. Our failure to acknowledge and discuss feelings derails a startling number of difficult conversations. And the inability to deal openly and well with feelings can undermine the quality and health of our relationships.

Max and his daughter Julie are negotiating about how much to spend on Julie's upcoming wedding. Should this conversation be about money alone? If so, then Max and Julie can simply list what they want and look for ways to accommodate these desires. "That's it. We'll spend two thousand dollars on the ballroom, fifteen hundred on the band, seventy-two hundred on food," and so forth. End of conversation.

But it isn't that easy. The conversation feels difficult and stressful for both dad and daughter. Each is feeling impatient, sensitive, and ready to find fault with the other. It is not, after all, just a matter of money. It is also about feelings. For example, Max experiences a deep sense of both sadness and joy when he thinks of the event — sadness because he will be receiving less of Julie's attention from now on, and joy because she has matured into such a wonderful woman. To Max, the planning of the event represents a final opportunity for his daughter to be just his daughter, and not also someone's wife. He'd like her to ask questions and to seek advice from him, the way she did when she was younger.

For better or worse, *this conversation will not go well unless these feelings are surfaced*. Why? Because you can't have an effective conversation without talking about the primary issues at stake, and in this conversation feelings are at the heart of what's wrong. No matter how skillfully dad and daughter negotiate about how much money to spend, the outcome will not leave them feeling satisfied unless they also talk about how they are feeling.

## We Try to Frame Feelings Out of the Problem

Max originally described his problem to us by saying, "My daughter and I are having trouble deciding how much we should spend on her wedding. She'd like to do certain things, and I respect that, but I believe there are cheaper options available." It was only after talking with him that we learned that what was really at stake for each of them were the feelings involved in the event.

This is a common pattern: we frame the problem exclusively as a substantive disagreement and believe that if only we were more skilled at problem-solving, we'd be able to lick the thing. Solving problems seems easier than talking about emotions.

Framing feelings out of the problem is one way we cope with the dilemma of whether to raise something or avoid it. The potential costs involved in sharing feelings makes raising them feel like too big a gamble. When we lay our feelings on the table, we run the risk of hurting others and of ruining relationships. We also put ourselves in a position to get hurt. What if the other person doesn't take our feelings seriously or responds by telling us something we don't want to hear? By sticking to the "business at hand," we appear to reduce these risks.

The problem is that when feelings are at the heart of what's going on, they *are* the business at hand and ignoring them is nearly impossible. In many difficult conversations, it is really only at the level of feelings that the problem can be addressed. Framing the feelings out of the conversation is likely to result in outcomes that are unsatisfying for both people. The real problem is not dealt with, and further, emotions have an uncanny knack for finding their way back into the conversation, usually in not very helpful ways.

## Unexpressed Feelings Can Leak into the Conversation

Emma was stunned to learn that her friend and mentor, Kathy, had told the Executive Committee that she didn't think Emma was mature enough to handle the responsibility her new promotion required. "I felt so betrayed," says Emma. "I was hurt that Kathy would think such a thing, and furious that she'd say something to management rather than to me." Upon further reflection, Emma also admitted some self-doubt. "What if I'm *not* ready?" she worried.

Late that afternoon, Emma and Kathy had a brief exchange about the situation:

EMMA: I heard you told the Executive Committee that I couldn't handle the new responsibility.

KATHY: Wait a second. I didn't say you couldn't handle responsibility. I simply said I thought you were being promoted awfully fast. I don't want them to set you up to fail.

EMMA: Well you should have come to me if you had doubts.

KATHY: I was going to talk to you about it. But I also have an obligation to talk to management.

EMMA: You have an obligation to talk to me first. I can't believe you would jeopardize my career like this.

KATHY: Emma, I've always supported your career! This is a question of *when* you should be promoted, not *if*.

Rather than share her feelings, Emma provokes an argument about the rules of professional communication. At no point does Emma say "I feel hurt" or "I feel angry" or "I'm terrified that you might be right," yet these feelings have a significant effect on the conversation.

Unspoken feelings can color the conversation in a number of ways. They alter your affect and tone of voice. They express themselves through your body language or facial expression. They may take the form of long pauses or an odd and unexplained detachment. You may become sarcastic, aggressive, impatient, unpredictable, or defensive. Studies show that while few people are good at detecting factual lies, most of us can determine when someone is distorting, manufacturing, or withholding an emotion. That's because, if clogged, your emotional pipes will leak.

Indeed, unexpressed feelings can create so much tension that you disengage: you choose not to work with a particular colleague because you have so many unresolved feelings about them, or you become distant from your spouse, children, or friends.

## Unexpressed Feelings Can Burst into the Conversation

For some of us, the problem is not that we are unable to express our feelings, but that we are unable not to. We get angry and show it in ways that are embarrassing or destructive. We cry or explode when we would rather act composed and capable. Of course, there are many possible explanations for anger or tears, some of which have deep psychological roots. One common explanation, however, is just the opposite of what we might expect. We don't cry or lose our temper because we express our feelings too often, but because we express them too rarely. Like finally opening a carbonated drink that has been shaken, the results can be messy.

Edward, for example, had the troubling habit of shouting at his wife when he was feeling frustrated. He told us he was working on learning to control his feelings. No matter how upset he felt by his wife's behavior, he desperately tried not to let his emotions show. But eventually he'd explode. His explanation for this pattern was that he was simply too emotional, yet his efforts to contain himself only made the habit worse.

## Unexpressed Feelings Make It Difficult to Listen

Unexpressed feelings can cause a third, more subtle problem. The two hardest (and most important) communication tasks in difficult conversations are expressing feelings and listening. A significant pattern we've observed in our coaching involves the sometimes elusive relationship between the two skills. When people are having a hard time listening, often it is not because they don't know how to listen well. It is, paradoxically, because they don't know how to express themselves well. Unexpressed feelings can block the ability to listen.

Why? Because good listening requires an open and honest curiosity about the other person, and a willingness and ability to keep the spotlight on them. Buried emotions draw the spotlight back to us. Instead of wondering, "How does what they are saying make sense?"

and "Let me try to learn more," we have a record playing in our mind that is stuck in the groove of our own feelings: "I'm so angry with him!" "I feel like she just doesn't seem to care about me," "I feel so vulnerable right now." It's hard to hear someone else when we are feeling unheard, even if the reason we feel unheard is that we have chosen not to share. Our listening ability often increases remarkably once we have expressed our own strong feelings.

## Unexpressed Feelings Take a Toll on Our Self-Esteem and Relationships

When important feelings remain unexpressed, you may experience a loss of self-esteem, wondering why you don't stick up for yourself. You deprive your colleagues, friends, and family members of the op-portunity to learn and to change in response to your feelings. And, perhaps most damagingly, you hurt the relationship. By keeping your feelings out of the relationship you are keeping an important part of yourself out of the relationship.

# A Way Out of the Feelings Bind

There are ways to manage the problem of feelings. Working to get feelings into the conversation is almost always helpful as long as you do so in a purposive way. While the drawbacks of avoiding feelings are inevitable, the drawbacks of sharing feelings are not. If you are able to share feelings with skill, you can avoid many of the potential costs associated with expressing feelings and even reap some unex-pected benefits. This is the way out of the feelings bind.

By following a few key guidelines you can greatly increase your chances of getting your feelings into your conversations and into your relationships in ways that are healthy, meaningful, and satisfy-ing: first, you need to sort out just what your feelings are; second, you need to negotiate with your feelings; and third, you need to share your actual feelings, not attributions or judgments about the other person.

# Finding Your Feelings: Learn Where Feelings Hide

Most of us assume that knowing how we feel is no more complicated than knowing whether we are hot or cold. We just know. But in fact, we often don't know how we feel. Many of us know our own emotions about as well as we know a city we are visiting for the first time. We may recognize certain landmarks, but fail to understand the subtle rhythms of daily life; we can find the main boulevards, but remain oblivious to the tangle of back streets where the real action is. Before we can get to where we're going, we need to know where we are. When it comes to understanding our own emotions, where most of us are is lost.

This isn't because we're dumb, but because recognizing feelings is challenging. Feelings are more complex and nuanced than we usually imagine. What's more, feelings are very good at disguising themselves. Feelings we are uncomfortable with disguise themselves as emotions we are better able to handle; bundles of contradictory feelings masquerade as a single emotion; and most important, feelings transform themselves into judgments, accusations, and attributions.

## Explore Your Emotional Footprint

As we grow up, each of us develops a characteristic "emotional footprint" whose shape is determined by which feelings we believe are okay to have and express and which are not. Think back to when you were growing up. How did your family handle emotions? Which feelings were easily discussed, and which did people pretend weren't there? What was your role in the emotional life of the family? What emotions do you now find it easy to acknowledge and express, and with whom? Which do you find more difficult? As you consider your responses to these questions, the contours of your emotional footprint will begin to emerge.

Each of us has a unique footprint. You may believe that it's okay to feel longing or sadness, but not okay to feel anger. Anger may be easy for me to express, while feelings of shame or failure are off-limits. And it is not only so-called negative feelings that are implicated. Some of us find it easy to express disappointment, but difficult to express affection, pride, or gratitude.

While there may be common themes, your emotional footprint will be different in different relationships. Your awareness of and ability to express emotions will vary depending on whether you are with your mother, your best friend, your boss, or the person sitting next to you on the plane. Exploring the contours of your footprint across a variety of relationships can be extremely helpful in raising your awareness of what you are feeling and why.

**Accept That Feelings Are Normal and Natural.** One assumption many of us incorporate into our footprint is the assumption that there is something inherently wrong with having feelings. As Rick, a retired judge, observed, "In my family we were taught not to talk about our problems, or the feelings that accompany them." For some of us, merely *having* feelings, any feelings, is enough to cause us shame.

Depending on how we handle them, feelings can lead to great trouble. But the feelings themselves just *are*. In that sense, feelings are like arms or legs. If you hit or kick someone, then your arms or legs are causing trouble. But there's nothing inherently wrong with arms or legs. The same with feelings.

**Recognize That Good People Can Have Bad Feelings.** A second assumption many of us incorporate into our footprint is that there are certain emotions "good people" should never feel: good people don't get angry at people they love, they don't cry, they don't fail, and they are never a burden. If you are a good person, we've got good news: everyone feels anger, everyone experiences the urge to cry, everyone fails, and everyone needs other people.

You won't always be *happy* with what you're feeling. For example, you assume you should feel sad at your brother's funeral but find instead that you feel only rage. You know you should be excited about finally getting your dream job, but instead you're unmotivated and weepy. Whether or not it makes sense, you *are*. And while it might be more pleasant to have only good feelings toward your mother, there will be times when you feel irritated or resentful or ashamed. We all experience such conflict, and it has nothing to do with whether or not we are a good person.

There are times when denying feelings serves a deeper psychological function: in the face of overwhelming anxiety, fear, loss, or trauma, removing yourself from your feelings can help you cope with daily life. As the saying goes, "Don't knock down a wall until you know why it was put up." At the same time, the reality is that unacknowledged feelings are going to have an effect on communication. All things being equal, it is better to strive toward an understanding of your feelings, perhaps over time with a therapist or a trusted friend. As you begin to feel things that were there all along and begin to deal with the underlying causes of these feelings, your interactions with others — including difficult conversations — will become increasingly easy to handle.

**Learn That Your Feelings Are as Important as Theirs.** Some of us can't see our own feelings because we have learned somewhere along the way that other people's feelings are more important than ours.

For example, it was always assumed that your father would move in with your family when his health began to fail. But now that he has, his constant demands and crankiness are beginning to take a toll, especially on top of managing his medications and frequent doctor's visits. You are exhausted and frustrated, and wonder why your brother isn't willing to do his share. Yet you don't raise it with parent or sibling. "It's hard, but it's not *that* hard," you reason. "Besides, I don't want to rock the boat."

Your girlfriend calls and says she can't have dinner on Friday after all. She's wondering whether Saturday is okay. She says a friend of hers is in town and wants to see a movie on Friday. You say, "Sure, if that's better for you." Although you said yes, Saturday is actually not as good for you, because you had planned to go to a baseball game. Still, you'd rather see your girlfriend, so you give your ticket away.

In each of these situations, you've chosen to put someone else's feelings ahead of your own. Does this make sense? Is your father's frustration or your brother's peace of mind more important than yours? Is your girlfriend's desire to see a movie with her friend more important than your desire to see a baseball game? Why is it that they express their feelings and preferences, but you cope with yours privately?

There are several reasons why you may choose to honor others' feelings even when it means dishonoring your own. The implicit rule you are following is that you should put other people's happiness before your own. If your friends or loved ones or colleagues don't get their way, they'll feel bad, and then you'll have to deal with the consequences. That may be true, but it's unfair to you. Their anger is no better or worse than yours.

"Well, it's just easier not to rock the boat," you think. "I don't like it when they're mad at me." If you're thinking this, then you are undervaluing your own feelings and interests. Friends, neighbors, and bosses will recognize this and begin to see you as someone they can manipulate. When you are more concerned about others' feelings than your own, you teach others to ignore your feelings too. And beware: one of the reasons you haven't raised the issue is that you don't want to jeopardize the relationship. Yet by *not* raising it, the resentment you feel will grow and slowly erode the relationship anyway.

## Find the Bundle of Feelings Behind the Simple Labels

Brad and his mother were often at odds over Brad's job search. Brad's mother called frequently to prod her son to send off résumés, to go to interviews, to network. For his part, Brad wasn't much interested. He tuned his mother out or tried to change the subject.

He talked to a friend about the problem, and she counseled him not to withdraw but instead to tell his mother how he was feeling. "What good will that do?" Brad asked. "All I'm feeling is angry. She drives me crazy." But Brad's friend persisted, encouraging him to consider what he felt in addition to anger. Brad took on his friend's challenge, and that evening he made a list of all the things he was feeling — about the job search, about his mother, and about himself.

He was stunned. About the job search, he was feeling hopeless, confused, and afraid. Putting off the search was Brad's way of putting off some of the anxiety. About his mother, Brad's feelings were more complex. On the one hand, he did indeed experience her constant prodding as a great annoyance. On the other hand, he also experienced it as a form of love and caring, and that meant a great deal to him.

About himself, Brad felt mostly shame. He believed he was letting his mother down and that, at least up until now, he was wasting his potential and his college education. But even as he felt shame, he felt some pride as well. Several of his friends had gotten jobs in management training, and Brad too could have taken this route. But that wasn't what he wanted, and he was willing to accept the pressure of the search to hold out for something that fit him better. In the meantime, he was supporting himself with odd jobs, and had never asked for a penny from his mother.

By suggesting that Brad felt more than just anger, Brad's friend offered him a powerful insight. Where he had originally seen only one emotion, Brad was able to find an entire spectrum of emotions.

In many situations, we are blinded to the complexity of our feelings by one strong feeling that trumps all the others. In Brad's case it was anger. In other situations, and for different people, it may be a different emotion.

Simply becoming familiar with the spectrum of difficult-to-find feelings may trigger a flash of recognition for you. On p. 96, there is a partial list of some feelings that, though quite familiar in the abstract, are sometimes difficult for people to identify in themselves or express to others.

**Don't Let Hidden Feelings Block Other Emotions.** Another common pattern is the existence of a feeling we are not even aware of, but that interferes with our experiences nonetheless.

Jamila had difficulty expressing her feelings of love toward her husband. "I know I love him," she said. "He's been generous and a good husband, putting up with all my stuff. But I have such a hard time letting him know that I love him." Something was acting as a block, and she wasn't exactly sure what it was.

At first, Jamila blamed herself: "Maybe this is just another way that I'm inadequate. A good wife can tell her husband she cares about him." In our effort to coach her, we asked Jamila if she ever expressed other feelings about her husband. We

---

### A Landscape of Sometimes Hard-to-Find Feelings

**Love**
Affectionate, caring, close, proud, passionate

**Anger**
Frustrated, exasperated, enraged, indignant

**Hurt**
Let down, betrayed, disappointed, needy

**Shame**
Embarrassed, guilty, regretful, humiliated, self-loathing

**Fear**
Anxious, terrified, worried, obsessed, suspicious

**Self-Doubt**
Inadequate, unworthy, inept, unmotivated

**Joy**
Happy, enthusiastic, full, elated, content

**Sadness**
Bereft, wistful, joyless, depressed

**Jealousy**
Envious, selfish, covetous, anguished, yearning

**Gratitude**
Appreciative, thankful, relieved, admiring

**Loneliness**
Desolate, abandoned, empty, longing

---

were specifically interested in whether she expressed anger or disappointment. "You're missing the point," she asserted. "I'm trying to learn to express love. If anyone has the right to be angry, it's my husband, for having to put up with me all the time."

This comment raised some flags. In any marriage, in any relationship, each person will feel at least some anger toward the other. "Have you ever felt anger toward your husband?" we asked. "I suppose on occasion," she finally said. "What would you say to your husband," we asked, "if you could let your guard down completely, if you could vent at him — get everything off your chest — with absolutely no consequences attached?"

After a slow start, Jamila was surprisingly forthcoming: "Sure, I'm not the best wife, but it's no wonder I run from you every chance I get! I'm sick of you playing the victim all the time, sick of your petty fears and constant complaining! I may not be perfect, but you're not God's gift either, pal! Do you ever stop to think of the impact your constant sniping has on me?!"

As soon as she finished, Jamila added, "Of course, I would never say any of that, and, really, I don't know if any of it is very fair. . . ." It doesn't matter if it's fair or reasonable or rational. What matters is that it is there. You can imagine the effect her buried anger was having on Jamila's ability to express love for her husband. Or, for that matter, on her attempts to express any feelings at all. The anger, though she kept it hidden even from herself, was getting in the way. Jamila put it well: "If I could just share some of that, it would be easy to balance it with the love I feel."

Let's hold for a moment the important question of whether and how to express feelings such as anger. We'll return to this example in the section below on negotiating with your feelings.

## Find the Feelings Lurking Under Attributions, Judgments, and Accusations

Peanuts aren't nuts. Whales aren't fish. Tomatoes aren't vegetables. And attributions, judgments, and accusations aren't feelings.

**Lift the Lid on Attributions and Judgments.** As we have seen, one danger of making attributions about the intentions of others is that it can lead to defensiveness and misunderstandings. A second danger is that the attributions themselves are so consuming that we fail to see the real feelings that are motivating them.

This happened to Emily in her relationship with her friend Roz. "Roz just isn't warm," Emily explains. "I helped her through her divorce, talked with her all the time, kept her company when she was feeling lonely. I was always there for her. And she never said a word of thanks." Emily claims that she has already shared her feelings with Roz and that it didn't help.

What, exactly, had Emily said to Roz? "I told Roz exactly how I felt. I was honest. I told her that at times she can be self-absorbed and thoughtless. And true to form, she went on the attack. She told me I was being oversensitive. That's what you get when you talk about your feelings with someone like Roz. It's not worth it."

Notice what Emily has communicated. She said, "You are self-absorbed. You are thoughtless." Both of these are judgments about Roz. Neither of them is a statement of how Emily feels. Prodded by this observation, Emily is able to focus more clearly on her own feelings: "I guess I feel hurt. I feel confused about the friendship. I feel angry at Roz. At some level I feel sort of embarrassed that I put all this work into a friendship that obviously wasn't that important to her. How stupid can I be?"

---

**We Translate Our Feelings Into**

**Judgments**
"If you were a good friend you would have been there for me."

**Attributions**
"Why were you trying to hurt me?"

**Characterizations**
"You're just so inconsiderate."

**Problem-Solving**
"The answer is for you to call me more often."

---

The difference between judgments about others and statements of our own feelings is sometimes difficult to see. Judgments *feel* like feelings when we are saying them. They are motivated by anger or frustration or hurt, and the person on the receiving end understands very clearly that we are feeling something. Unfortunately, that person probably isn't sure what we are feeling, and more important, is focused on the fact that we are judging, attributing, and blaming. That's only natural.

While they may feel similar, there is a vast difference between "You are thoughtless and self-absorbed" and "I feel hurt, confused, and embarrassed." Finding the feelings that are lurking around and under angry attributions and judgments is a key step in bringing feelings into a conversation effectively.

**Use the Urge to Blame as a Clue to Find Important Feelings.** A common complaint when we encourage people to talk in terms of joint contribution rather than blame is that the ensuing conversation leaves them feeling unsatisfied. It is as if they are stuck with a bowl of fat-free yogurt when they're craving real ice cream. As a result, they tend to conclude that talking about contribution is not the real thing, that they really need to blame the other side.

What is unsatisfying, though, is not the failure to express blame, but the failure to express feelings. The urge to blame arises when the contribution system is explored in a feelings vacuum. When we can't seem to get past needing to say, "Admit it! This was your fault!" we should recognize that as an important clue that we are sitting on unexpressed emotions. The sense of incompleteness that sometimes accompanies a conversation about contribution should not be a stimulus to blame, but a stimulus to search further for hidden feelings. Once those feelings are expressed ("Here's what I've contributed, here's what I think you've contributed, and, more important, I ended up feeling abandoned"), the urge to blame recedes.

# Don't Treat Feelings as Gospel: Negotiate with Them

A colleague of ours has two rules for expressing feelings. He begins by explaining rule number two: try to get everything you are feeling into the conversation. Most people are horrified by this rule. Surely, we think to ourselves, there are plenty of feelings that are better left unexpressed. Which brings our friend to rule number one: before saying what you are feeling, *negotiate* with your feelings.

Most of us assume that our feelings are static and nonnegotiable, and that if they are to be shared authentically, they must be shared "as is." In fact, our feelings are based on our perceptions, and our perceptions (as we have seen in the preceding three chapters) *are* negotiable. As we see the world in new ways, our feelings shift accordingly. Before sharing feelings, then, it is crucial to negotiate — with ourselves.

What does it mean to negotiate with our feelings? Fundamentally, it involves a recognition that our feelings are formed in response to our thoughts. Imagine that while scuba diving, you suddenly see a shark glide into view. Your heart starts to pound and your anxiety skyrockets. You're terrified, which is a perfectly rational and understandable feeling.

Now imagine that your marine biology training enables you to identify it as a Reef Shark, which you know doesn't prey on anything as large as you. Your anxiety disappears. Instead you feel excited and curious to observe the shark's behavior. It isn't the shark that's changed; it's the story you tell yourself about what's happening. In any given situation our feelings follow our thoughts.

This means that the route to changing your feelings is through altering your *thinking*. As we saw in the "What Happened?" Conversation, our thinking is often distorted in predictable ways, providing rich ground for negotiating with our emotions. First, we need to examine our own story. What is the story we are telling ourselves that is giving rise to how we feel? What is our story missing? What might the other person's story be? Almost always, an increased awareness of the other person's story changes how we feel.

Next, we need to explore our assumptions about the other person's intentions. To what extent are our feelings based on an untested assumption about their intentions? Might the other person have acted unintentionally, or from multiple and conflicting intentions? How does our view of their intentions affect how we feel? And what about our own intentions? What was motivating us? How might our actions have impacted them? Does that change how we feel?

Finally, we should consider the contribution system. Are we able to see our own contribution to the problem? Are we able to describe the other person's contribution without blaming? Are we aware of the ways that each of our contributions forms a reinforcing pattern that magnifies the problem? In what way does this shift how we feel?

We don't need definitive answers to these questions. Indeed, until we have had a conversation with the other person, we can only hypothesize. But it is enough to raise the questions, to grapple with them, to walk around the sculpture of our feelings and observe it from different angles. If we are thoughtful, if we are honest, if we approach the questions openly and with a spirit of fairness, our feelings will begin to shift. Our anger may lose its edge; our hurt may run less deeply; our feelings of betrayal or abandonment or shame or anxiety may feel more manageable.

Consider again Jamila's situation with her husband. Venting to us helped Jamila get in touch with her feelings of anger. But anger was not all she was feeling, nor upon reflection did she think of herself as a victim or her husband as entirely pathetic. When she considered the situation from his point of view, when she asked herself what his intentions might have been, when she focused not on blame but on what each of them had contributed, her portrait of the situation became more complex, as did her feelings.

She was able to take the And Stance and keep several things in her head at once, and to share all of those things with her husband. "I know I've contributed to the problems we're having," she told him. "I think that the anger and frustration I've been feeling in reaction to your contributions has made me focus more on our problems than on our strengths. But when I step back from that, what's also clear to me is that I love you very much, and I'd like for things to get better." Jamila realized that by working, however slowly, to express some of her feelings of anger, she would be clearing the way to express the love that originally motivated her to seek help.

# Don't Vent: *Describe* Feelings Carefully

Once you have found your feelings and negotiated with them, you
face the task of deciding how to handle those feelings. There will be
times when you decide that sharing your feelings is unnecessary or
unhelpful. At other times, of course, your feelings will take center
stage in the conversation.

Too often we confuse being emotional with expressing emotions
clearly. They are different. You can express emotion well without being emotional, and you can be extremely emotional without expressing much of anything at all. Sharing feelings well and clearly
requires thoughtfulness. Below are three guidelines for expressing
your feelings that should help ease your anxiety and make an effective conversation more likely.

## 1. Frame Feelings Back into the Problem

Step one in expressing feelings well involves simply remembering
that they're important. Almost every difficult conversation will involve strong feelings. It is always possible to define a problem without
reference to feelings. But that's not true problem-solving. If feelings
are the real issue, then feelings should be addressed.

Your feelings need not be rational to be expressed. Thinking that
you *shouldn't* feel as you do will rarely change the fact that you do.
Your feelings, at least for the moment, are an important aspect of the
relationship. You can preface their expression with an admission that
you are uncomfortable with these feelings, or that you aren't sure
they make sense, but follow that preface by expressing them. Your
purpose here is simply to get them out. You can decide what, if anything, to do about them later.

## 2. Express the Full Spectrum of Your Feelings

Let's return to the conversation between Brad and his mother about Brad's job search. It's easy to see why Brad would be hesitant to express his emotions when he's aware only of his anger. He imagines himself telling his mother he's angry at her, only to have her say the same back. At best, the conversation won't go anywhere. More likely, they will each feel even angrier than before.

But what if Brad took the time to paint a more complete picture? Instead of saying, "Mom, you're driving me crazy!" Brad might say, "When you ask me how the job search is going, I feel a couple of things. One thing I feel is angry. I suppose that's because I've asked you not to bring it up, and you do anyway. But at the same time, part of me is appreciative, and reassured that things will be okay. It means a lot that you're looking out for me and that you care."

And when his mother asks why he's not being more aggressive about looking for a job, rather than saying, "Stop bugging me," Brad might say, "It's hard for me to talk with you about this. Whenever I think about it, I end up feeling ashamed, like maybe I'm wasting my potential or letting you down."

By putting the broader spectrum of his feelings into the conversation, Brad has changed the nature of the conversation. It's no longer a battle of anger. Brad has brought some depth and complexity to the discussion, and given his mother some things to reflect on. She better understands what is motivating her son's behavior, and the impact of her actions on him. The conversation doesn't end with Brad's expression of feeling; indeed, that's just the beginning. Nor does expressing the full range of emotion make the conversation "easy." But it may well be less contentious, lead to greater understanding and engagement, and point the way toward different patterns of interacting that are more mutually supportive.

## 3. Don't Evaluate — Just Share

Getting everyone's feelings on the table, heard and acknowledged, is essential before you can begin to sort through them. If you say, "I felt hurt," and they say, "You're overreacting," the process of struggling toward deeper understanding of each other and of the problem is short-circuited. Premature evaluation of whether feelings are legitimate will undermine their expression and, ultimately, the relationship. You can establish an evaluation-free zone by respecting the following guidelines: share pure feelings (without judgments, attributions, or blame); save problem-solving until later; and don't monopolize.

**Express Your Feelings Without Judging, Attributing, or Blaming.** People often say, "I've expressed my feelings, and all it did was cause a fight." Remember the story of Emily and Roz. Emily told Roz that she thought Roz was "thoughtless and self-absorbed," because Roz had not thanked Emily for being a good friend during Roz's divorce. Not surprisingly, Roz became defensive and angry.

After realizing that she had expressed judgments about Roz rather than her own feelings, Emily started over: "Instead of judging her, I just explained that I felt hurt. And confused about the state of our friendship. I was amazed. She was very contrite, and couldn't stop thanking me for how I had helped her."

Talking successfully about feelings requires you to be scrupulous about taking the judgments, attributions, and statements of blame out of what you are saying, and putting the statement of feeling in. It is crucial to look at the actual words you are using to see whether those words really convey what you want them to. For example, the statement "You are so damn undependable!" is a judgment about the other person's character. There is no reference in the statement to how the speaker feels. We should not be surprised if the response is "I am *not* undependable!"

In contrast, the statement "I feel frustrated. You didn't send the letter out," removes the blame and focuses on the feelings underneath. Such a formulation won't make all of your problems disappear, but it is more likely to lead to a productive discussion.

A more subtle but equally common difficulty occurs when we mix a pure statement of feelings with a statement of blame. We say, "You didn't call me like you said. It's your fault that I felt hurt." This statement contains a feeling — "I felt hurt" — but it also contains a conclusion about causation, of who is to blame for my being hurt. The person you are talking with is likely to focus on the fact that you are blaming them rather than focus on your feelings. A better way to express this is to state the pure feeling first — "When you didn't call, I felt hurt" — and to explore joint contribution (not blame) later.

**Don't Monopolize: Both Sides Can Have Strong Feelings at the Same Time.** If you and your significant other are grocery shopping, it is unlikely that only one of you will be putting food into the grocery cart. Instead, you'll both be tossing in your favorite items. The same is true when discussing feelings. You can feel angry at your boss for the way she treated you when you arrived at work late, and she can feel annoyed with you for not getting the memo done on time. If you have strong feelings, it's quite likely that the other person does too. And just as your own ambivalent feelings don't cancel each other out, their feelings don't cancel yours, or vice versa. What's important is to get both parties' strong and perhaps conflicting emotions into the conversational cart before you head for the checkout.

**An Easy Reminder: Say "I Feel . . . ."** It is surprising how many people would prefer to have a cavity filled without novocaine than to utter the simple words "I feel." Yet these words can have a powerful effect on your listener.

Beginning with "I feel . . . ." is a simple act that carries with it extraordinary benefits. It keeps the focus on feelings and makes clear that you are speaking only from your perspective. It avoids the translation trap of judging or accusing. "Why do you insist on undermining me in front of the kids?!" for example, is a promising start — for an argument. Your spouse will obviously hear that you are upset or angry, but you haven't expressed an emotion at all — only a judgment about your spouse's intentions and parenting skills. If you begin instead with, "When you disagree with me about child-rearing in front of the kids, I feel betrayed, and also worried about the message it sends to them," your spouse cannot argue with how you feel. Your spouse is less likely to feel defensive and more likely to engage in a conversation about your feelings, theirs, and disciplinary strategies you can develop together.

## The Importance of Acknowledgment

Describing feelings is an important first step along the road toward getting things resolved, but you can't leap from there directly into problem-solving. Each side must have their feelings *acknowledged* before you can even start down that road. Acknowledgment is a step that simply cannot be skipped.

What does it mean to acknowledge someone's feelings? It means letting the other person know that what they have said has made an impression on you, that their feelings matter to you, and that you are working to understand them. "Wow," you might say, "I never knew you felt that way," or, "I kind of assumed you were feeling that, and I'm glad you felt comfortable enough with me to share it," or, "It sounds like this is really important to you." Let them know that you think understanding their perspective is important, and that you are trying to do so: "Before I give you a sense of what's going on with me, tell me more about your feeling that I talk down to you."

It's tempting to jump over feelings. We want to get on with things, to address the problem, to make everything better. We often seek to get feelings out of the way by "fixing" them: "Well, let's see. If you're feeling lonely, I guess I'll try to spend more time with you." Or even: "You're right. What can I say?" This may be the other person's honest response to your feelings, and it is good they are sharing their reaction. But they're doing it too soon.

To avoid this short circuit, direct the conversation back to the purpose of understanding: "I'm not saying you intended to hurt me. I don't know whether you did or not. What's important to me is that you understand how I felt when you criticized my work in front of the department." Before moving on to problem-solving, you have a responsibility to yourself and to the other person to ensure that they appreciate the importance of this topic to you; that they truly understand your feelings; and that they value your having shared them. If they aren't getting how important something is to you and you don't flag it, then you are letting yourself down.

Acknowledging feelings is crucial in any relationship, and particularly so in what are sometimes referred to as "intractable conflicts." In one case, the simple act of acknowledging feelings helped transform a community divided by racial tensions. A small group of police officers, political leaders, businesspeople, and neighborhood residents gathered to discuss a series of recent incidents between police officers and minority community members. When asked afterward whether he thought he had changed any minds, a black teenager, in tears, responded, "You don't understand. I don't want to change their minds. I just wanted to share my story. I didn't want to hear that everything will be okay or to hear that it wasn't their fault, or to have them tell me that their stories are just as terrible. I wanted to tell my story, to share my feelings. So why am I crying? Because now I know: they care enough about me to just listen."

## Sometimes Feelings Are All That Matter

As soon as Max, our bride-to-be's father, shared his feelings of loss and pride with his daughter, resolving issues about how to spend money on the wedding became easy. The troubling subtexts of their previous conversations — feelings of rejection on Max's part, or resentment at Max's apparent need to be in control on his daughter's part — were discussed explicitly and ceased to get in the way of further logistical problem-solving. And the two of them began to form a relationship based on an honest expression of who they were and what they wanted to be to each other.

Sometimes, however, feelings aren't all that matter. Sometimes they are difficult and troubling, and you still have a job to do together or kids to raise. The process of working on your relationship, or solving the problem you face, can be a long and hard one. Even so, it's one where being able to communicate effectively with the other person — about your feelings and about the problem — will be critical.

# The Identity
# Conversation

• • • • •

# 6

# Ground Your Identity:
## *Ask Yourself What's at Stake*

I've already accepted a job elsewhere, and all that's left for me to do is tell my boss I'm leaving. I don't need any references or future business, and no one can influence my decision. And still, when I think of telling my boss, I'm *terrified*.

— Ben, software company vice president

Viewed from the outside, Ben would seem to have nothing to fear; he holds all the cards. Even so, Ben isn't getting any sleep.

He explains: "My father worked for one company his whole life, and I always admired his loyalty. In my own life, I've tried to do the right thing, and for me a big part of that is sticking by the people around me — my parents, my wife, my children, and my colleagues. Telling my boss I'm leaving raises this loyalty issue directly. My boss was also my mentor, and has been very supportive. The whole thing is making me wonder: Am I really the loyal soldier I like to think I am, or just another greedy jerk willing to betray someone for the right price?"

## Difficult Conversations Threaten Our Identity

Ben's predicament highlights a crucial aspect of why some conversations can be so overwhelmingly difficult. Our anxiety results not just from having to face the other person, but from having to face *ourselves*. The conversation has the potential to disrupt our sense of who we are in the world, or to highlight what we hope we are but fear we are not. The conversation poses a threat to our identity — the story we tell ourselves about ourselves — and having our identity threatened can be profoundly disturbing.

## Three Core Identities

There are probably as many identities as there are people. But three identity issues seem particularly common, and often underlie what concerns us most during difficult conversations: Am I competent? Am I a good person? Am I worthy of love?

- **Am I Competent?** "I agonized about whether to bring up the subject of my salary. Spurred on by my colleagues, I finally did. Before I could even get started, my supervisor said, 'I'm surprised you want to discuss this. The truth is, I've been disappointed by your performance this year.' I felt nauseous. Maybe I'm not the talented chemist I thought I was."

- **Am I a Good Person?** "I had intended to break up with Sandra that night. I began in a roundabout way, and as soon as she got the drift, she started to cry. It hurt me so much to see her in such pain. The hardest thing for me in life is hurting people I care about; it goes against who I am spiritually and emotionally. I just couldn't bear how I was feeling, and after a few moments I was telling her how much I loved her and that everything would work out between us."

- **Am I Worthy of Love?** "I began a conversation with my brother about the way he treats his wife. He talks down to her and I know it really bothers her. I was hugely nervous bringing it up, and my words were getting all twisted. Then he shouted, 'Who are you to tell me how to act?! You've never had a real relationship in your whole life!' After that, I could hardly breathe, let alone talk. All I could think about was how I wanted to get out of there."

Suddenly, who we thought we were when we walked into the conversation is called into question.

## An Identity Quake Can Knock Us Off Balance

Internally, our Identity Conversation is in full swing: "Maybe I *am* mediocre," "How can I be the kind of person who causes others pain?" or "My brother's right. No woman has ever loved me." In each case, it is what this conversation seems to be saying about us that rips the ground from beneath our feet.

Getting knocked off balance can even cause you to react physically in ways that make the conversation go from difficult to impossible. Images of yourself or of the future are hardwired to your adrenal response, and shaking them up can cause an unmanageable rush of anxiety or anger, or an intense desire to get away. Well-being is replaced with depression, hope with hopelessness, efficacy with fear. And all the while you're trying to engage in the extremely delicate task of communicating clearly and effectively. Your supervisor is explaining why you're not being promoted; you're busy having your own private identity quake.

## There's No Quick Fix

You can't "quake-proof" your sense of self. Grappling with identity issues is what life and growth are all about, and no amount of love or accomplishment or skill can insulate you from these challenges. Seeing your husband cry when you tell him you don't want to have another child, or hearing your coach say "Grow up" when you raise the issue of discriminatory treatment on the team, *will* test your sense of who you are in these relationships and in the world.

Not all identity challenges are earthshaking, but some will be. A difficult conversation can cause you to relinquish a cherished aspect of how you see yourself. At its most profound, this can be a loss that requires mourning just as surely as the death of a loved one. There's no use pretending there's a quick fix, or that you will never again lose your balance, or that life's toughest challenges can be overcome by mastering a few easy steps.

But there is some good news. You can improve your ability to recognize and cope with identity issues when they hit. Thinking clearly and honestly about who you are can help reduce your anxiety level during the conversation and significantly strengthen your foundation in its aftermath.

## Vulnerable Identities: The All-or-Nothing Syndrome

Getting better at managing the Identity Conversation starts with understanding the ways in which we make ourselves vulnerable to being knocked off balance. The biggest factor that contributes to a vulnerable identity is "all-or-nothing" thinking: I'm either competent or incompetent, good or evil, worthy of love or not.

The primary peril of all-or-nothing thinking is that it leaves our identity extremely unstable, making us hypersensitive to feedback. When faced with negative information about ourselves, all-or-nothing thinking gives us only two choices for how to manage that information, both of which cause serious problems. Either we try to deny the information that is inconsistent with our self-image, or we do the opposite: we take in the information in a way that exaggerates its importance to a crippling degree. All-or-nothing identities are about as sturdy as a two-legged stool.

### Denial

Clinging to a purely positive identity leaves no place in our self-concept for negative feedback. If I think of myself as a supercompetent person who never makes mistakes, then feedback suggesting that I have made a mistake presents a problem. The only way to keep my identity intact is to deny the feedback — to figure out why it's not really true, why it doesn't really matter, or why what I did wasn't actually a mistake.

Recall the chemist who asked for a raise. Her boss responded by saying, "I'm surprised you want to discuss this. The truth is, I've been disappointed by your performance this year." The chemist must now decide how to internalize this information, and what this says about her identity. The denial response might sound like this: "My boss knows business, but not chemistry. He doesn't understand how important my contributions have been. I wish I had a boss who could appreciate just how good I am."

Working to keep negative information out during a difficult conversation is like trying to swim without getting wet. If we're going to engage in difficult conversations, or in life for that matter, we're going to come up against information about ourselves that we find unpleasant. Denial requires a huge amount of psychic energy, and sooner or later the story we're telling ourselves is going to become untenable. *And the bigger the gap between what we hope is true and what we fear is true, the easier it is for us to lose our balance.*

## Exaggeration

The alternative to denial is exaggeration. In all-or-nothing thinking, taking in negative feedback requires us not just to adjust our self-image, but to *flip* it. If I'm not completely competent, then I'm completely *in*competent: "Maybe I'm not as creative and special as I thought I was. I'll probably never amount to anything. Maybe I'll even get fired."

**We Let Their Feedback Define Who We Are.** When we exaggerate, we act as if the other person's feedback is the *only* information we have about ourselves. We put everything up for grabs, and let what they say dictate how we see ourselves. We may turn in a hundred memos on time, but if we are criticized for being late with the 101st memo, we think to ourselves, "I can never do *anything* right." This one piece of information fills our whole identity screen.

This example may seem ridiculous, but we all think like this on occasion, and not only around dramatic or traumatic events. If the waitress gives you a funny look as she collects her tip, you're cheap. If you don't help your friends paint their house, you're selfish. If your brother says you don't visit his children enough, you're an uncaring aunt. It's easy to see why exaggeration is such a debilitating reaction.

# Ground Your Identity

Improving your ability to manage the Identity Conversation has two steps. First, you need to become familiar with those identity issues that are important to you, so you can spot them during a conversation. Second, you need to learn to integrate new information into your identity in ways that are healthy — a step that requires you to let go of all-or-nothing thinking.

## Step One: Become Aware of Your Identity Issues

Often during a difficult conversation we are not even aware that our identity is implicated. We know we feel anxious, fearful, or tentative, and that our ability to communicate skillfully has deserted us. Usually articulate, we stumble and stammer; usually empathetic, we can't stop interrupting and arguing; usually calm, we boil over with anger. But we aren't sure why. The connection to our identity is not obvious. It's easy to think, "I'm talking with my brother about how he treats his wife. What does this have to do with my identity?"

What triggers an identity quake for you may not trigger one in someone else. We each have our own particular sensitivities. To become more familiar with yours, observe whether there are patterns to what tends to knock you off balance during difficult conversations, and then ask yourself why. What about your identity feels at risk?

What does this mean to you? How would it feel if what you fear were true?

It may take some digging. Consider Jimmy's story. Growing up, Jimmy developed a reputation for being emotionally distant. This posture helped protect him from all the emotional shrapnel he was exposed to in his home life. Everyone else might be quick to fly off the handle, but not Jimmy. He'd be rational to a fault.

But after years on his own, Jimmy changed. He began to see the value of acknowledging and sharing his emotions, and doing so with friends and colleagues added to the richness of his life. He wanted to reveal this change to his family, but was afraid. The patterns of who he was with them were deeply etched and, though far from perfect, were comfortable and predictable. His detachment had costs, but they were familiar costs.

He discussed his fears with a friend, who asked Jimmy some hard questions: "What are you really afraid of? What's the downside?" Jimmy's first response was that he was acting out of obligation to his family: "Someone in my family has to be the rational one. Otherwise, it will be chaos. The way things are now, everything more or less works."

All true, but Jimmy continued to consider his friend's questions and pushed himself for deeper answers. Eventually he discovered the fear that at some level he knew was there all along: "What if they reject me? What if they laugh? What if they think, 'What's gotten into him?'" Jimmy knew he'd be in for a serious identity shake-up if his parents responded badly, and he wasn't sure he wanted to risk it.

Jimmy's increased awareness of his identity concerns wasn't the end of the story. He determined he would show greater emotion around his family, and at first, the going was not smooth. There were awkward moments, and some members of his family wondered why he was acting differently. But Jimmy persisted, and in time a more genuine set of relationships replaced the old ones.

## Step Two: Complexify Your Identity (Adopt the And Stance)

Once you've identified which aspects of your identity are most important to you or seem most vulnerable, you can begin to complexify your self-image. This means moving away from the false choice between "I am perfect" and "I am worthless," and trying to get as clear a picture as you can about what is actually true about you. As for everyone, what is true about you is going to be a mix of good and bad behavior, noble and less noble intentions, and wise and unwise choices you've made along the way.

For even the best and worst among us, all-or-nothing identities oversimplify the world. "I'm always there for my children." "When it comes to dating, I just have bad judgment." "I'm always a good listener." No one is *always* anything. We each exhibit a constellation of qualities, positive and negative, and constantly grapple with how to respond to the complicated situations life presents. And we don't always respond as competently or compassionately as we'd like.

Ben's fear of telling his boss that he has accepted another job is a good example of this. Is Ben loyal or is he a sellout? Both of those are simplifying labels that can't capture the complexity of the endless interactions Ben has had with the many people in his life. He has made many sacrifices for his family and many for his boss. He has worked weekends, turned down other job offers, worked hard to help the company recruit top talent. The list of things Ben has done that indicate loyalty is long indeed.

*And*, Ben *is* leaving his job for higher paying work elsewhere. It's reasonable for his boss to feel abandoned. That doesn't mean Ben is a bad person. It doesn't mean Ben has made a choice based on greed. He wants to put his children through college; he has been under-compensated for years and not complained.

What, then, is the bottom line on Ben? The bottom line is that there is no bottom line. Ben can feel good about many of his actions and choices, and ambivalent or regretful about others. Life is too complex for any reasonable person to feel otherwise. Indeed, a self-image that allows for complexity is healthy and robust; it provides a sturdy foundation on which to stand.

## Three Things to Accept About Yourself

No doubt, there are some aspects of who you are that you will struggle with for a lifetime. When you look inside, you won't always like what you see, and you'll find that accepting those parts of yourself takes serious work. But as you move away from an all-or-nothing identity and toward a more complex view of who you are, you'll notice that it is easier to accept certain parts of yourself that have given you trouble in the past.

There are three characteristics that are particularly important to be able to accept about yourself in difficult conversations. The more easily you can admit to your own mistakes, your own mixed intentions, and your own contributions to the problem, the more balanced you will feel during the conversation, and the higher the chances it will go well.

**1. You Will Make Mistakes.** If you can't admit to yourself that you sometimes make mistakes, you'll find it more difficult to understand and accept the legitimate aspects of the other person's story about what is going on.

Consider what happened between Rita and Isaiah. "It's important to me to be trustworthy — someone friends can really talk to," Rita explains. "That's part of being a good friend. Isaiah, one of my co-workers, confided in me that he was struggling with alcoholism, and I promised to keep it confidential. But I knew that a mutual friend had faced many of the same issues in the past, and so I talked with her about Isaiah's problem, to get some advice.

"Then Isaiah found out, and he was really furious. At first, I kept trying to explain that I was trying to help, and that my friend could be a valuable resource. Eventually I realized that the reason I was arguing was that I couldn't admit to myself that I had violated his trust, plain and simple. I didn't live up to my word. Once I was able to admit to myself that I made a mistake, Isaiah and I began to get somewhere in our conversation."

When you hold yourself to an all-or-nothing standard, even a small mistake can seem catastrophic and almost impossible to admit. If you are busy trying to shore up your "no mistakes, no failures" identity, you won't be able to engage in a meaningful learning conversation. And if you can't do that, you are likely to make the same mistakes again.

One reason people are reluctant to admit mistakes is that they fear being seen as weak or incompetent. Yet often, generally competent people who take the possibility of mistakes in stride are seen as confident, secure, and "big enough" not to have to be perfect, whereas those who resist acknowledging even the possibility of a mistake are seen as insecure and *lacking* confidence. No one is fooled.

**2. Your Intentions Are Complex.** Sometimes we get nervous about upcoming conversations because we know that our past behavior was not always motivated by good intentions.

Consider the situation that Sally and her boyfriend, Evan, find themselves in. Sally wants to break up with Evan, but is afraid that he will accuse her of just using him to get through a lonely period. Before Sally claims that her intentions were purely positive, she should think honestly about whether they actually were. Although in the big picture Sally didn't want to hurt Evan and wasn't acting maliciously, there was at least a bit of selfishness in Sally's behavior.

By being honest with herself about the complexity of her motivations, Sally has a better chance of staying on her feet if the accusation of having bad intentions arises. And she can respond in a way that is genuine: "As I think about it, some of what you're saying makes sense. I *was* lonely, and being with you helped. I don't think that was my only reason for wanting to be with you. I did hope it would work out. There are lots of pieces to what was going on for me."

**3. You Have Contributed to the Problem.** A third crucial step for grounding yourself involves assessing and taking responsibility for what you've contributed to the problem.

This is not always easy to do. Walker recently learned that his daughter Annie Mae is struggling with an eating disorder. Her college advisor called, letting Walker know that Annie Mae had checked herself into the university health clinic. Walker called to see how Annie Mae was, but couldn't seem to get past the surface exchange of "How are you doing, kiddo?" and "I'll be okay, Dad."

Walker wants to have a more genuine conversation, but he's afraid. He suspects that at least some of the issues Annie Mae is dealing with are connected to their relationship. He suspects Annie Mae thinks he was not a good father, and he fears that she might for the first time tell him so. And that prospect terrifies him.

Up until now, without knowing for sure what his daughter thinks, Walker has been able to live with the hope that he's been a good father. He'd like nothing more than for that to be true. But he suspects that the truth is more complex. After all, he was away a lot, he wasn't as supportive as he might have been, and he made promises to Annie Mae that he didn't always keep.

Walker has two options. He can try to tiptoe through the conversations with his daughter, hoping against hope that Annie Mae doesn't raise the issue of how he has contributed to their troubled relationship and her current illness. Or he can work through some of his identity issues in advance and accept in his own heart his contribution to their problems.

It won't be easy. In fact, it may be the toughest thing Walker ever does. But if he's able to accept himself and his actions for what they are, and to take responsibility for them, both in his own mind and when talking with Annie Mae, he'll probably find that over time his conversations with his daughter become easier. And, more important, Walker will find that he no longer needs to hide. His conversations with Annie Mae won't be fraught with the potential to strike at his all-or-nothing identity as a good father. He can say to his daughter, "I wish I'd been there for you more often. I'm so sorry and sad that I wasn't," and can approach her with compassion instead of fear.

# During the Conversation: Learn to Regain Your Balance

After observing O Sensei, the founder of Aikido, sparring with an accomplished fighter, a young student said to the master, "You never lose your balance. What is your secret?"

"You are wrong," O Sensei replied. "I am constantly losing my balance. My skill lies in my ability to regain it."

So it is with difficult conversations. Working through your identity issues is extremely helpful. And still, the conversation will bring its share of surprises, testing your self-image in ways you hadn't counted on. The question is not whether you will get knocked over. You will. The real question is whether you are able to get back on your feet and keep the conversation moving in a productive direction.

Four things you can do before and during a difficult conversation to help yourself maintain and regain your balance include: letting go of trying to control their reaction, preparing for their response, imagining the future to gain perspective, and if you lose your balance, taking a break.

## Let Go of Trying to Control Their Reaction

Especially in conversations that implicate important identity issues, you may already feel conflicted or ashamed, and you may want to avoid the extra pressure of a bad reaction from the other person. "Whatever happens," you think, "I just don't want them to get upset, and I especially don't want them to be upset at me." You feel bad enough about yourself; a bad reaction from them would make things unbearable. As a result, you may hold as one of your primary goals getting through the conversation without the other person having a "bad" reaction.

There's nothing wrong (and plenty right) with not wanting to hurt someone, or wanting them to like you even after you convey bad news. Yet holding this as a *purpose* in the conversation leads to trouble. Just as you can't change another person, you can't control their reaction — and you shouldn't try.

When you tell your kids that you and their mother are getting a divorce, they are likely to be upset. How could they not be? Because you care for them, it is natural to want to minimize their hurt at this news. But there is also likely to be an element of *self*-protection in this urge: "I just hope they don't cry or get angry or withdraw or argue," you think, in part because of how that would make you feel about yourself: "Maybe I'm a rotten dad, as well as a lousy husband." Trying to control their reaction can seem like a way to avoid the difficult work of accepting your contribution to what's happening — with the resulting painful impact on your identity.

But trying to smooth over or stifle the other person's reaction will make things worse, not better. It's understandable that you'd want the kids to feel that the divorce won't be all that bad, or to persuade your employee that being fired is really an opportunity for her to find a better fit for her skills. Yet even if your rosy predictions turn out to be true in the longer term, dismissing the feelings that the other person is experiencing in the moment is disastrous. You may intend the message "Everything will be all right," but the message the other person is likely to hear is "I don't understand how you feel" or worse, "You're not allowed to be upset by this."

When delivering bad news — indeed, in any difficult conversation — rather than trying to control the other person's reaction, adopt the And Stance. You can come in with the purpose of letting your children know about the divorce, letting them know how much you love and care about them, letting them know that you honestly believe things will be okay, *and* giving them space to feel however they are feeling and letting them know their feelings make sense and are okay to feel. This gives you control over everything you can actually control (yourself), and gives them space to be honest in response.

The same dynamic applies to giving bad news at work. When you fire someone, that person will likely be upset, and possibly upset at you. Don't measure the success of the conversation by whether or not they get upset. It's their right to be upset, and it's a reasonable response. Better instead to go in with the purposes of giving them the news, of taking responsibility for your part in this outcome (but not more), of showing that you care about how they feel, and of trying to be helpful going forward.

Learning that you can't control the other person's reaction, and that it can be destructive to try, can be incredibly liberating. It not only gives the other person the space to react however they need to, but also takes a huge amount of pressure off you. You will learn things about yourself based on their reaction, but if you are prepared to learn, you'll feel free from the desperate need for their reaction to go one certain way.

## Prepare for Their Response

Instead of trying to control the other person's reaction, *prepare* for it. Take time in advance to imagine the conversation. Instead of focusing on how badly it will go — which may be your tendency when you are fretting late at night over whether to raise it — focus on what you can learn about how the other person might respond. Are they likely to cry? Sulk and withdraw? Pretend everything is fine? Attack or reject you?

And then consider whether any of these responses implicate identity issues for you. If so, imagine they respond in the most difficult manner possible, and ask yourself, "What do I think this says about me?" Work through the identity issues in advance: "Is it okay for me to make someone cry? How will I respond? What if they attack my character or motivations? Then how would I respond?" The more prepared you are for how the other person might react, the less surprised you'll be. If you've already considered the identity implications of how they might react, you are far less likely to be knocked off balance in the moment.

## Imagine That It's Three Months Or Ten Years From Now

Getting some perspective on yourself is hard when the world is looking bleak and you're feeling confused, dejected, unlovable, or unemployable. Sometimes projecting yourself into your own future can help you feel better about what's happening now with the reassurance that eventually you'll feel better, and that someday it may not seem so important.

Thinking of your future self looking back can also give you some direction. If you're in the midst of a particularly painful time, think about what it will feel like to look back on this period in your life from thirty years hence. What do you think you'll have learned from the experience? How will you feel about how you handled it? What advice can the you of thirty years from now give to the you that is facing the pain?

## Take a Break

Sometimes you'll find that you are just too close to the problem and too overwhelmed by your internal identity quake to engage effectively in the conversation. You're not at a place where you can take in more information or untangle your thoughts. Maintaining the charade of participation in the conversation at times like this is unlikely to be helpful to anyone.

Ask for some time to think about what you've heard: "I'm surprised by your reaction to this and would like some time to think about what you've said." Even ten minutes can help. Take a walk. Get some air. Check for distortions. Spend some quiet time weighing their attack on your judgment or arrogance against other information you have about yourself. Check for denial. In what ways is what they are saying true? Check for exaggerations. What is the worst that could happen here? And what might you do right now to turn the conversation around?

Some people find asking for a break embarrassing. But postponing the conversation until you've regained your balance may save you from worse things than embarrassment down the road.

## Their Identity Is Also Implicated

When we're wrapped up in our own Identity Conversation it can be difficult to remember that the other person may be grappling with identity issues of their own. Certainly as Walker tries to talk with Annie Mae about her illness, she'll be absorbed in her own Identity Conversation. Simply being in the clinic because something is "wrong" with her may in her mind confirm her greatest fear — that she will never be good enough or achieve enough to please her father.

One important way Walker can help his daughter is to lead her away from all-or-nothing thinking. He can help provide balance to her self-image by letting her know that everyone needs help sometimes. And he can remind her of the positive things that are true about her and important to him: "I'm proud of you for getting help," he might say to Annie Mae. And he can remind her that he loves her not because she gets all A's in school, but because she's his daughter. And that won't change no matter what.

## Raising Identity Issues Explicitly

Sometimes your identity issues will be important to you, but not terribly relevant to the person you are talking to, or to the relationship generally. You don't need to tell your new colleague that he reminds you of a former boyfriend with whom you had a bad sexual experience. It's useful for you to be aware of it, but talking about it explicitly probably won't move your conversations forward. You can identify the issue in your own mind and recognize that it's something for you to work out on your own.

Other times, making the Identity Conversation explicit can help you get directly to the heart of what is going on: "What I'm sensing this is all about is whether I'm a good spouse or not. Is that how you're feeling too?" "I've always regretted not saying something at Dad's funeral. That's why it's so important for me to speak at Mom's." "I'm sensitive to criticism of my writing style. I know I need the feedback, but it's something for both of us to be aware of as we work through these memos."

You'll be astounded how often difficult conversations are wrapped up in both people reacting to what the conversation seems to be saying about them.

## Find the Courage to Ask for Help

Sometimes life deals us a blow that we can't cope with on our own. What constitutes such a blow is different for each of us. It may be something as undermining as rape or as horrifying as war. It may be a physical or mental illness, an addiction, or a profound loss. Or it may be something that would not disturb most other people but does disturb you.

We sometimes ascribe valor to those who suffer in silence. But when suffering is prolonged or interferes with accomplishing what we want with our lives, then such suffering may be more reckless than brave. Whatever it is, if you've worked to get over it and can't, we encourage you to ask for help. From friends, from colleagues, from family, from professionals. From anyone who might be able to offer a hand.

For many of us, that's not easy. Our Identity Conversation tells us loud and clear that asking for help is not okay — that it is shameful or weak and creates burdens on others. These thoughts are powerful, but ask yourself this: If someone you loved — an uncle or daughter, a favorite colleague — were in the situation you find yourself in, would you think it was okay for *them* to ask for help? Why should you be held to a different standard?

If part of your identity is believing that you don't need help, then asking for it is never going to be easy. And when you do ask, not everyone will come through for you, and that will be painful. But many people will. And by trusting them enough to ask, you offer them an extraordinary opportunity to do something important for someone they care about. Then one day, you may have the opportunity to return the favor.

# Create a
# Learning
# Conversation

• • • • •

# 7

# What's Your Purpose?
## *When to Raise It and*
## *When to Let Go*

You can't have every difficult conversation you come across. Life is too short, the list too long. So how do you decide when to have a conversation, for the first time or the fifteenth? And how do you let go of the issues you decide not to raise?

These are the questions that torment us as we lie awake listening to that barking dog next door. We've spent the first half of this book talking about *what* you might raise. We'll spend the next half outlining *how*. But before we get to that, is there anything we can say about *when?*

## To Raise or Not to Raise: How to Decide?

It would be easy if there were some hard-and-fast rules about when to raise issues and when to leave well enough alone. "Never talk politics at the dinner table," "Whatever you do, don't raise anything before 8 a.m.," and "Never disagree with your boss" have the advantage of being clear rules. They're also nonsense, and so not particularly helpful.

Whether or not you should raise an issue with your husband or your agent or your mechanic is ultimately something only you can decide. Because the specifics of each situation are different, there is no simple rule we can offer to guide you in making a wise decision. What we *can* offer are a few questions and suggestions to help you sort through whether and how you might initiate a conversation.

## How Do I Know I've Made the Right Choice?

When we're trying to decide whether or not to raise something, we often think, "I wish I were better at making up my mind. If only I were smarter, this wouldn't be so hard for me." The truth is, there is no "right choice." There is no way to know in advance how things will really turn out. So don't spend your time looking for the one right answer about what to do. It's not only a useless standard, it's crippling.

Instead, hold as your goal to *think clearly* as you take on the task of making a considered choice. That is as good as any of us can do.

## Work Through the Three Conversations

In every case, work through the Three Conversations as best you can. Get a better handle on your feelings, key identity issues, and possible distortions or gaps in your perceptions. Think clearly about what you do know (your own feelings, your own experiences and story, your identity issues), and what you don't know (their intentions, their perspective, or feelings).

This approach will help you become more aware of the process of communication and gain insight into what's making your conversations difficult. Sometimes the insights you find will present a clear answer: "Raising this is important, and now I have some ideas about how to do it differently" or "Now I'm starting to see why having a conversation probably won't help."

# Three Kinds of Conversations That *Don't* Make Sense

As you consider whether to engage, you'll find that while it often makes sense to initiate a conversation, sometimes it doesn't. In making that choice wisely, three key questions stand out.

## Is the Real Conflict Inside You?

Sometimes what's difficult about the situation has a whole lot more to do with what's going on inside you than what's going on between you and the other person. In that case, a conversation focused on the interaction isn't going to be very illuminating or productive, at least until you've had a longer conversation with yourself.

Insight into her Identity Conversation helped Carmen resolve a running dispute with her husband over responsibility for managing a variety of kid-related activities, such as carpool schedules, doctor's appointments, and piano lessons:

> Despite the fact that I was working full-time to support the family while Tom stayed home with the kids, I was still doing much of the scheduling and running around. I felt like Tom wasn't responsible enough. As I saw it, he kept dropping the ball; I had to pick it up to make sure things ran smoothly.
>
> But when I began sorting through my Identity Conversation, I started seeing the ways in which I was *keeping* control of this part of the kids' lives — perhaps because of my ambivalence about working full-time. I love my job. I'm good at it, and I make decent money. But I'm still nagged by guilt, and there are times when I'm jealous that my daughter often goes to Tom with problems before she comes to me.

Once Carmen realized that taking responsibility for the scheduling was her way of assuring herself that she was still a good mother — still involved and essential to her children's well-being — she was able to let go of the resentment she felt when things got hectic: "I both turned some things over to Tom and shifted the way I thought about these responsibilities. They are things I've chosen to take on to stay involved, rather than things he's let slide."

## Is There a Better Way to Address the Issue Than Talking About It?

As you sort out your feelings or identify your contribution to a situation it may become clear that what's called for is not a conversation about the interaction, but a change in your behavior. Sometimes actions are better than words.

Walter had endured a series of difficult conversations with his mother over the family farm, located in northern Missouri. He tells the following story:

> Since dad died, my brothers have been helping my mother run the place. Whenever I talk with her she asks when I'm going to come home and join the family business — or at least take old Doc Denny's job as the town doctor.
>
> I enjoy living in St. Louis, where I have a terrific pediatric practice, so the conversation I thought I needed to have more successfully was telling my mother to leave the issue alone, to accept that I'm not coming back — at least not anytime soon.
>
> But as I sorted through the Three Conversations, I discovered some things. I realized that in addition to feeling frustrated and resentful when my mother raises this issue, I also felt appreciative that she misses me, and grateful that I have roots and the option to return. And I felt sad that my kids weren't developing the close relationship with their grandmother that my nieces have, and were missing out on the chance to grow up on a farm, which was a wonderful experience for me.
>
> One of the most important insights came from imagining my mother's perceptions and feelings. Suddenly it occurred to me that what my mom was really saying was that she missed knowing what was going on with me — being a part of our lives. She wanted me to

bring my family back so that she could be more connected and involved with us. But when she would express this by asking when I'd be coming home, I usually reacted by cutting the conversation short. Then I wouldn't call her for weeks on end, simply because I dreaded having to discuss the issue again. So I ended up contributing to her feeling even *more* disconnected — which in turn would prompt her to express how much she missed us, and we'd go around again.

Once Walter sorted out this contribution system and the complexity of his feelings, he realized that he didn't need to have a conversation with his mother about how often she asked if he was coming home. He first needed to change his contribution to the problem.

I began phoning mom more often, sending her short notes about the kids' activities, and inviting her to visit in St. Louis just for fun, rather than for a holiday or family event. When she raised the question of when I might come home, instead of cutting the conversation short, I shared how satisfying my practice was. I also described my feelings of regret and confusion about not getting to spend more time with the family, and wishing the kids could spend more time with her. This prompted an invitation for my daughters to spend the summer with their cousins on the farm. Slowly, the questions about my return decreased.

And, not surprisingly, Walter grew closer to his mother.

Sometimes a conversation is simply not worth the time, or not even possible. But you still want to do something. Fran, who is a successful workers' rights lobbyist, had an upsetting exchange with a toll collector on her daily commute. Fran prefers to keep only quarters in her change drawer to pay the fifty-cent toll, so she doesn't have to search in the dark and take her eyes off the road to find the right change. Accordingly, on those occasions when she pays with a dollar bill, she prefers to receive quarters as change. When a toll collector offers nickels and dimes as change, Fran gives it back and asks for quarters.

Generally the collectors are fine about this, but yesterday the man collecting snapped, "Where do rich people like you get off feeling so high-and-mighty entitled? Doesn't it even occur to you that I might be giving you dimes for a reason?" Flustered, Fran responded, "Well, yes, but it just seems to me that you're in a better position to have change than I am." To which the collector replied as he slapped two quarters in her hand, "You don't have the first idea what my job is like. And you don't care either! Go on." Speechless and furious, Fran drove on.

Reflecting on this exchange at home, Fran realized that her anger stemmed largely from denial of several unpleasant truths: she definitely was feeling entitled, even a little righteously so, when she demanded her quarters; it *hadn't* occurred to her to wonder what constraints the collector was operating under; and from the collector's point of view she does appear wealthy. All of which conflicts with important aspects of how she likes to see herself. She still didn't like how the collector had behaved, but she could imagine being in his shoes at the end of a long day with an endless line of cars stretched out before him.

The upshot for Fran was that she no longer felt angry, and stopped fantasizing about defending herself to this man when she next met him at the toll booth. She also saw her experience as part of a more complex picture. She still wanted to do something about the situation, but a different approach seemed in order. So she wrote the Turnpike Authority a letter explaining her interests in being able to receive quarters as change without putting the toll collectors in a difficult situation, and asking what could be done to ensure that. To her pleasant surprise, she got a reply explaining that the toll collectors were allowed to bring only a certain amount of change to the booth and were prohibited from leaving the booth except at designated times. The Toll Authority thanked her for raising the issue, and explained how they had found a creative solution to meet her request and ease the dilemma for their collectors.

## Do You Have Purposes That Make Sense?

Imagine asking the head of NASA about the purpose of a particular space mission, and getting the answer: "Um, I don't know. We thought we'd launch someone into space and figure things out from there."

Not likely. Yet we often launch into our conversations in much the same way. We find ourselves in the middle of the conversation, and neither person is quite sure what the point is or what a good outcome would look like.

Other times we try having conversations when our purposes are simply off-base. When that happens, whatever you say or do is not going to help (and might even make things worse), because you've chosen a destination that is impossible to reach.

**Remember, You Can't Change Other People.** In many situations, our purpose in initiating a conversation is to get the other person to change. There's nothing wrong with hoping for change. The urge to change others is universal. We want them to be more loving, to show more appreciation for our hard work, to give us more personal space, or to be more social at parties. To accept our career choice or our sexual orientation. To believe in our God or our views on important issues of the day.

The problem is, *we can't make these things happen.* We can't change someone else's mind or force them to change their behavior. If we could, many difficult conversations would simply vanish. We'd say, "Here are the reasons you should love me more," and they'd say, "Now that I know those reasons, I do."

But we know things don't work that way. Changes in attitudes and behavior rarely come about because of arguments, facts, and attempts to persuade. How often do *you* change your values and beliefs — or whom you love or what you want in life — based on something someone tells you? And how likely are you to do so when the person who is trying to change you doesn't seem fully aware of the reasons you see things differently in the first place?

We can have an influence, but here we need to be especially careful. The paradox is that trying to change someone rarely results in change. On the other hand, engaging someone in a conversation where mutual learning is the goal often results in change. Why? Because when we set out to try to change someone, we are more likely to argue with and attack their story and less likely to listen. This approach increases the likelihood that they will feel defensive rather than open to learning something new. They are more likely to change if they think we understand them and if they feel heard and respected. They are more likely to change if they feel free *not* to.

**Don't Focus on Short-Term Relief at Long-Term Cost.** Another common mistake is acting to relieve psychological tension in the short term at the cost of creating a worse situation in the future.

Janet learned this the hard way. With twenty years of experience in nonprofit financial management, she never thought she'd be brought to tears by a board member questioning her competence. But here she was. Finally, sick of feeling attacked each time she presented the budget numbers, she decided to confront the board member, a woman named Sylvie. It did not go well. Janet explains:

> Looking back, although I was saying some of the right things — taking responsibility for my contribution and so forth — I think what I really wanted to do was tell her off. I wanted her to feel as small as I had. And I wanted to let her know that she couldn't treat me this way.
>
> Oh, I let her have it. And I walked out of the meeting feeling great . . . for about fifteen minutes. Then I started to regret some of the things I'd said, and realized that I'd just made the situation worse by feeding the antagonism between us. The fact was, she *could* treat me this way, and I'd just made it more likely that she would.

If your purpose is to change the other person or their behavior, to vent or tell them off, then having this conversation is quite likely to produce many of the negative consequences you fear. Saying "You are insensitive/unreliable/unacceptable" *will* jeopardize the relationship. You will probably hurt the other person's feelings, provoke a defensive reaction, or get yourself fired.

This is not to say that Janet is stuck being mistreated by Sylvie without any way to address the situation. Janet might have a constructive conversation with Sylvie if she can shift her purposes a bit. If Janet can negotiate herself into a place of curiosity about why Sylvie reacts as she does, this could be a worthwhile conversation. Janet can see it as an opportunity to learn Sylvie's story, share her own, and then figure out how they might work together better. Is it something Janet is doing? Is Sylvie aware of the impact she's having on Janet? Is this the way Sylvie has gotten results in the past? What advice can Janet offer Sylvie on how to get a better reaction from her?

If Janet can come into the conversation with this kind of curiosity stance toward Sylvie's view, the conversation is much less likely to provoke a bad reaction or to damage the relationship. Janet would be investing in the relationship by trying to work with Sylvie in figuring out why things have been so difficult.

Negotiating with yourself to shift your purposes can *lower the threshold* of how risky the conversation is likely to be and improve the odds of a constructive outcome.

**Don't Hit-and-Run.** Often, when we have something important to say, we say it now because now is when it's causing us frustration. Most of us are thoughtful enough to avoid the most egregious errors of bad timing. If someone tells us they've just returned from the doctor's office and are going to have to have that operation after all, few of us would say, "I'm sorry to hear that. Oh, by the way, you still owe me $500."

However, there's another error around timing that we do make. It's the hit-and-run. An employee wanders into work late, something you've been meaning to talk to them about, so you say, "Late again, eh?" and leave it at that. Or you visit your son for the weekend, notice the empty beer bottles in the garbage, and say, "I see you're still drinking up a storm."

These comments are intended to help. You hope your employee

or your son will take the message to heart. But while your comments may help *you* feel a bit better ("At least I've said something"), they make the other person defensive and frustrated, which is unlikely to produce the kind of change you had in mind.

A good rule to follow is: If you're going to talk, talk. Really talk. And if you're really going to talk, you can't do it on the fly. You have to plan a time to talk. You have to be explicit about wanting ten minutes or an hour to discuss something that is important to you. You can't have a real conversation in thirty seconds, and anything less than a real conversation isn't going to help. If hit-and-run is all you can muster, it's better not to raise the issue at all.

## Letting Go

The approach in this book can help you accomplish a number of astonishing results. You'll make better decisions about when bringing something up just doesn't make sense, at least until you've sorted through some of your own issues or tried changing your own contribution. And when you choose to engage, you'll slowly get better at staying out of your own way — spotting and side-stepping the ways you used to trip yourself up. Over time, you'll lessen your own anxiety and deepen your most important relationships.

But this approach is not magic. Sometimes — despite our very best efforts — nothing helps. You can't force the other person to want to invest in the relationship or work things out. No matter how many times you explain to your son how worried you are when he doesn't call, he may not call. Your boss may continue to lose his temper. Your mother may never come to understand how emotionally abandoned you felt when you were young.

Sometimes you consider your purposes and some possible strategies, and decide not to have the conversation. Holding onto the issues inside the relationship becomes too painful or too exhausting, so you move on. You are able to let go.

Other times, it's not that easy. For one reason or another, even though you think it's the better choice not to engage with the issue, the situation has you by the throat. The story inside your head still carries emotional punch; you experience a flood of emotions every time you think about it. You've decided to move on, but your emotions have dug in their heels.

Some people say letting go is a choice. Others think it happens only when the conditions are right — after contrition has been shown, after you've found a new relationship, or after *you've* been forgiven. What does it take to be able truly to let go? To open your palm and let the bitterness and exasperation and hurt and shame sift through your fingers?

We don't presume to know. And we're suspicious of anyone who thinks there's an easy formula. Probably, it is something different for each of us.

What we do know is that letting go usually takes time, and that it is rarely a simple journey. It's not easy to find a place where you can set free the pain, or shame, you carry from your experiences. A place where you can tell the story differently in your head — where you can relinquish the role of victim or villain, and give yourself and the other person roles that are more complex and liberating. A place where you can accept yourself for who you've been and who you are.

If someone tells you that you *should* have gotten over something or someone by now, don't believe it. Believing there's some appropriate time frame for getting over something is just one more way to keep yourself stuck. But neither should you believe that there's nothing you can do to enable yourself to let go, or that it just takes time. There's plenty you can do to help yourself down that road.

## Adopt Some Liberating Assumptions

A good place to start is in the Identity Conversation, challenging some of the common assumptions that can get in the way of letting go and being at peace with our choices. Four liberating assumptions are presented below.

**It's Not My Responsibility to Make Things Better; It's My Responsibility to Do My Best.** For Karenna, the key to closure was letting go of the fantasy that things could be better:

> I've failed at relationships before, and I so wanted this one to work. But I didn't just want it to work. Somewhere along the way, I decided it *had* to work, no matter what, and that it was my job to make it happen. I tried everything, and maybe I should have gotten out of the relationship sooner. But it was hard to let go of the idea that things between Paul and me might have worked out, if only I'd been a better person, or said the right thing at the right time, or worked harder at it, or something.

In Karenna's situation, part of the process of letting go of the guilt and sadness she carried was accepting that sometimes there are limits — you cannot always make a relationship more comfortable or more nourishing or more intimate or more durable. The best you can do is try.

**They Have Limitations Too.** Sometimes you'll tell the other person about your feelings and perspectives, or about the impact they are having on you, and they say they understand, and you each agree to change your behavior. Then they do whatever annoys you yet again, and you think, "Well, now they know that this aggravates me. So what's the story? Am I not important enough to them? Are they trying to drive me nuts? What am I to make of this?"

One thing you can make of it is that they are as imperfect as you are. No matter how clearly you share how much their drinking hurts you, their forgetfulness aggravates you, or their unresponsiveness saddens you, they may not have the capacity to be different, at least not right now.

After a lifetime of being a big sister, Alison couldn't change being bossy overnight even if she wanted to. At some point, her younger brother may find it easier to accept her as her imperfect, bossy self than to continue to fight with her. He can work through the identity issues that make it easy for Alison to get to him, and love her for the things about her that he likes and admires.

**This Conflict Is Not Who I Am.** An important barrier to letting go occurs when we integrate the conflict into our sense of who we are. In our mind's eye, we *are* the least favorite son, the long-suffering wife, part of the oppressed group. We define ourselves in relation to our conflict with others.

Over the last four years the leadership in Rob's firm has split over several key strategic questions. Part of the "losing" faction, Rob's professional identity has been all but consumed by being one of the few still holding out, standing up to management. Now in the wake of a sudden merger, Rob's faction has been handed control, and the satisfaction he feels is mingled with uneasiness. No longer playing the opposition, Rob is not sure how to see himself. Rob's sense of self was perhaps too aligned with his role in the conflict.

Such dynamics play an important part in ethnic conflict. Our sense of who we are as a community is often defined in terms of who we are *not*, who we are against, and what hardships we've endured. Tragically, we can feel threatened by the prospect of reconciliation, because it can rob us not only of our role, but also of our communal identity.

These kinds of situations are notoriously difficult to manage because we don't want to give up who we are unless there is something better to replace it. If you find yourself being swallowed up by a conflict, if you begin to see your very identity as tied to the fight, try to take a step back and remember why you are fighting. You are fighting for what is right and fair, not because you need the conflict to survive.

**Letting Go Doesn't Mean I No Longer Care.** Often we are unable to let go because we fear that if we do, it will mean we no longer care. If you and your sister weren't at odds, how would you show how important she is to you, or know that you're just as significant in her life? Is it possible to let go and still care enormously?

David has wrestled with this issue more deeply than most:

When my brother was murdered, I didn't think I could ever forgive the man who shot him — over something as stupid as a drink in a poker game. And I have to admit that I was also angry with my brother for being there.

I didn't attend the trial. I couldn't. For years every time I would be reminded of my brother, the fury and pain of the injustice of his death would surge through me. In my mind, I would have conversations with my brother in which I'd tell him not only how sad I was, but how angry I was at him for being so foolish, and for abandoning me.

It's only recently that I've begun to see the power in forgiving each of them — my brother *and* the man who murdered him. Letting go of my rage and indignation doesn't mean I have to let go of my love for my brother or my sense of loss. There's nothing I can do about it, and I've finally accepted that. I'll never get over losing my brother. I still talk to him. But the conversations aren't so hard. I can miss him terribly without the clutter of so many other feelings.

David's story shows us the power of being able to let go of anger while still holding on to love and memories. David can't and doesn't want to forget what happened. He's learned a great deal from the experience, painful as it was, that he applies to his relationships with his children and others. And yet in letting go and forgiving, some of the emotional burden he's carried since the tragedy has eased.

Even in situations much more mundane than David's, letting go of the emotions and identity issues wrapped up in a difficult conversation can be one of the most challenging things you do. Difficult conversations operate at the core of our being — where the people and the principles we care about most intersect with our self-image and self-esteem. Letting go, at heart, is about how to handle with skill and grace *not* having a difficult conversation.

Of course, the better you become at engaging difficult conversations, the less there will be for you to let go of. One key to improving is having sound purposes.

# If You Raise It: Three Purposes That Work

We've talked about purposes that will get you into trouble. But how about purposes that make sense? The gold standard here is working for mutual understanding. Not mutual agreement, necessarily, but a better understanding of each of your stories, so that you can make informed decisions (alone or together) about what to do next.

Anytime you think a conversation might be difficult, keep the following three purposes front and center in your consciousness.

## 1. Learning Their Story

Exploring the other person's perspective takes us into each of the Three Conversations. What information do they see that we missed or don't have access to? What past experiences influence them? What is their reasoning for why they did what they did? What were their intentions? How did our actions impact them? What do they think we are contributing to the problem? What are they feeling? What does this situation mean to them? How does it affect their identity? What's at stake?

## 2. Expressing Your Views and Feelings

Your goal should be to express your views and feelings to your *own* satisfaction. You hope that the other person will understand what you are saying, and perhaps be moved by it, but you can't count on that. What you can do is say, as well as you can, what is important for you to say about your views, intentions, contributions, feelings, and identity issues. You can share your story.

## 3. Problem-Solving Together

Given what you and the other person have each learned, what would improve the situation going forward? Can you brainstorm creative ways to satisfy both of your needs? Where your needs conflict, can you use equitable standards to ensure a fair and workable way to resolve the conflict?

## Stance and Purpose Go Hand in Hand

These three purposes accommodate the fact that you and the other person see the world differently, that you each have powerful feelings about what is going on, and that you each have your own identity issues to work through. Each of you, in short, has your own story. You need purposes that can reckon with this reality.

These are the purposes that emerge from a learning stance, from working through the Three Conversations and shifting your internal orientation from certainty to curiosity, from debate to exploration, from simplicity to complexity, from "either/or" to "and." They may seem simple — perhaps even simplistic. But their straightforwardness masks both the difficulty involved in doing them well and the power they have to transform the way you handle your conversations.

Working from a learning stance with these purposes in mind, the rest of this book explores in detail how to conduct a learning conversation, from getting started to getting unstuck.

# 8

# Getting Started:
## *Begin from the Third Story*

The most stressful moment of a difficult conversation is often the beginning. We may learn in the first few seconds that the news for us is not good, that the other person sees things very differently, that we aren't likely to get what we want. They may become angry or distraught or we may discover that they don't want to talk to us at all.

But while the beginning is fraught with peril, it is also an opportunity. It's when you have the greatest leverage to influence the entire direction of the conversation. Sure, you can begin in a way that sends things careening into a brick wall; we've all done that. But it doesn't have to go that way. What you say at the outset can put you squarely on the road toward understanding and problem-solving. There are techniques you can learn for how to take advantage of the opportunity the beginning presents, and simple principles for understanding why your usual approaches so often go awry.

How to begin a conversation? Let's first consider how *not* to.

## Why Our Typical Openings Don't Help

One way or another, if we are going to have a conversation, we have to start by saying *something*. So, perhaps recalling advice from a childhood swimming coach, we close our eyes, take a deep breath, and jump in:

If you contest Dad's will, it's going to tear the family apart.

I was very upset by what you said in front of our supervisor.

Your son Nathan can be difficult in class — disruptive and argumentative. You've said in the past that things at home are fine, but something must be troubling him.

Before we know it, we're in over our heads. The other person becomes hurt or angry, we feel defensive, our preparation goes out the window, and we wonder why we thought having this conversation was a good idea in the first place.

What went wrong?

## We Begin Inside Our Own Story

When we jump into conversations we typically begin inside our story. We describe the problem from our own perspective and, in doing so, trigger just the kinds of reactions we hope to avoid. We begin from precisely the place the other person thinks is causing the problem. If they agreed with our story, we probably wouldn't be having this conversation in the first place. Our story sends up flares, warning them to defend themselves or to counterattack.

## We Trigger Their Identity Conversation from the Start

Our story invariably (though often unintentionally) communicates a judgment about them — the kind of person they are — and the fact that inside our version of the events, they are the problem. Something as simple as an opening sentence can give us away. Let's take a look at the lines offered above:

| Opening Lines | Implicit Message About Them |
|---|---|
| If you contest Dad's will, it's going to tear the family apart. | You're selfish, ungrateful, and don't care about the family. |
| I was very upset by what you said in front of our supervisor. | At worst, you betrayed me — at best, you were stupid. |
| Your son Nathan can be difficult in class — disruptive and argumentative. You've said in the past that things at home are fine, but something must be troubling him. | Your son is a troublemaker, probably because you're a bad parent who's created a lousy home environment. What are you hiding? |

We could imagine even worse ways to begin, but it's not hard to see why these provoke defensiveness. We trigger the other person's Identity Conversation from the outset, and there's no room in our agenda for their story. It's natural that they would reject our version and want to get their own on the table: "I'm not trying to tear the family apart, I'm just sticking up for what Dad wanted." Or, "Nathan is not a problem child. People who know how to handle children see that he's a very sweet boy."

By leaving their story out, we implicitly set up a trade-off between their version of events and our version, between our feelings and theirs.

The question is what to do instead. Below, we lay out two powerful guidelines for starting the conversation off in the right direction: (1) begin the conversation from the "Third Story," and (2) offer an invitation to explore the issues jointly.

## Step One: Begin from the Third Story

In addition to your story and the other person's story, every difficult conversation includes an invisible Third Story. The Third Story is the one a keen observer would tell, someone with no stake in your particular problem. For example, in the battle between bicycles and cars for the streets of the city, the Third Story would be the one told by city planners, who can understand each side's concerns and see why each group is frustrated with the other. When tensions arise in a marriage, the Third Story might be the one offered by a marriage counselor. In a dispute between friends, the Third Story may be the perspective of a mutual friend who sees each side as having valid concerns that need to be addressed.

## Think Like a Mediator

The urban planner, marriage counselor, and mutual friend each have the vantage point of a neutral observer, or mediator. Mediators are third parties who help people solve their problems. Unlike judges or arbitrators, though, mediators have no power to impose a solution; they are there to help the two sides communicate more effectively, and to explore possible ways of moving forward.

One of the most helpful tools a mediator has is the ability to identify this invisible Third Story. This means describing the problem between the parties in a way that rings true for both sides simultaneously. It's easy to describe the problem so that only one of the disputants would agree with it — in fact, that's what each of us does when we begin inside our own story. The trick is being able to get two people with different stories to sign on to the same description of what is going on.

Mediators don't possess some magical intuition that allows them to do this. They are relying on a formula (and a lot of practice), and this formula can be learned by anyone. You don't have to be an impartial third party to begin from the Third Story. You can begin your own conversations this way.

## Not Right or Wrong, Not Better or Worse — Just Different

The key is learning to describe the gap — or difference — between your story and the other person's story. Whatever else you may think and feel, you can at least agree that you and the other person see things differently. Consider an example.

**Jason's Story.** Jason's roommate, Jill, leaves dishes in the sink for days on end. This drives Jason crazy, and means that he ends up doing much of the cleaning up, since he can't stand to let them sit. In the past, Jason has raised the issue with Jill by saying, "Do I have to do *everything* around here? You can't let dishes sit this long — it's a health risk."

Obviously, Jason is speaking from inside his story. Jill is not going to be thrilled with this start to a conversation, and will likely respond by defending herself or attacking Jason. This would be true even if Jason began with more tact, offering something like, "Jill we need to talk about your problem with getting the dishes done." Tact or not, it's still *his* story.

**Jill's Story.** If Jill were to raise the problem, she would begin differently: "Jason, we need to talk about the fact that you are so annoyingly anal about the dishes. Last night you practically cleared the table before I was finished eating. You need to relax." This, of course, suits Jill but not Jason.

**The Third Story.** The Third Story would remove the judgment from the description, and instead describe the problem as a *difference* between Jason and Jill. It might go like this: "Jason and Jill have different preferences around when the dishes are done, and different standards for what constitutes appropriate or obsessive cleanliness. Each is unhappy with the other's approach." That's how a mediator or observant friend might describe the problem. Both Jason and Jill can sign on to this difference.

Clearly, there is a difference, and in the Third Story there is no judgment about who is right or even whose view is more common. The Third Story simply captures the difference. That's what allows both sides to buy into the same description of the problem: each feels that their story is acknowledged as a legitimate part of the discussion.

Once you find it, you can begin with the Third Story yourself. So Jason might say, "Jill, you and I seem to have different preferences about when the dishes get done or beliefs about when they should be done. I wonder if that's something we could talk about?" Jason can offer that without sacrificing his own views (soon enough, he'll ask about Jill's story, and describe his own), and Jill can sign on without defensiveness.

Importantly, you don't have to know what the other person's story entails to include it in initiating the conversation this way. All you have to do is acknowledge that it's there: that there are probably lots of things you don't understand about their perspective, and that one of the reasons you want to talk is that you want to learn more about their view. You can begin from the Third Story by saying, "My sense is that you and I see this situation differently. I'd like to share how I'm seeing it, and learn more about how you're seeing it."

### Opening Lines

*From Inside Your Story: If you contest Dad's will, it's going to tear our family apart.*

**From the Third Story:** I wanted to talk about Dad's will. You and I obviously have different understandings of what Dad intended, and of what's fair to each of us. I wanted to understand why you see things the way you do, and to share with you my perspective and feelings. In addition, I have strong feelings and fears about what a court fight would mean for the family; I suspect you do too.

---

*From Inside Your Story: I was very upset by what you said in front of our supervisor.*

**From the Third Story:** I wanted to talk to you about what happened in the meeting this morning. I was upset by something you said. I wanted to explain what was bothering me, and also hear your perspective on the situation.

> **From Inside Your Story:** *Your son Nathan can be difficult in class —*
> *disruptive and argumentative. You've said in the past that things at*
> *home are fine, but something must be troubling him.*
>
> **From the Third Story:** I wanted to share with you my concerns
> about Nathan's behavior in class, and hear more about your sense of
> what might be contributing to it. I know from our past conversation
> that you and I have different thinking on this. My sense is that if a
> child is having trouble at school, something is usually bothering
> him at home, and I know you've felt strongly that that's not true in
> this case. Maybe together we can figure out what's motivating
> Nathan and how to handle it.

Most conversations can be initiated from the Third Story to include both perspectives and invite joint exploration. Consider the
openings we looked at earlier, and how they might sound if begun
from the Third Story:

Stepping out of your story doesn't mean giving up your point of
view. Your purpose in opening the conversation is to invite the other
person into a joint exploration. In the course of that exploration
you'll spend time in each side's perspective, and then come back to
adjust your own views based on what you've learned and what you've
shared.

After talking with your brother about how you each think your father's estate should be divided, where those views come from, and
how you feel about the current conflict, it may be that your view of
what's fair changes. Your brother's view may also shift. And the two of
you may find a way to settle the issue that feels fair to both of you.

Or the two of you may still disagree. You think that the estate
should be evenly divided among the three kids. Your brother says Dad
meant it to be divided equally among the seven grandchildren — so
that his branch of the family with its three grandsons gets more than
you and your only daughter. Even if you disagree on the substance of
the dispute, you've had the chance to express how upsetting, sad, and
worrisome the conflict is for you, and to gain a deeper understanding
of why your brother sees it as he does. You may be able to find a
process for working through the differences while protecting your

family relationships from being ravaged by a nasty fight. Keeping communication open and understanding the feelings and perspectives involved sends an important message that even when we disagree, we care about each other. That we are going to stay in communication with each other, even while we take the questions we can't agree on to an arbitrator or probate court to be decided. If nothing else, you will be better able to separate the substantive disagreements from the importance of the relationships.

## If They Start the Conversation, You Can Still Step to the Third Story

Of course, you won't always have the chance to reflect on how you want to begin the conversation. Sometimes difficult conversations will simply descend upon you — presenting themselves in your office or on your doorstep — whether you are ready for them or not.

You can follow the Third Story guidelines even when you are not the initiator of the conversation. Here's what you do. You take whatever the other person says and use it as their half of a description from the Third Story. Since the Third Story includes their story, starting the conversation with their view doesn't mean you're off track.

If Jill comes to Jason and says, "We need to talk about how you ruin all our meals by being so obsessive about the dishes," Jason might find himself wanting to respond from inside his story: "What? You're the one with the problem. You're the biggest slob I know!" But if he does, he'll send the conversation headlong toward that brick wall.

Instead, Jason can treat Jill's opening as her part of the Third Story. He might say, "It sounds like you're pretty unhappy with how I handle the dishes. I have trouble with how you deal with the dishes too, so I think we each have different preferences and assumptions around that. It seems like that would be a good thing for us to talk about. . . ."

Jason has not only acknowledged Jill's story as an important part of the conversation, but also included his own as part of the process of understanding the problem. And in doing so Jason has succeeded in shifting the purpose of the conversation from arguing toward understanding.

## Step Two: Extend an Invitation

The second step in getting off to a good start is to offer a simple invitation: I've described the problem in a way we can each accept. Now I want to propose mutual understanding and problem-solving as purposes, check to see if this makes sense to you, and invite you to join me in a conversation.

### Describe Your Purposes

If the other person is going to accept your invitation, they need to know what it is they are agreeing to do. Letting them know up front that your goal for the discussion is to understand their perspective better, share your own, and talk about how to go forward together makes the conversation significantly less mysterious and threatening. Knowing that their perspective has a place in the conversation, and that this isn't a campaign to change them, makes it more likely that they will accept your invitation.

### Invite, Don't Impose

An invitation, of course, can be turned down. Neither person can force the other to engage in a conversation. If you conceptualize your task as "setting *the* description of the problem and purposes for the conversation," even a well-crafted opening may meet with some resistance, because this is now your version of the Third Story. So your offer should be open to modification by the other person.

Think of the goal rather as "offering and discussing a possible description and purpose" for your conversation. In other words, the task of describing the problem and of setting purposes is itself a joint task.

## Make Them Your Partner in Figuring It Out

Your invitation is more likely to be accepted if you offer the other person an appealing role in managing the problem. You need to side-step the temptation to cast them as "the problem," or in an unappeal-ing light, since this will trigger their Identity Conversation and stop the conversation cold. So if, in a stalled contract negotiation, you were to say, "I can see that we have different ideas about what salary makes sense here," so far so good. But if you then add, "and since you're new at this, I can tell you how it's usually done," you cast them as the neophyte, and sink the ship.

If accepting your invitation requires the other person to acknowl-edge that they are naive, callous, manipulative, or in any other way unsavory or inadequate, they are substantially less likely to accept. If, on the other hand, you say, "Can you help me understand . . . ?" you offer the role of advisor. "Let's work on how we might . . . ." invites a partnership. "I wonder whether it's possible to . . . ." throws out a chal-lenge, one which offers the other person the potential role of hero.

The role you offer has to be genuine. But don't be fooled into thinking that your original depiction — the story that casts the other person as the villain, for example — is any more genuine than other roles you can find for them. It may be that recasting them into a more attractive role requires recognizing that if you are going to gain a more complete picture of what's going on — and make any real progress — you need their help.

Sometimes the most genuine thing you can do is share your in-ternal struggle to cast them in a more positive role. You can say some-thing like, "The story I'm telling in my head about what is going on is that you are being inconsiderate. At some level I know that's unfair to you, and I need you to help me put things in better perspective. I need you to help me understand where you are coming from on this." It's honest and, at the same time, offers them the role of "someone who can help me get my perspective back."

## Be Persistent

Being persistent is not inconsistent with the advice to invite rather than impose. It may take a little work to help them understand what it is you are proposing.

Ruth wants to have a conversation with her ex-husband about the time he spends with their daughter, Alexis. In the past, their conversations have resulted in fights. This time, Ruth begins from the Third Story and offers some useful purposes. Even so, it takes some negotiating to get her ex-husband to understand:

> RUTH: Brian, it seems to me that we're having a hard time being clear with each other about how likely it is that you'll make it for your time with Lexi.
>
> BRIAN: I know, I know. I'm sorry, okay? We had a crisis on the shop floor and I was tied up in meetings trying to address it.
>
> RUTH: I understand that things sometimes come up. I guess I was thinking about the bigger picture, since there have been several times in the last few months when I thought we'd confirmed plans for you to spend the day with Lexi, and later learned that you understood our plans to be more tentative. You thought the plan was that you'd come by *if* you could get away.
>
> BRIAN: That was what I said. *If* I could get away, I'd visit.
>
> RUTH: See, and I thought we'd agreed to a definite plan — that you'll be here no matter what. So you and I are misunderstanding each other. I'd like to sort this out, because it's awfully hard on Alexis when you and I get our signals crossed. Can we spend some time trying to figure this thing out?
>
> BRIAN: Sure. I don't want to upset Lexi. . . .

Notice that Brian didn't accept or perhaps even understand Ruth's description of the problem or purposes at the beginning. He expected to be yelled at for not showing up, and reacted accordingly. But Ruth does a nice job of being both persistent and open to Brian's response.

## Some Specific Kinds of Conversations

In addition to the general advice to open the conversation from the Third Story, we can offer more specific advice on getting started, depending on the nature of the difficult conversation you are anticipating.

### Delivering Bad News

As we said in Chapter 2, even delivering bad news should be a conversation, and it's usually best to put the bad news up front. Don't try to trick the other person into saying it first, by asking, for example, "So, what do you think of the relationship?" when what you mean is "I want to break up." And don't talk for two hours about some of the "issues" you've been having with the relationship, if you know that in the end what you want to do is break up.

If you are letting your parents know that you and your family won't be coming for Christmas, you might say, "We've talked a lot about how important it is to you for us to come home for the holidays, and also how difficult it is financially and emotionally for us to do that. I'm calling because Juan and I have talked a lot about it, and have decided that we are going to spend this Christmas here with the kids. It was a really difficult decision, and I feel bad about disappointing you. I wanted to let you know as early as I could, and to talk a little bit, if you'd like, about your reactions and our thinking."

This doesn't mean that if you have both good news and bad news that you necessarily have to start with the bad. Rather, be clear that you have both. Indeed, you might discuss where to start with the recipient. Or there may be a logical order to follow that you can share.

## Making Requests

Some difficult conversations center on our desire to get something. A common example is asking for a raise. How to begin?

**"I Wonder If It Would Make Sense . . . ?"** The simple advice about making requests is this: Don't make it a demand. Instead, invite an exploration of whether a raise is fair, whether it makes sense. That's not being unassertive, that's being in better touch with reality. Your boss has information about you and your colleagues that you don't have. It may sound like nitpicking, but in fact you can't know that you deserve a raise until you've explored the issue with your boss.

At some level you know this, which is one of the big reasons asking for a raise causes anxiety. Try replacing "I think I deserve a raise" with "I'd like to explore whether a raise for me might make sense. From the information I have, I think I deserve one. [Here's my reasoning.] I wonder how you see it?" This seemingly small change in how you begin should not only reduce stress but also get the conversation off on an even keel. In the end, you may learn that you don't deserve a raise, or that you deserve an even bigger one than you initially thought you did.

## Revisiting Conversations Gone Wrong

Sometimes you know, perhaps from past experience, that the other person is likely to react negatively the minute you raise an especially sensitive topic. Your son doesn't want to talk about his grades, your wife doesn't want to talk about the finances, and the minute you raise the question of racism in the department your colleagues roll their eyes. How can you open a more constructive conversation when conversations haven't gone well in the past and the simple fact of raising the old issue casts you as the nag?

**Talk About How to Talk About It.** The easiest approach is first to talk about how to talk. Treat "the way things usually go when we try to have this conversation" as the problem, and describe it from the Third Story: "I know that in the past when I've raised the question of who's getting promoted and what role race plays in that process, people have sometimes felt accused or exasperated. I don't mean to accuse anyone, or to make people feel uncomfortable. At the same time, it feels important to me to discuss. I'm wondering whether we could talk about how we each react to that conversation, and whether there's a better way we could address these issues?"

Or imagine that you have a friend who you think is so overbooked with commitments that it's affecting her health. Only she doesn't see it that way, and whenever you try to bring it up, she gets defensive. Raising it by talking about how you talk might sound like this: "I definitely get the sense that you don't like discussing your schedule, at least not the way I bring it up. The problem for me is that I feel worried and I would like to share why in a way that's helpful. I don't seem to know how to do that, and I was wondering if you had any advice."

Your friend may still tell you to butt out. But it's also possible that she'll engage: "You know what, I more or less agree with you. But so many people are hitting me with this from so many angles right now that what I really need is someone who'll just be supportive without trying to give me advice. Just listen while I think things through and decide what to cut out. You know what I mean?"

## A Map for Going Forward: Third Story, Their Story, Your Story

Beginning from the Third Story gets you safely to the base of the mountain. But then there's the mountain itself to climb. Once a description of the problem is on the table, and your purposes are clear, then you will need to spend time exploring the Three Conversations from each of your perspectives. The other person will share their views and feelings, and you'll step back into your story and share yours.

## What to Talk About: The Three Conversations

As you share your stories, each of the Three Conversations offers a useful path to explore. You can talk about the past experiences that have led each of you to see the current situation the way you do: "I think the reason I reacted so strongly is that the last time we didn't receive payment from a vendor, the situation only went from bad to worse."

You can ask about the other person's intentions, and share the impact of their behavior on you: "I don't know whether you realize this or not, but when you didn't call, I was frantic with worry." You can empathize with how they might be feeling: "If I were you, I'd be pretty frustrated at this point." Or share what's going on with your Identity Conversation: "I think the reason I find this so hard is that being fair is so important to me. It's upsetting to think that the way I handled this situation might not have been fair to you." Ultimately, what

---

**What to Talk About**

**Explore where each story comes from**
"My reactions here probably have a lot to do with my experiences in a previous job. . . ."

**Share the impact on you**
"I don't know whether you intended this, but I felt extremely uncomfortable when . . . ."

**Take responsibility for your contribution**
"There are a number of things I've done that have made this situation harder. . . ."

**Describe feelings**
"I'm anxious about bringing this up, but at the same time, it's important to me that we talk about it. . . ."

**Reflect on the identity issues**
"I think the reason this subject hooks me is that I don't like thinking of myself as someone who . . . ."

you choose to share will depend upon the context and the relationship and what feels appropriate and helpful.

## How to Talk About It: Listening, Expression, and Problem-Solving

The Three Conversations provide a useful map for *what* to talk about; the next few chapters delve more deeply into *how* to talk about it.

To be able to see the other person's story from the inside you'll need some specific skills in inquiring, listening, and acknowledgment. To share your own story with clarity and power, you need to feel entitled and be precise in speaking only for yourself. Chapters 9 and 10 explore these challenges and offer guidelines for effectiveness. Of course, it will never be as tidy as moving from the *Third Story*, to *Their Story*, to *Your Story*. A real conversation is an interactive process — one where you are constantly going to be listening, sharing your view, asking questions, and negotiating to get the conversation back on track when it starts to go off the rails. Chapter 11 provides guidance on how to manage this interactive process and how to move toward problem-solving. Finally, Chapter 12 returns to our original story of Jack and Michael and offers an extended example illustrating how it all works in practice.

# 9

# Learning:
## *Listen from the Inside Out*

Andrew is visiting his Uncle Doug. While Doug is on the phone, Andrew tugs on his uncle's pant leg, saying, "Uncle Doug, I want to go outside."

"Not now, Andrew, I'm on the phone," says Doug.

Andrew persists: "But Uncle Doug, I want to go outside!"

"Not now Andrew!" comes Doug's response.

"But I want to go out!" Andrew repeats.

After several more rounds, Doug tries a different approach: "Hey, Andrew. You really want to go outside, don't you?"

"Yes," says Andrew. Then without further comment, Andrew walks off and begins playing by himself. Andrew, it turns out, just wanted to know that his uncle understood him. He wanted to know he'd been heard.

Andrew's story demonstrates something that is true for all of us: we have a deep desire to feel heard, and to know that others care enough to listen.

Some people think they are already good listeners. Others know they are not, but don't much care. If you're in either group you might be tempted to skip this chapter. Don't. Listening well is one of the most powerful skills you can bring to a difficult conversation. It helps you understand the other person. And, importantly, it helps them understand you.

## Listening Transforms the Conversation

A year ago, Greta's mother learned she had diabetes and was ordered to follow a strict regimen of medication, diet, and exercise. Greta is concerned that her mother is not following the regimen, but Greta has had little success encouraging her mother to do so. A typical conversation between them goes like this:

> GRETA: Mom, you need to stay on the exercise plan. I worry that you don't understand how important it is.
>
> MOM: Greta, please stop hounding me about this. You don't understand. I'm doing the best I can.
>
> GRETA: Mom, I do understand. I know that exercising can be difficult, but I want you to stay well. I want you to be around for your grandchildren.
>
> MOM: Greta, I really don't like these conversations. It's all very hard for me, the diet, the exercise.
>
> GRETA: I know it's hard. Exercising is no fun, but the thing is, after a week or two, it gets easier, and you start to look forward to it. We can find you some sort of activity that you'll really enjoy.
>
> MOM: [choked up] You don't realize . . . . It's very stressful. I'm just not going to talk about it anymore. That's all there is to it!

Not surprisingly, these conversations leave Greta feeling frustrated, powerless, and deeply sad. Greta wonders how she might be more assertive, how she can persuade her mother to change.

But assertiveness isn't Greta's problem. What's missing from her stance is curiosity. In a follow-up conversation, Greta shifts her goal from persuasion to learning. To do this she limits herself to listening, asking questions, and acknowledging her mother's feelings:

> GRETA: I know you don't like talking about your diabetes and exercising.

MOM: I really don't. It's very upsetting to me.

GRETA: When you say it's upsetting, what do you mean? In what ways?

MOM: Greta, the whole thing! Do you think it's fun for me?

GRETA: No, Mom, I know it's really hard. I just don't know much about what you think about it, what it means to you, what you feel about it.

MOM: I'll tell you, if your father were alive, it would be different. He was so sweet when I would get sick. Having to follow all these complicated rules, that's what he would have been good at. He would have taken care of the whole thing. Being sick, it just makes me miss him so much.

GRETA: It sounds like you've been feeling really lonely without Dad.

MOM: I have friends, and you've been wonderful, but it's not the same as having your father here to help. I suppose I really do feel lonely, but I hate to talk about that. I don't want to be a burden on you kids.

GRETA: You feel like if you tell us you're lonely, it will be a burden? We'll worry?

MOM: I just don't want you to have to go through what my mother went through. You know *her* mother died of diabetes.

GRETA: I didn't know. Wow.

MOM: It's scary to be told you have what your grandmother died of. It's hard for me to accept. I know the medications are better now, which is why I should be following all those rules, but if I follow all those rules, it just makes me feel like some sick old lady.

GRETA: So keeping to the regimen would feel like accepting something that you don't really totally accept yet?

MOM: It's irrational. I'm not saying it's not. [choked up] It's just very frightening and overwhelming.

GRETA: I know it is, Mom.

MOM: I'll tell you something else. I don't even understand what I'm supposed to be doing. The eating, the exercise. If you do one, it affects the other, and you have to keep track. It's

> complicated, and the doctor isn't terribly helpful in explaining it. I don't know where to begin. Your father would know.
>
> GRETA: Maybe that's something I could help you with.
>
> MOM: Greta, I don't want to be a burden.
>
> GRETA: I want to help. It would actually make me feel better. Not so powerless.
>
> MOM: If you could, that would take a big load off my mind. . . .

Greta was astonished and delighted at how much better her conversations became after she began truly listening to her mother. She came to see the issues from her mother's point of view, how much deeper they ran than she suspected, and how she might be able to help her mother in ways that her mother wanted to be helped. This is perhaps the most obvious benefit of listening: learning about the other person. But there is a second, more surprising benefit as well.

## Listening to Them Helps Them Listen to You

Ironically, when Greta shifted away from trying to persuade her mother to exercise and toward simply listening and acknowledging, she ended up achieving the goal that had eluded her up to that point. This is not an accident. One of the most common complaints we hear from people engaged in difficult conversations is that the other person won't listen. And when we hear that, our standard advice is "*You* need to spend more time listening to *them*."

When the other person is not listening, you may imagine it is because they're stubborn or don't understand what you're trying to say. (If they did, they'd understand why they should listen to it.) So you may try to break through that by repeating, trying new ways to explain yourself, talking more loudly, and so forth.

On the face of it, these would seem to be good strategies. But they're not. Why? Because in the great majority of cases, the reason the other person is not listening to you is not because they are stubborn, but because *they* don't feel heard. In other words, they aren't listening to you for the same reason you aren't listening to them: they think *you* are slow or stubborn. So they repeat themselves, find new ways to say things, talk more loudly, and so forth.

If the block to their listening is that they don't feel heard, then the way to remove that block is by helping them feel heard — by bending over backwards to listen to what they have to say, and perhaps most important, by demonstrating that you understand what they are saying and how they are feeling.

If you don't quite believe this, try it. Find the most stubborn person you know, the person who never seems to take in anything you say, the person who repeats himself or herself in every conversation you ever have — and listen to them. Especially, listen for feelings, like frustration or pride or fear, and acknowledge those feelings. See whether that person doesn't become a better listener after all.

## The Stance of Curiosity: How to Listen from the Inside Out

What, specifically, does Greta do differently in the second conversation? She asks questions. She paraphrases what her mother says to make sure she understands it, and to make sure her mother understands that Greta understands. Greta is also listening for the feelings that might be behind what her mother is saying, and acknowledges them when she hears them.

Each of these is enormously important to good listening. But none is enough. The single most important thing Greta has done is to shift her internal stance from "I understand" to "Help me understand." Everything else follows from that.

### Forget the Words, Focus on Authenticity

Scores of workshops and books on "active listening" teach you what you should *do* to be a good listener. Their advice is relatively similar — ask questions, paraphrase back what the other person has said, acknowledge their view, sit attentively and look them in the eye — all good advice. You emerge from these courses eager to try out your new skills, only to become discouraged when your friends or colleagues complain that you sound phony or mechanical. "Don't use that active listening stuff on me," they say.

The problem is this: you are taught what to say and how to sit, but the heart of good listening is authenticity. People "read" not only your words and posture, but what's going on inside of you. If your "stance" isn't genuine, the words won't matter. What will be communicated almost invariably is whether you are genuinely curious, whether you genuinely care about the other person. If your intentions are false, no amount of careful wording or good posture will help. If your intentions are good, even clumsy language won't hinder you.

Listening is only powerful and effective if it is authentic. Authenticity means that you are listening because you are curious and because you care, not just because you are supposed to. The issue, then, is this: Are you curious? Do you care?


## The Commentator in Your Head:
## Become More Aware of Your Internal Voice

You can tell what's going on inside of you by listening to *yourself*. Finding and paying attention to your own internal voice — what you're thinking but not saying — is the crucial first step in overcoming the biggest barrier to inauthentic listening. Left unattended, that voice blocks good listening; to the extent you're listening to your own internal voice, you're at best only half listening to the other person.

Take a moment to locate the commentator in your head. It's saying something like "Hmm, this internal voice is an interesting concept" or "What are they talking about? I don't have an internal voice" (*that's* the voice).

## Don't Turn It Off, Turn It Up

Perhaps surprisingly, our advice is not to turn off your internal voice, or even to turn it down. You can't. Instead, we urge you to do the opposite — turn *up* your internal voice, at least for the time being, and get to know the kinds of things it says. In other words, listen to it. Only when you're fully aware of your own thoughts can you begin to manage them and focus on the other person.

There are endless thoughts and feelings you might have while you're listening, but by now you know the patterns: your voice will be chattering away in each of the Three Conversations. In the "What Happened?" Conversation, you'll find yourself thinking things like "I'm right," "I did not intend to hurt you," and "This isn't my fault." You'll also notice plenty of feelings ("I can't believe she thinks that about me! I'm so furious!") and identity issues ("Was I really that thoughtless? I couldn't have been"). Or not uncommonly, you may simply be daydreaming ("I wonder if there's enough meatloaf for the in-laws") or beginning to prepare your response ("When it's my turn to talk, there are four points I'm going to make").

No wonder the person you're listening to doesn't feel they have your full attention.

## Managing Your Internal Voice

How then can you give the other person your full attention and listen with curiosity when your internal commentator is chattering away? You can try two things. First, see if you can negotiate your way to curiosity. See if you can get your internal voice into a learning mode. If this doesn't work, and sometimes it won't, you may first have to express your internal voice before trying to listen to the other person.

**Negotiate Your Way to Curiosity.** It's a mistake to think your internal voice can't change. If you find your curiosity failing, you can work to rev it up. Remind yourself that the task of understanding the other person's world is always harder than it seems. Remind yourself that if you think you already understand how someone else feels or what they are trying to say, it is a delusion. Remember a time when you were *sure* you were right and then discovered one little fact that changed everything. There is always more to learn. Remind yourself of the depth, complexities, contradictions, and nuances that make up the stories of each of our lives.

Audrey's six-year-old daughter, Jocie, woke her up in the middle of the night. Jocie was scared because of a movie they'd seen about a puppy's mother who ran away and never came back. Audrey assumed Jocie was worried about being abandoned herself, and she explained to Jocie that "I would never run away and leave you by yourself."

But it turned out that that wasn't what Jocie was worried about at all. She was anxious about her new turtle. The movie had caused her to wonder whether her turtle might be someone's mother, and whether there was a baby turtle somewhere that needed its mother back. In fact, Jocie's turtle was itself a baby, but Jocie didn't know that and was consumed with fear and guilt. Audrey had fallen into the trap of listening to her internal voice rather than to her daughter. Her internal voice was saying, "I know what this is all about," and that was the end of her curiosity.

Another way to rekindle your curiosity is to keep focused on your purpose in the conversation. If your purpose is to persuade or win or get the other person to do something, your internal voice will be saying things in line with those purposes, such as, "Why don't you just do this — it's obviously the best answer." If, instead, you hold as one of your primary purposes understanding the other person, it motivates your internal voice to ask questions, such as "What else do I need to know for that to make more sense?" or "I wonder how I can understand the world in such a way that that would make sense?"

**Don't Listen: Talk.** Sometimes you'll find that your internal voice is just too strong to take on. You try to negotiate your way to curiosity, but you just can't get there. If you're sitting on feelings of pain or outrage or betrayal, or, conversely, if you're overcome with joy or love, then listening may be a hopeless task.

Listening certainly feels out of reach for Dalila as she learns that Heather, her roommate of six months, is bisexual. As Heather talks, Dalila sits feeling confused, embarrassed, even a little angry. Rather than pretending to listen, Dalila needs to do the opposite. To remain authentic in the conversation she needs first to be honest about what she is thinking and feeling: "I'm glad you trust me enough to tell me this, and I really want to listen. At the same time, this is very upsetting for me. I'm feeling awkward, like I'm not sure how to act around you right now, and I'm just overwhelmed about what this means."

Dalila and Heather have a tough conversation ahead. Not only will each of them have strong feelings to sort through and share, but they have very different views about sexuality. As they talk about their friendship and how to handle their ongoing rooming situation, it will be critically important that each has the ability to listen to the other. At times, to be able to listen they'll need first to speak.

When you find yourself in this situation, let the other person know that you want to listen and that you care about what they have to say, but that you can't listen right now. Often it's enough to give a headline of what you're thinking: "I'm surprised to hear you say that. I think I disagree, but say more about how you see it," or "I have to admit that as much as I want to hear what you have to say, I'm feeling a little defensive right now." With that on the table, you can get back to listening, knowing that you've signaled your difference and will get back to your view in time.

In some cases, you may decide that you can neither listen nor talk. This may be because you're too upset or confused, or simply because you need to be doing something else. Rather than give the other person half your attention, it's better to say, "This is important to me, I want to find a time to talk about it, and right now I'm not able to."

Managing your internal voice is not easy, especially at first. But it is at the heart of good listening.

# Three Skills: Inquiry, Paraphrasing, and Acknowledgment

While your internal stance is the key to good listening, there are some specific techniques we can pass along, some how-tos that people find helpful. In addition to the stance of curiosity, there are three primary skills that good listeners employ: inquiry, paraphrasing, and acknowledgment. Below are some dos and don'ts relating to each.

## Inquire to Learn

The heading says it all: inquire to learn. And only to learn. You can tell whether a question will help the conversation or hurt it by thinking about why you asked it. The only good answer is "To learn."

### Don't Make Statements Disguised as Questions

Anyone who has ever been a kid in a car has uttered the cranky words "Are we there yet?" You know you're not there yet, and your parents know you know, and so they respond in a tone as cranky as yours. What you really meant was "I'm feeling restless" or "I wish we were there" or "This is a long trip for me." Any of these would likely elicit a more productive response from Mom and Dad.

This illustrates an important rule about inquiry: If you don't have a question, don't ask a question. Never dress up an assertion as a question. Doing so creates confusion and resentment, because such questions are inevitably heard as sarcastic and sometimes mean-spirited. Consider some examples of assertions disguised as questions:

> "Are you going to leave the refrigerator door open like that?" (Instead of "Please close the refrigerator door" or "I feel frustrated when you leave the refrigerator door open.")

"Is it impossible for you to focus on me just once?" (Instead of "I feel ignored" or "I'd like you to pay more attention to me.")

"Do you have to drive so fast?" (Instead of "I'm feeling nervous" or "It's hard for me to relax when I'm not in control.")

Notice that these examples of disguised assertions are either about feelings or about requests. This should not be surprising. Sharing our feelings and making requests are two things that many of us have difficulty doing directly. They can make us feel vulnerable. Turning what we have to say into an attack — a sarcastic question — can feel safer. But this safety is an illusion, and we lose more than we gain. Saying "I'd like you to pay more attention to me" is more likely to produce a conversation (and a satisfying outcome) than "Is it impossible for you to focus on me just once?"

Why? Because instead of hearing the underlying feeling or request, the other person focuses on the sarcasm and the attack. Instead of hearing that you feel lonely, they hear that you think they are thoughtless. The real message doesn't get through, because they are distracted by the need to defend themselves. In fact, they are likely to respond in kind: "Well, sure, I can focus on you just *once*." And things deteriorate from there.

## Don't Use Questions to Cross-Examine

A second error that gets us into trouble is using questions to shoot holes in the other person's argument. For example:

"You seem to think this is my fault. But surely you'd agree that you made more mistakes than I did, wouldn't you?"

"If it's true that you did everything you could have done to make the sale, how do you explain the fact that Kate was able to make the sale so soon after you gave up?"

These questions are wrong-footed from the start. They emerge from a purpose of trying to persuade the other person that you are right and they are wrong, rather than trying to learn.

To use the ideas in these questions constructively, pull out the statements embedded in the questions and express them — but not as facts. Rather than asserting them as true, share them as open questions or perceptions, and ask for the other person's reaction. Rather than assuming that this is an argument they have ignored, assume that they *have* thought about it and have reason to tell a different story. You might say, for example, "I understand that you feel you did everything you could to make the sale. To me, that seems inconsistent with the fact that Kate made the sale right after you gave up. What's your thinking about that?"

## Ask Open-Ended Questions

Open-ended questions are questions that give the other person broad latitude in how to answer. They elicit more information than yes/no questions or offering menus, such as, "Were you trying to do A or B?" Instead ask "What were you trying to do?" This way you don't bias the answer or distract the other person's thinking by the need to process your ideas. It lets them direct their response toward what is important to *them*. Typical open-ended questions are variations on "Tell me more" and "Help me understand better . . . ."

## Ask for More Concrete Information

To understand where the other person's conclusions came from and enrich your understanding of what they envision going forward, it helps to ask them to be more explicit about their reasoning and their vision. "What leads you to say that?" "Can you give me an example?" "What would that look like?" "How would that work?" "How would we test that hypothesis?"

Consider the situation Ross ran into with his boss. He received a flyer for a professional seminar he wanted to take. It would help him in his job as a product manager, so he figured the conversation with his boss about getting the time off and the course paid for would be a cinch.

He was wrong. The conversation went like this:

> Boss: For me even to consider having the company pay for you to go to that seminar I'd need more evidence that you're dedicated to working here for the long term, and right now I just don't see it.
>
> Ross: What? I'm totally dedicated to the company. I've told you that. That's the whole point of me wanting to take this seminar.
>
> Boss: I don't see it that way. I get the sense you view this job as a stepping stone to something else.
>
> Ross: Well, I don't know what else I can say, except that I love it here and plan to stay. And the seminar would be very helpful for the work I do. . . .

It's not hard to see why this is an unproductive exchange. There's virtually no information being transferred back and forth except "Am so!" and "Are not!" In essence, Ross's boss is saying, "I don't think you're dedicated, but I'm not going to tell you why." And unfortunately, Ross isn't asking.

After some coaching, Ross took up the issue again, but this time asked for more concrete information:

> Ross: Say more about how you judge dedication, and what you've observed in me that suggests to you that I'm not as dedicated as you'd like me to be.
>
> Boss: Well, obviously it's a lot of things. One piece of it is that you seem uninterested in the social events here. In my experience that has always been a pretty good indicator of dedication. People who are in this for the long haul know the

importance of building and maintaining good relationships with their coworkers, and they make sure to get to as many social events as possible.

Ross: Huh. I'm totally surprised to hear you say that. I was assuming you measured dedication based on things like working late and doing a lot of assignments well.

Boss: That's very important too. But sometimes people do that to build a good record for when they decide to move on to the next job. In my experience the socializing aspect is the most tightly correlated to long-term interest. . . .

Finally, Ross and his boss were getting somewhere. By the end of the conversation, they had a much deeper understanding of why they each reached a different conclusion about Ross's commitment to the company, important information for Ross to know.

## Ask Questions About the Three Conversations

Each of the Three Conversations provides fertile ground for curiosity:

- Can you say a little more about how you see things?

- What information might you have that I don't?

- How do you see it differently?

- What impact have my actions had on you?

- Can you say a little more about why you think this is my fault?

- Were you reacting to something I did?

- How are you feeling about all of this?

- Say more about why this is important to you.

• What would it mean to you if that happened?

If the answers aren't entirely clear, keep digging. If necessary, say what's still unclear or inconsistent to you, and ask for clarification: "Okay, so your view is that Kate made the sale because she could offer a reduced price on the service contract. I can see how that would make a difference. What I'm still not clear on, though, is why you couldn't offer that or get permission to offer that. Can you say more about that?"

## Make It Safe for Them Not to Answer

Sometimes even the most skillful question provokes defensiveness. You ask a question out of genuine caring toward the other person and a genuine desire to learn, and still they react by shutting down, defending, counterattacking, accusing you of bad intentions, or changing the subject.

One response is to say that you are trying to help and that there is no need to be defensive, and then continue to press for an answer. But this can be experienced as an attempt to control them, provoking further resistance. It's better to make your question an invitation rather than a demand, and to make that clear. The difference is that an invitation can be declined without penalty. This offers a greater sense of safety and, especially if the other person declines to respond and your reaction makes that okay, it builds trust between you.

Whether you are talking with your boss or your eight-year-old daughter, giving them the choice of whether to answer increases the chance that they will respond and respond honestly. Even if they don't answer now, they may later, after they think about it. Knowing that it's their choice underscores your caring intent and frees them to think about the question.

## Paraphrase for Clarity

The second skill a good listener brings to the conversation is paraphrasing. Paraphrasing is when you express to the other person, in your own words, your understanding of what they are saying. There are two significant benefits to paraphrasing.

### Check Your Understanding

First, paraphrasing gives you a chance to check your understanding. Difficult conversations are made harder when an important misunderstanding exists, and such misunderstandings are more common than we imagine. Paraphrasing gives the other person the chance to say, "No, that's not quite what I meant. What I really meant was . . . ."

### Show That You've Heard

Second, paraphrasing lets the other person know they've been heard. Usually the reason someone repeats himself or herself in a conversation is because they have no indication that you've actually taken in what they've said. If you notice that the other person is saying the same thing over and over again, take it as a signal that you need to paraphrase more. Once they feel heard, they are significantly more likely to listen to *you*. They will no longer be absorbed by their internal voice, and can focus on what you have to say.

Consider this conversation between Rachel and Ron, a married couple who frequently argue about how strictly to observe Shabbat (the Jewish Sabbath) and its traditional rules restricting travel:

RON: I told Chris I'd come by tomorrow.
RACHEL: Ron, tomorrow's Saturday. You know you can't drive

over to Chris's on Shabbat. Besides, we've got temple in the
morning.

RON: I know, but I told Chris I'd come. It's the only day he had
available.

RACHEL: Well, I think it's important that we go to services as a
family. Why don't you go over there on Sunday?

RON: Chris can't do it on Sunday — he's got church and
stuff.

RACHEL: Oh, so his religious practices are more important than
ours?

Neither Rachel nor Ron feels heard in this conversation. If they
are going to break this cycle, one of them has to decide to listen and
to paraphrase. Let's assume that Ron decides to try:

RON: I told Chris I'd come by tomorrow.

RACHEL: Ron, tomorrow's Saturday. You know you can't drive
over to Chris's on Shabbat. Besides, we've got temple in the
morning.

RON: It sounds like my making plans is frustrating to you.

RACHEL: You bet it's frustrating. I assumed we were going.

RON: So part of the problem is that I made plans without consulting you?

RACHEL: No, it's more that I hate being the one who always nags
us to go to temple.

RON: You feel like I make you the one responsible for our religious life.

RACHEL: Yeah. I hate feeling like the Shabbat police. Plus, I
worry about the message it sends to the kids.

RON: So you're afraid that if the kids see me breaking the Sabbath they won't take it seriously?

RACHEL: That's part of it, but it's a lot of things. It's lonely when
I go by myself. And I want you to go to temple because you
want to go, not because I'm making you go.

RON: I can see how that would be lonely. I do want to go for

myself. I think that sometimes when I feel pressured to go, I
resist because I don't like being told what to do. Also, sometimes I feel like I am following the spirit of the law by doing
other things.

RACHEL: [skeptical] Like what?

RON: Well, like helping out Chris. He's having a really rough
time in his marriage right now, and I wanted to try to spend
some time with him. That makes me feel like I'm connecting with people in our community, which is part of what I
get out of services. And I'd like the kids to see that caring for
people is a big part of what this is all about. Maybe we could
talk to them about this.

RACHEL: Well, that would help. . . .

RON: But that might not meet your interest in going to services together, or not wanting to carry the weight of responsibility for
it in our family. Can you say more about that? . . .

This time Rachel and Ron are starting to get somewhere in a
complex and emotionally charged issue. Ron's paraphrasing lets Rachel know that he is trying to understand her and that he cares about
her feelings. He stops repeating himself, and she starts listening.

## Acknowledge Their Feelings

Notice that Ron begins paraphrasing by responding not to what
Rachel says, but to what she doesn't say: that she's frustrated. It is a
fundamental rule: feelings crave acknowledgment. Like free radicals,
feelings wander around the conversation looking for some acknowledgment to hook onto. They won't be happy until they get it,
and nothing else will do. Unless they get the acknowledgment they
need, feelings will cause trouble in the conversation — like a kid desperate for attention, positive or negative. And if you provide that
acknowledgment, you give the other person and the relationship
something quite precious, something, perhaps, that they can only get
from you.

## Answer the Invisible Questions

Why is acknowledgment so important? Because attached to each expression of feelings is a set of invisible questions: "Are my feelings
okay?" "Do you understand them?" "Do you care about them?" "Do
you care about me?" These questions are important, and we have
trouble moving on in the conversation until we know the answers.
Taking time to acknowledge the other person's feelings says loud and
clear that the answer to each question is yes.

## How to Acknowledge

An acknowledgment is simply this: any indication that you are struggling to understand the emotional content of what the other person
is saying. If the other person says to you, "I'm confused by the fact
that you lied to me," you might say any of the following:

> Well, it won't happen again.

> I should explain that I did *not* lie.

> It sounds like you're overreacting a bit here.

> Each of these is an understandable response. The first two re-
spond to the substance of what is being said; the third judges the feeling. But none simply acknowledges the feeling, or responds to the
invisible questions. In contrast, any of the following would count as
an acknowledgment:

> It sounds like you're really upset about this.

> This seems really important to you.

> If I were in your shoes I'd probably feel confused too.

There is no one perfect thing to say. In fact, you may not need to say anything. Sometimes you can acknowledge the other person with a simple nod, or even by the look in your eyes.

## Order Matters: Acknowledge Before Problem-Solving

Ultimately, of course, people want their problems addressed. Questions like "What are we going to do about this?" "Why did you do what you did?" "How do you explain what happened?" are important. But order matters. Whether they say it or not, often people need some acknowledgment of feelings before they can move on to the "What Happened?" Conversation.

Too often in difficult conversations and with the best of intentions, we skip right to problem-solving without acknowledging, and the loss is significant. "You're working too hard," says your husband. "I never see you anymore." You realize he's right, and say, "Well, for the next month, my workload is a lot lighter. I'll make a real effort to be home every night by six o'clock." Your husband doesn't seem satisfied, and you are left wondering what more you could have said.

But your husband's complaint is not a math problem. You may think you've "solved" the problem, but his invisible questions haven't been addressed. Your husband wants his feelings acknowledged. "It's been a tough time, these last few months, hasn't it?" or "It sounds like you're feeling abandoned" would be more appropriate. Problem-solving is important, but it has to wait.

## Acknowledging Is Not Agreeing

The most common concern that arises around the issue of acknowledging is this: What if I don't agree with what the other person is saying? This is an important concern. It is useful to distinguish here between the Feelings Conversation and the "What Happened?" Conversation. While you may not agree with the substance of what the other person is saying, you can still acknowledge the importance of their feelings.

For example, a supervisor has transferred one of her subordinates to a different department, and he comes into her office to complain. Notice how the supervisor acknowledges his feelings without agreeing with his conclusion:

> SUBORDINATE: I have worked so hard for you and now you're shipping me out. It's just not fair. I've been a loyal team player and now what's going to happen to me?
>
> SUPERVISOR: Sounds like you feel really hurt and betrayed. I can see why that would be upsetting.
>
> SUBORDINATE: So you agree with me that this is unfair?
>
> SUPERVISOR: What I'm saying is that I can see how upset you're feeling, and it hurts me to see you so upset. I also think I understand why you think this transfer is unfair, and why it could feel like I've betrayed your loyalty. Those factors made the decision to transfer you very difficult for me. I fought hard to make this work. I feel badly about how it's turned out, but I do think it's the right decision, and overall I don't think it's unfair. We should talk about why.

It requires thought to make these kinds of distinctions, but it can help immensely. Too often we assume that we either have to agree or disagree with the other person. In fact, we can acknowledge the power and importance of the feelings, while disagreeing with the substance of what is being said.

## A Final Thought: Empathy Is a Journey, Not a Destination

The deepest form of understanding another person is empathy. Empathy involves a shift from my observing how you seem on the outside, to my imagining what it feels like to be you on the inside, wrapped in your skin with your set of experiences and background, and looking out at the world through your eyes.

As an empathetic listener, you are on a journey with a direction but no destination. You will never "arrive." You will never be able to say, "I truly understand you." We are all too complex for that, and our skills to imagine ourselves into other people's lives too limited. But in a sense this is good news. Psychologists have found that we are each more interested in knowing that the other person is *trying* to emphathize with us — that they are willing to struggle to understand how we feel and see how we see — than we are in believing that they have actually accomplished that goal. Good listening, as we've said, is profoundly communicative. And struggling to understand communicates the most positive message of all.

# 10

# Expression:
## *Speak for Yourself*
## *with Clarity and Power*

Beginning from the Third Story is a productive way to open a conversation. Listening to the other person's story with a real desire to learn what they are thinking and feeling is a crucial next step. But understanding them is rarely the end of the matter; the other person also needs to hear *your* story. You need to express yourself.

## Orators Need Not Apply

Expressing yourself well in a difficult conversation has nothing to do with how big your vocabulary is or how eloquent or quick-witted you are. Winston Churchill and Martin Luther King, Jr. were great orators, but in difficult conversations their powers of oration would be of no particular assistance.

In a difficult conversation your primary task is not to persuade, impress, trick, outwit, convert, or win over the other person. It is to express what you see and why you see it that way, how you feel, and maybe who you are. Self-knowledge and the belief that what you want to share is important will take you significantly further than eloquence and wit.

In the first part of this chapter we take up the issue of entitlement. To communicate with clarity and power, you must first negotiate yourself into a place where you truly believe that what you want to express is worthy of expression — a belief that your views and feelings are as important as anyone else's. Period. In the second part of the chapter, we look at how to figure out *what* you want to express and *how* you might best express it. We'll examine several common but significant expression errors, ways to avoid them, and methods for expressing yourself well.

## You're Entitled (Yes, You)

John, a second-year law student, was preparing to meet with a well-respected federal judge to discuss several concerns he had about his upcoming clerkship. The judge had a reputation for being a some-times prickly and argumentative fellow, and John was anxious about losing his courage once he stepped into the judge's chambers.

John's favorite professor offered advice: "Whenever I have felt intimidated or mistreated by someone above me, I remember this — we are all equal in the eyes of God."

## No More, But No Less

Regardless of our spiritual orientation, we can all benefit from the message: No matter who we are, no matter how high and mighty we fancy ourselves, or how low and unworthy we may feel, we all deserve to be treated with respect and dignity. My views and feelings are as legitimate, valuable, and important as yours — no more, but no less. For some people, that's utterly obvious. For others, it comes as important news.

In an essay in her book, *Sister Outsider*, poet and activist Audre Lorde pondered the question of expression and entitlement shortly after she learned she had breast cancer:

I have come to believe . . . . that what is most important to me must be spoken, made verbal and shared, even at the risk of having it bruised or misunderstood. . . .

In becoming forcibly and essentially aware of my mortality, and of what I wished and wanted for my life, however short it might be, priorities and omissions became strongly etched in a merciless light, and what I most regretted were my silences. . . . I was going to die, if not sooner then later, whether or not I had ever spoken myself. My silences had not protected me. Your silence will not protect you. . . .

We can learn to work and speak when we are afraid in the same way we have learned to work and speak when we are tired. For we have been socialized to respect fear more than our own needs for language and definition, and while we wait in silence for that final luxury of fearlessness, the weight of that silence will choke us.

Lorde sees substantial risks in expressing oneself. But she recognizes that the costs of silence are even greater. Recognizing *your* entitlement can help you find your voice in a conversation and the courage to stand up for yourself when you feel frightened or powerless.

## Beware Self-Sabotage

Sometimes we can feel trapped between the belief that we should stand up for ourselves and a hidden feeling that we don't deserve to be heard, that we're not entitled. In this situation our unconscious mind can offer a devious — and illusory — "solution": We go through the motions of trying, but incompetently, so that in the end we fail. We wait to speak until there's not enough time to deal with our concerns. We conveniently forget our materials. All our points suddenly disappear from our head. And voilà! All of our interests are satisfied: we can feel good about trying, and secretly satisfied that we didn't succeed. This is the art of self-sabotage.

If this feels like a familiar trick in your repertoire, then you may need to pay more attention to when you are feeling ambivalent. When you sense that vaguely sick or confused feeling, imagine an enormous STOP sign to halt you in your tracks. Before proceeding, you need to engage your Identity Conversation. Why aren't you entitled? Whose voice from your past do you hear in your head telling you you're not? What would you need to feel fully entitled to speak up?

## Failure to Express Yourself Keeps You Out of the Relationship

The ferry tickets to the island of Martha's Vineyard, Massachusetts, read like many transportation tickets. Perforated in the middle, the ticket carries a warning that it will be "void if detached."

We run the same risks in difficult conversations. When we fail to share what's most important to us, we detach ourselves from others and damage our relationships.

Most of us actually prefer being with someone who will speak their mind. Angela broke off her engagement because her fiancé was "too nice." He never stated a preference, never argued, never raised his voice, never asked for anything. While she appreciated his kindness, she felt something was missing: him.

If you are sometimes lonely or despondent and never share this with those close to you, then you deny them the chance to come to know a part of you. You presume that they will not respect or like or admire you as much if they knew the way you really think and feel. But it's hard to present only this sanitized version of yourself. Often, to hide parts of who we are, we end up hiding all of who we are. And so we present a front that appears lifeless and removed.

Expressing yourself can be difficult and trying, but it gives the relationship a chance to change and to become stronger. Callie, a Native American woman, did not feel particularly close to her co-workers at a tutoring program for troubled teens. Partly because they were white, she suspected they wouldn't really understand her; indeed, she often found them to be insensitive.

But one day she took a risk and shared some stories. She described how she had been called names and teased when she was younger, and how for years she yearned to be "normal." These revelations significantly changed her relationship with her colleagues, who came to have great admiration for her. Her colleagues, in turn, felt encouraged to share their own stories of feeling left out or awkward. If Callie had not shared her story, she would have deprived her colleagues of the chance to rebut a stereotype she herself harbored — that "white people don't understand and don't care." And she wouldn't have offered them the opportunity, perhaps for the first time, to understand and care about her.

A relationship takes hold and grows when both participants experience themselves and the other as being authentic. Such relationships are both more comfortable (it's more relaxing to be yourself) and nourishing to the soul ("My boss knows some of my vulnerabilities and still thinks I'm okay").

## Feel Entitled, Feel Encouraged, But Don't Feel Obligated

You are entitled to express yourself. If you do not believe this to your core then you've got some work to do.

But being entitled doesn't mean you're obligated. That turns entitlement into another way to beat yourself up: "I should be saying what's on my mind, but I'm too afraid. I can't do anything right!" Expressing yourself is often extremely difficult. Finding the courage to do it is a lifelong process. If you aren't doing it as much as you'd like, it's something to work on, but not something to punish yourself about.

## Speak the Heart of the Matter

The first step toward expressing yourself is finding your sense of entitlement to speak up; the next step is figuring out what, exactly, you want to say.

## Start with What Matters Most

There's no better place to begin your story than with what is at the very heart of the matter for you: "For me, what this is really about is . . . . What I'm feeling is . . . . What is important to me is . . . ."

Sharing what is important to you is common sense, and yet it's advice we often neglect. Consider the story of Charlie, the oldest of four brothers, who wants to improve his relationship with his youngest brother, sixteen-year-old Gage. Gage is dyslexic, which is especially tough since his older brothers all graduated near the top of their high school classes and went to college on academic scholarships. Gage struggles in school, is prone to act out, and has increasingly turned to drinking for solace.

Charlie wants to help by offering the benefit of his experience and advice: "You should definitely do the debate team. The coach is great, and it will help your college applications." And, "You know, Gage, don't overdo the drinking thing. It can really be bad news." But whatever Charlie says makes Gage feel criticized, defensive, and patronized. As a result, the two brothers have grown increasingly distant.

When we asked Charlie why the relationship is important to him, the story took a different turn. Charlie admires the way Gage works so hard to succeed. He feels bad about how he treated Gage when they were younger. And ultimately, it turns out that Charlie needs deeply to feel like a good brother, who loves and is loved in turn. As he revealed this, Charlie cried.

When Charlie finally shared these things with his brother, Gage was riveted. Charlie needed *him*. Charlie needed Gage's help in being a good brother. It proved a turning point in their relationship.

Gage would have had to be a mind reader to perceive even a hint of these meanings in Charlie's original communication. The heart of the message simply wasn't there. Nor was there a hint of the enormous depth of feelings at stake. Instead, there was a completely different message in its place: "You're a screw-up who needs my help and is too dumb to ask for it."

This is unfortunately all too typical of many difficult conversations. We say the least important things, sometimes over and over again, and wonder why the other person doesn't realize what we really think and how we really feel.

As you embark upon a difficult conversation, ask yourself, "Have I said what is at the heart of the matter for me? Have I shared what is at stake?" If not, ask yourself why, and see if you can find the courage to try.

## Say What You Mean: Don't Make Them Guess

One way we often skirt sharing things that are important to us is by embedding them in the subtext of the conversation rather than simply stating them outright.

**Don't Rely on Subtext.** Think back to the Introduction, where we discussed the dilemma of whether to engage in a conversation or to try to avoid it. One common way to manage this dilemma — especially when you're not sure you're really entitled to bring something up — is to communicate through subtext. You try to get your message across indirectly, through jokes, questions, offhand comments, or body language.

Bringing it up by not quite bringing it up seems a happy medium between avoiding and engaging. It is a way of doing neither and doing both. The problem is, to the extent you are doing both, you're doing both badly. You end up triggering all of the problems you worried you'd create by bringing it up, without getting the benefit of clearly saying what you want to say.

Imagine that you and your husband have usually spent Saturdays sleeping in, puttering around the house, walking the dog, or doing errands together. Recently, however, he has discovered golf, and has begun playing eighteen holes every Saturday morning. Your Saturday regime has never been particularly important — it's not like it was a date or something — but now that it's gone, you're missing it. The two of you don't spend much time alone together during the rest of the week, and as a result, you're feeling more and more irritated with his new hobby.

You could avoid conflict altogether by simply saying nothing, though as we've seen, your unhappiness would probably still leak out in spite of yourself. Or you might try to bring it up indirectly: "Honey, there's really a lot to be done around the house this weekend." "Is golf so important that you need to play it this often?" "Honey, you are simply playing too much golf!"

None of these comments conveys what you really mean, which is: "I want to spend more time with you." Let's consider the text and subtext of what each statement is saying:

**"Honey, there's really a lot to be done around the house this weekend."** This comment falls short on several grounds. First, it's simply the wrong subject. Working around the house is related to but different from spending time together. Second, even if work were the issue, the statement is shared as "truth." Your husband can reply, "There's not that much to do, and we'll talk about it when I get back."

**"Is golf so important that you need to play it this often?"** This is a classic example of a statement masquerading as a question. It's obvious that the meaning of the comment is conveyed in the subtext. What is less obvious is what the meaning is supposed to be. Your tone conveys anger or frustration. But it's not clear what is causing the anger or what your husband is supposed to do about it. Are you angry that your husband is engaged in a meaningless sport rather than community service or household chores? Are you angry that he's not taking you along? Are you angry that you aren't spending enough time together? How would he know?

**"Honey, you are simply playing too much golf!"** This statement is an opinion couched as a fact. Your husband is left to wonder, "Too much golf in relation to what?" "How much golf is too much golf?" "How much would be an appropriate amount of golf?" "Even if I am playing too much golf, so what?" Of course, even if he knew the answers to these questions, he would not have received the message intended. The gap between "You are playing too much golf" and "I would like to spend more time with you" is just too great.

To do better, you need to figure out what you are really thinking and feeling, and then say it directly: "I'd like to spend more time with you, and Saturday morning was one of the few times we had to spend together. As a result, I'm finding your interest in golf irritating."

Sometimes, you'll find yourself wishing you didn't have to be explicit. You wish the other person already knew that there was a problem and would do something about it. This is a common and understandable fantasy — our ideal mate or perfect colleague should be able to read our mind and meet our needs without our having to ask. Unfortunately, such people don't exist. Over time, we may come to know better how we each think and feel, but we will never be perfect. Being disappointed that someone isn't reading our mind is one of *our* contributions to the problem.

**Avoid Easing In.** A related and often destructive way to communicate through subtext is what Professor Chris Argyris of Harvard Business School has called *easing in*. Easing in is where you try to soften a message by delivering it indirectly through hints and leading questions. This is all too common in performance reviews: "So, how do *you* think you've done?" "Do you think you've really done as much as you could have?" "I have the same problem, but it probably would have been a little better to . . . . Wouldn't you agree?"

Easing in conveys three messages: "I have a view," "This is too embarrassing to discuss directly," and "I'm not going to be straight with you." Not surprisingly, these messages increase both sides' anxiety and defensiveness. And the recipient's imagination almost always conjures up a message worse than the real one.

A better approach is to make the subject clear and discussable by stating your thoughts straight out, while also indicating, honestly, that you are interested in whether the other person sees the situation differently and, if so, how: "Based on what I know, it seems to me that you might have gotten more done. However, you know more about what happened. In what ways would you see it differently?" Then if you disagree, you can talk directly about how to test or otherwise reconcile or deal with your different views.

## Don't Make Your Story Simplistic: Use the "Me-Me" And

We've all learned that for others to understand us, we need to make what we say clear and simple. Fair enough, as far as it goes. The problem is this: What's going on in our heads is often a jumble of complex thoughts, feelings, assumptions, and perceptions. When we try to be simple, we often end up being incomplete.

Imagine that you receive a memo from a co-worker that leaves you confused. You are thinking, "This memo shows incredible creativity, and at the same time is so badly organized that it makes me crazy." In your attempt to be clear, you say, "Your memo is so badly organized it makes me crazy," or worse, "Your memo makes me crazy."

You can avoid oversimplifying by using the Me-Me And. The And Stance recognizes that each of various perceptions, feelings, and assumptions is important to talk about. This is true of the other person's perceptions *and* your perceptions, the other person's feelings *and* yours. It's also true of the various perceptions, feelings, and assumptions that are going on *just inside you*. The "and" in this case is connecting two aspects of what you think or feel. And though complex, it's both clear and accurate. Me-Me And statements sound like this:

I do think you are bright and talented, *and* I think you're not working hard enough.

I feel badly for how rough things have been for you, *and* I'm feeling disappointed in you.

I'm upset with myself for not noticing that you were so lonely. *And* I also was having problems during that time.

I feel relieved and happy that I finally went through with the divorce — it was the right decision. *And* I do miss him sometimes.

The Me-Me And is also useful for overcoming a common obstacle to starting a difficult conversation: the fear of being misunderstood. You think your team would be the best one to take on a new client, but fear that it will sound self-serving, that you're in it only for the glory and the bonus. If this is the fear, share it along with your argument: "I have a view on this that I want to share, and I have to say that I'm nervous about doing so because I'm afraid it may sound self-serving. So if you see anything in what I say that doesn't seem legitimate, please say so and let's discuss it." Or, in a different situation, "I'm having a strong reaction here that I'd like to share, and I'm worried about feeling embarrassed if I'm not able to be clear or unemotional at first. I hope if that happens that you'll bear with me and help me stay with it until I can put it succinctly."

## Telling Your Story with Clarity: Three Guidelines

Obviously, how you express yourself makes a difference. How you say what you want to say will determine, in part, how others respond to you, and how the conversation will go. So when you choose to share something important, you'll want to do so in a way that will maximize the chance that the other person will understand and respond productively. Clarity is the key.

## 1. Don't Present Your Conclusions as *The* Truth

Some aspects of difficult conversations will continue to be rough
even when you communicate with great skill: sharing feelings of vulnerability, delivering bad news, learning something painful about
how others see you. But presenting your story as the truth — which
creates resentment, defensiveness, and leads to arguments — is a
wholly avoidable disaster.

It is an easy mistake to make. It's based on an error of thought: we
often experience our beliefs, opinions, and judgments as facts. When
you're arguing about a favorite movie or food or sports hero, sharing
judgment as the truth is fine. But in difficult conversations it doesn't
wash. Facts are facts. Everything else is everything else. And you
need to be scrupulously vigilant about the distinction.

If you and your friend disagree about whether it is ever okay to
spank your child, you add to the conflict if you state your view as the
truth: "Spanking children is just plain wrong." This statement mud-
dies the already turbulent waters, and your friend may hear it as accusatory or presumptuous. Instead of engaging you on the issue, your
friend may react by saying, "Who are *you* to proclaim what's right
and wrong?!"

Far better to say any of these: "I believe spanking children is
wrong," "I've read several books that say spanking children is harmful
to them," "I was spanked as a child and I feel sad and frightened
when I hear of a child being spanked," or even "I'm not sure why I
feel this way, but I just feel so strongly that spanking children is
wrong." Each of these clearly distinguishes between what your view
or feeling is and what the facts are.

Some words — like "attractive," "ugly," "good," and "bad" — carry
judgments that are obvious. But be careful with words like "inappropriate," "should," or "professional." The judgments contained in
these words are less obvious, but can still provoke the "Who are you
to tell me?!" response. If you want to say something is "inappropriate," preface your judgment with "My view is that . . . ." Better still,
avoid these words altogether.

This is not an argument that there is no truth, or that all opinions are equally valid. It simply distinguishes opinion from fact, and allows you to have a careful discussion that leads to better understanding and better decisions rather than to defensiveness and pointless fighting.

## 2. Share Where Your Conclusions Come From

The first step toward clarity, then, is to share your conclusions and opinions as *your* conclusions and opinions and not as the truth. The second step is to share what's beneath your conclusions — the information you have and how you have interpreted it.

As we saw in Chapter 2, often we merely trade our conclusions back and forth, and never get into the process of exploring where these views come from. You have information about yourself that the other person has no access to. That kind of information can be important; consider sharing it. And you have life experiences that are influencing what you think and why, as well as how you feel. When you tell these stories, it puts some meat onto the bones of your views.

You and your wife argue about whether to send your daughter, Carol, to private school. Your wife says, "I really think we should do it this year. It's an important age and I know we can come up with the money." You say in response, "I think she's doing fine in public school. I think we should keep her there."

If this conversation is going to get anywhere, the two of you need to share where these conclusions come from: What specific information is in your heads? What past experiences influence how you're thinking about this? You need to share your own experience in private school — the fear you felt the first few months, the sense of never quite fitting in. How guilty you felt that your parents weren't able to buy a car because they were paying your tuition for so many years. Tell that story with all the vividness and detail that's in your head as you discuss your concerns about the decision. Nothing else you say will make sense if your wife is unaware of the experiences that inform your feelings on this subject.

## 3. Don't Exaggerate with "Always" and "Never": Give Them Room to Change

In the heat of the moment, it's easy to express frustration through a bit of exaggeration: "Why do you *always* criticize my clothes?" "You *never* give one word of appreciation or encouragement. The only time anyone hears anything from you is when there's something wrong!"

"Always" and "never" do a pretty good job of conveying frustration, but they have two serious drawbacks. First, it is seldom strictly accurate that someone criticizes *every* time, or that they haven't at some point said *something* positive. Using such words invites an argument over the question of frequency: "That's not true. I said several nice things to you last year when you won the interoffice new idea competition" — a response that will most likely increase your exasperation.

"Always" and "never" also make it harder — rather than easier — for the other person to consider changing their behavior. In fact, "always" and "never" suggest that change will be difficult or impossible. The implicit message is, "What is wrong with you such that you are driven to criticize my clothes?" or even "You are obviously incapable of acting like a normal person."

A better approach is to proceed as if (however hard it may be to believe) the other person is simply unaware of the impact of their actions on you, and, being a good person, would certainly wish to change their behavior once they became aware of it. You could say something like: "When you tell me my suit reminds you of wrinkled old curtains, I feel hurt. Criticizing my clothes feels like an attack on my judgment and makes me feel incompetent." If you can also suggest what you would wish to hear instead, so much the better: "I wish I could feel more often like you believed in me. It would really feel great to hear even something as simple as, 'I think that color looks good on you.' Anything, as long as it was positive."

The key is to communicate your feelings in a way that invites and encourages the recipient to consider new ways of behaving, rather than suggesting they're a schmuck and it's too bad there's nothing they can do about it.

# Help Them Understand You

It's not easy to step into someone else's story. It's especially hard when the issues are emotionally charged or when your views are rooted in a different generation or radically dissimilar corporate culture. You'll need their help in understanding them. And they'll need your help in understanding you.

If you feel overwhelmed with anxiety when leaving your children with a babysitter, and your husband says that you should "just learn to relax," you can express your anxiety in terms he might understand: "It's like your fear of flying. You know how when I try to tell you to re-lax during take-off it has no impact, and in fact it makes it worse? Well this is the same sort of thing."

And recognize that different people take in information at differ-ent speeds and in different ways. For example, some people are visu-ally oriented. For them, you may want to use visual metaphors and refer to pictures or, in a business setting, charts. Some people prefer to get their arms around the whole problem first, and can't listen to anything else you say until they do. Others like all the details up front. Pay attention to these differences.

## Ask Them to Paraphrase Back

Paraphrasing the other person helps you check your understanding and helps them know you've heard. You can ask them to do the same thing for you: "Let me check to see if I'm being clear. Would you mind just playing back what you've heard me say so far?"

## Ask How They See It *Differently*—and Why

Explaining your story clearly is a first step toward being understood. But don't expect instant success. Real understanding may take some back and forth. If the other person seems puzzled or unpersuaded by your story, rather than putting it more forcefully or trying to tell it in a different way, ask how *they* see it. In particular, ask how they see it *differently*.

A common tendency is to ask for agreement, perhaps because it's reassuring: "Does that make sense?" "Wouldn't you agree?" But asking the other person how they see it differently is more helpful. If you ask for agreement, people may be reluctant to share their doubts and reservations. They aren't sure whether you really want to hear them. They say, "Yes, I suppose so," but you don't know whether they're actually thinking, "Yes, in a limited, warped kind of way that's just like you." If you ask explicitly for how they see it differently, you are more likely to discover their true reaction. Then you can begin to have a real conversation.

. . .

The secret of powerful expression is recognizing that you are the ultimate authority on you. You are an expert on what you think, how you feel, and why you've come to this place. If you think it or feel it, you are entitled to say it, and no one can legitimately contradict you. You only get in trouble if you try to assert what you are *not* the final authority on — who is right, who intended what, what happened. Speak fully the range of your experience and you will be clear. Speak for yourself and you can speak with power.

# 11

# Problem-Solving:
## *Take the Lead*

It may be that the person you're talking to has read this book and understands how to engage in a learning conversation. But don't count on it.

More likely, you'll talk about understanding, and they'll talk about who's right. You'll talk about contribution, while they're stuck in blame. You'll bend over backwards to listen and acknowledge their feelings, and in return you'll be attacked, interrupted, and judged. You're doing your best to improve the way the two of you communicate; they're doing their best to ensure that no constructive communication ever occurs between you. It may be that they are still worried about being blamed, or don't understand the terminology you're using. Perhaps they don't yet trust you and your new behavior, which after all is different from the last time you had this conversation.

What to do?

## Skills for Leading the Conversation

If your conversations are going to get anywhere, you're going to have to take the lead. There are a set of powerful "moves" you can make during the conversation — reframing, listening, and naming the dynamic — that can help keep the conversation on track, whether the other person is being cooperative or not.

When the other person heads in a destructive direction, *reframing* puts the conversation back on course. It allows you to translate unhelpful statements into helpful ones. *Listening* is not only the skill that lets you into the other person's world; it is also the single most powerful move you can make to keep the conversation constructive. And *naming the dynamic* is useful when you want to address a troubling aspect of the conversation. It is a particularly good strategy if the other person is dominating the conversation and seems unwilling to follow your lead.


## Reframe, Reframe, Reframe

Reframing means taking the essence of what the other person says and "translating it" into concepts that are more helpful — specifically, concepts from the Three Conversations framework. You are walking down a new path and inviting the other person to join you. You're illuminating the way.

Let's return to the situation between Miguel and Sydney from Chapter 4. Recall that Sydney is leading a team of engineers on a project in Brazil. After initially resisting her leadership, Miguel has become Sydney's most ardent supporter. Unfortunately for Sydney, Miguel's enthusiasm has apparently progressed to romantic interest as well. He has taken to following her around, expressing how much he likes spending time with her, and inviting her for quiet walks alone on the beach.

When Sydney steps away from her own focus on blame, she begins to see the mixed signals she may be sending to Miguel. She realizes that by not expressing her discomfort directly, she is contributing to the situation. Sydney decides to raise the issue with Miguel. She knows that for the conversation to be successful, she's going to have to be persistent in reframing the conversation from blame to contribution. We pick up the dialogue partway in:

SYDNEY: I should have brought this up with you earlier, which is why it's really important to me that we talk about it now. . . .

MIGUEL: Of course you should bring it up with me if you feel uncomfortable! This is the reason you are uncomfortable. A team leader should know how to handle this better.

SYDNEY: Whether I should or shouldn't, I guess I didn't. It makes sense to me that by not bringing it up, I probably exacerbated the problem. Rather than focus on which one of us is to blame, I'm trying to figure out how we got into this spot in the first place. I think we each did — or didn't do — some things that made the situation worse.

MIGUEL: Well, I think this whole thing is because you are American. American women are oversensitive to these issues and create problems where there aren't any.

SYDNEY: You and I could probably argue all day about whether or not American women are oversensitive. What's important is perhaps that you and I are coming at this from very different cultural perspectives. So I experienced your comments as suggestive and uncomfortable, and you seemed to see our interaction as not out of place in a working relationship. Is that right?

MIGUEL: That is true. For me, what I did was normal and not a big deal.

SYDNEY: When you say "normal," do you mean normal for two people in just a professional relationship? Or do you mean normal that two people in a professional relationship might choose to pursue something further?

MIGUEL: Either one. We can tease each other. I can tell you how much I like you. If you are not interested, you can ignore it. If you are, you can respond in kind. The problem here is that you are overreacting, and you should have brought this up sooner.

SYDNEY: As I said at the beginning, I agree with you that if I had brought it up, we might have avoided some of this. I think I felt frustrated that I was *trying* to ignore it, and you persisted.

Like when I kept turning down your invitations to have a drink in the bar or take a walk on the beach.

MIGUEL: You know, there were times I could tell something was wrong. I suppose I could have also asked you if things were okay, or if I had offended you for some reason. And maybe we should have just talked about our expectations of each other up front. . . .

With this last statement Miguel is finally starting to sense the difference between contribution and blame, and is starting to feel comfortable enough to begin to acknowledge his own contribution. But to get to this point, Sydney had to be persistent in redirecting him away from blame.

## You Can Reframe Anything

Reframing works on all fronts; you can reframe anything the other person says to move toward a learning conversation. Consider these examples:

THEY SAY: I'm right, and there are no two ways about it!

YOU REFRAME: I want to make sure I understand your perspective. You obviously feel very strongly about it. I'd also like to share my perspective on the situation.

| You Can Reframe | | |
| --- | --- | --- |
| Truth | ☞ | Different stories |
| Accusations | ☞ | Intentions and impact |
| Blame | ☞ | Contribution |
| Judgments, characterizations | ☞ | Feelings |
| What's wrong with you | ☞ | What's going on for them |

THEY SAY: You hurt me on purpose!

YOU REFRAME: I can see that you're feeling really angry about what I did, which is upsetting to me. It wasn't my intention. Can you say more about how you felt?

THEY SAY: This is all your fault!
YOU REFRAME: I'm sure I've contributed to the problem; I think we both have. Rather than focus on whose fault this is, I'd like just to look at how we got here — at what we each contributed to the situation.

THEY SAY: You are the nastiest person I've ever met.
YOU REFRAME: It sounds like you're feeling really badly.

THEY SAY: I am not a bad neighbor!
YOU REFRAME: Heavens, I don't think you are either. And I certainly hope you don't think I'm a lousy neighbor. I do think that we disagree about how this should be handled, and I think that's pretty normal between good neighbors. The question is whether we can work together to figure out how to address both of our concerns.

Of course, one sentence alone is unlikely to do the trick, but these examples give you a sense of where to start. Like Sydney, you'll need to be persistent, and you should expect to be constantly reframing the conversation to help keep it on a productive track.

## The "You-Me" And

A second reframing move you can make is from "either/or" to "and." If the other person is setting up a choice between what you think and what they think, between how you feel and how they feel, you can reject that choice by moving to the And Stance.

In the previous chapter, we took a look at the Me-Me And. In terms of managing the interactive conversation, it is the *You-Me And* that is crucial. This is not the "and" within us, but between us. It's the one that says, "I can listen and understand what you have to say, *and* you can listen and understand what I have to say."

Stacy found the You-Me And helpful in her quest to find her birth mother. Stacy's adoptive mother, Joyce, argued that Stacy's search was sure to be fruitless and painful. Stacy avoided engaging in an argument over whether or not that was true by using "and" to embrace both stories: "You might be right. It may be that all my efforts won't turn up anything, and even if I do find her, I might be disappointed. She might not want to see me at all. *And* it's still important to me to try. Here's why. . . ."

When Joyce said, "After all we've done to love you and raise you, what could you possibly need that your birth mother could provide?" Stacy responded with some Me-Me Ands *and* You-Me Ands. If this sounds complex, it is. And that's why Stacy's response was so constructive and effective: "It sounds like my search is really hard for you. You're the best mother in the world, and the only mother I'll ever have. That's not going to change. This is hard for me too, because it's hard for me to see you feeling hurt like this — sometimes I think I'm just being selfish or ungrateful. At the same time, I have questions that I really want to answer. I hope we can keep talking about what this means to each of us as I begin to pursue this." Stacy was able to assert herself without invalidating the power and importance of her mother's concerns.

## It's Always the Right Time to Listen

No matter how good you get at reframing, the single most important rule about managing the interaction is this: *You can't move the conversation in a more positive direction until the other person feels heard and understood.* And they won't feel heard and understood until you've listened. When the other person becomes highly emotional, listen and acknowledge. When they say their version of the story is the only version that makes sense, paraphrase what you're hearing and ask them some questions about why they think this. If they level accusations against you, before defending yourself, try to understand their view.

Whenever you feel overwhelmed or unsure how to proceed, remember that it is *always* a good time to listen.

## Be Persistent About Listening

We often assume that the listener is playing a passive role in the conversation, but that's not necessarily true. You can use listening to direct the conversation.

Consider this telephone conversation between Harpreet and his wife, Monisha. Monisha is a sales representative for a large pharmaceutical company and spends a significant amount of time on the road. The distance highlights what has been a tense issue throughout their relationship.

MONISHA: Okay, well, I better get some sleep. I've got a big presentation first thing in the morning.
HARPREET: So I'll see you on Thursday?
MONISHA: Yeah, Thursday night. I should be home around seven.
HARPREET: Okay, sleep tight. . . . [silence] I love you.
MONISHA: Good night. See you Thursday.

Harpreet hangs up hurt and frustrated. "She never tells me that she loves me," he complains. "Whenever I bring it up, she'll say something like, 'You know I love you, so why do I need to say it all the time?' "

This issue is obviously important to Harpreet. And for that reason, it makes sense that he should be persistent in raising it with Monisha. Many people think that being persistent means asserting your view — in other words, that Harpreet should just repeat himself. But that doesn't work.

You have to find a way to be persistent, while remembering that you are in a two-way conversation. Persistence in a difficult conversation means remaining as stubbornly interested in hearing the other person's views as you are in asserting your own.

In thinking through the Three Conversations, Harpreet began to be curious about why Monisha reacted the way she did. In the next conversation, Harpreet decided that his purpose was mainly to listen, ask questions, and try to understand how Monisha experienced this issue.

> HARPREET: When I say that I love you, what are you thinking?
>
> MONISHA: I'm thinking, "Okay, he's waiting for me to say it back to him." So it makes me not want to say it then, because I feel pressured into it. Besides, you know I love you.
>
> HARPREET: Sometimes I do feel confident that you love me. But sometimes I feel less sure. When you say that I know, how are you thinking I would know?
>
> MONISHA: Well, I'm still with you, right?
>
> HARPREET: That's a pretty low standard! Besides, my parents stayed together for years after they stopped loving each other. Maybe that's why I sometimes feel nervous about this. . . .
>
> MONISHA: Hmm. I guess I have the opposite experience. My parents were crazy about each other, and were always saying these sappy things in front of us. I thought it was embarrassing. It just seems like if you really love each other you don't have to say it all the time. You can just show it.
>
> HARPREET: Show it how?
>
> MONISHA: I don't know, like by being kind to each other. Like when I dropped everything and flew to Phoenix that weekend your mom was sick. I did it because I knew how hard it was for you, and I wanted to be there to help. . . .

Harpreet and Monisha have some distance to go. But simply by listening through the retorts and arguments for the feelings and stories, Harpreet is helping them have a much more interesting and constructive conversation on a topic that is hard for both of them.

# Name the Dynamic: Make the Trouble Explicit

Reframing and listening involve leading the conversation in the direction you want it to go. These tools are powerful, and most of your conversations will call on both. Sometimes, though, they are not enough. No matter how well you listen, no matter how many times you reframe, the other person will continue to interrupt, attack, or dismiss you. Every time you begin to get somewhere, they have another reason why the problem isn't a problem after all. Or perhaps they're *acting* upset, but each time you ask about it, they say, "No, no, I'm fine. I'm not upset at all."

At times like these, naming the dynamic can help. You put on the table as a topic for discussion what you see happening in the conversation itself. In a sense, you are acting as your own "conversation doctor," diagnosing the problem and prescribing a way back to health. These kind of diagnoses, and suggestions, sound like this:

> I've noticed that we keep running out of time whenever we start talking about this. Maybe we should designate an hour when we can both really focus on this and address it then.

> I've tried to say what I was thinking three times now, and each time you've started talking over me. I don't know whether you're aware that it's happening, but I'm finding it frustrating. If there's something important about what you're saying that I'm not understanding, please share it. And then I want to be able to finish what I'm saying.

> Here's what I'm noticing. I ask you if you are feeling hurt by what I said, and you say, "No, no, no, of course not. I'm not that kind of person." But then you keep acting toward me in ways that people act when they're hurt or mad at me. At least that's how I'm seeing this. It seems to me the best thing to do is to try to figure out what I'm doing that might be upsetting to you. Otherwise, I don't think we're going to get anywhere.

> Hang on a second. Several times now, when I've said the things that are important to me, you've gotten very angry to the point where I

feel threatened. I don't know what's causing your response. If you're upset, I'm interested to hear why. If you're trying to intimidate me into changing my mind, it won't work. I really do want to know what's upsetting you, *and* I want us to find a way to talk about it that doesn't feel intimidating to me.

Naming the dynamic between you can be enormously helpful in clearing the air. It draws what you are each really thinking and feeling but not saying onto the table for honest discussion. And it can stop frustrating interactions in their tracks; often the other person is not aware that they are doing something that is upsetting to you. However, it does take the conversation off the substance, and sometimes, it can escalate tension. So naming the dynamic is probably best thought of as something to try when nothing else has worked.

# Now What? Begin to Problem-Solve

Often simply sorting out the Three Conversations and bringing to light the heart of the matter for each person clears up the issues between you. But not always. You've come a long way in understanding each other's stories, and untangling what's happened. You have a better grasp on the feelings involved. But at the end of the day, you still need to decide how to go forward together, and you may not agree on how to do that.

This is the time for problem-solving. Fundamentally, problem-solving consists of gathering information and testing your perceptions, creating options that would meet both sides' primary concerns, and, where you can't, trying to find fair ways to resolve the difference.

## It Takes Two to Agree

Difficult conversations require a certain amount of compromise and mutual accommodation to the other's needs. If you find problem-solving difficult and anxiety producing, it may be because you are focused on persuading them. Those caught in this trap struggle like a fish on a hook, desperately trying to satisfy the seemingly insatiable demands of the other and reach some reasonable agreement on how to move forward. And no wonder. This frame gives the other side total control — until and unless they are satisfied, you must continue to struggle.

Describing the pattern this way illuminates its flaw: there are two people involved, and there will be no agreement unless both concur. You need to persuade them no more and no less than they need to persuade you. Thus, you always have the option to turn the tables, to invite them to persuade you and insist that they do. As long as you are open to persuasion, and prepared, if absolutely necessary, to live with no agreement, you can do this as firmly as you would like: "I understand that you are determined to have your article reviewed this week, and I'm still not persuaded that I should spend my vacation doing it."

For many people, realizing that they don't have to agree brings a sense of great liberation, relief, and empowerment.

## Gather Information and Test Your Perceptions

Henry had planned this weekend away with friends months ago. He worked extra hours all week finishing up the new displays and work schedules. It was Friday morning when Henry's boss, Rosario, approached him in the back room.

"Hank, I've got big problems with this supplier. We've got to get it figured out over the weekend, so that we're sure we've got the stock to handle the holiday rush next month," she explained. "I'm really sorry, because I know that you had plans this weekend. But I need you to stay. I'm sure you can reschedule with your friends, right?"

**Propose Crafting a Test.** Rather than explode or argue, Henry decided to learn more about why Rosario was so concerned. As Henry and Rosario sorted through their stories, they discovered that they had different assumptions about their relationship with the supplier in question. Henry believed that even if they ran into problems down the road, the supplier would work with them to rush their order overnight. Rosario has had too many bad experiences with suppliers over the years to believe that anything other than getting it right the first time would ensure that the holidays would go smoothly.

Divergent views are often rooted in one or more conflicting assumptions or hypotheses. If these can be identified, then you can discuss what would constitute a fair test of which assumption is empirically valid, or to what extent it is valid. Henry suggested that they call the supplier and ask about the availability of the stock in question, and whether someone would be willing to work with them if they ran into problems in the coming weeks. Rosario wanted to make sure they asked a series of what-if questions and established a personal relationship with someone on the other end who could take responsibility for making it work. To be persuasive, of course, such a test needs to satisfy both parties that it is fair and adequate.

**Say What Is Still Missing.** As you struggle with conflicting perceptions and conclusions, each of you needs to say unambiguously where the other person's story still doesn't make sense to you. As you follow *their* reasoning, what's missing that would make their version make sense? So Henry might say, "I think I understand now why stock problems caused us to lose money last year. It does seem that we need to get it sorted out early. Yet right now we've got a thirty-day head start on the problem, so I'm not understanding why this weekend is going to make the difference."

**Say What Would Persuade You.** Being open to persuasion is a powerful stance to have. It allows you to be honest and firm about your current views, and to listen to theirs. "Based on my understanding, it seems to me that my assistant manager, Bill, has the training to do the inventory this weekend, giving me a head start on the problem next week. Is your understanding different? Maybe you've got concerns about Bill that would be persuasive to me."

**Ask What (If Anything) Would Persuade Them.** "I have offered a number of what seem to me good reasons why it doesn't make sense for me to cancel my plans and work this weekend. Yet you remain adamant that I stay. Is there a reason I haven't heard? If not, I'm wondering if there is anything I could say that would persuade you otherwise and, if so, what it would be?"

**Ask Their Advice.** "Help me understand how you would feel and how you might think about the situation, if you were in my shoes. What would you do? Why? Could you imagine a way of staying that would not end up making it more likely that something like this would happen again?"

Our experience has been that people who understand that persuasion must be a two-way street rarely find themselves in situations like this. Their reputation for not being a pushover gains them both general respect and a wider berth from those who might otherwise be inclined to try taking advantage.

## Invent Options

Let's come back to your neighbors with the barking dog. When you finally raise the issue, you learn that they feel the dog's barking is important for security reasons, and that the reason he's left outside at night is that they fear he might accidentally hurt the new baby (whom he adores). This makes sense to you, *and* you are able nonetheless to share how frustrating and exhausting it is for you to be kept awake. When it comes time to figure out what to do about it, you may get stuck. Your answer (get rid of the dog) isn't so appealing to them, and their answer (wear earplugs or close the windows) seems ridiculous to you.

Many difficult situations are amenable to creative solutions that meet most of everyone's needs, but which may not be obvious and may take some effort to find. This calls for determined joint brainstorming. "I wonder if we can work to find a creative way to meet both interests here. What do you think? Are you willing to try?" Odds are, persistence will pay off.

Brainstorming might yield some useful ideas. For example, your son might spend time with the neighbors' dog so that the dog gets more exercise and attention during this busy period with the new baby. This might also meet some of your son's interests in getting a dog of his own. Or your neighbors might decide to get a second dog to keep the first one company, or to bring the dog indoors after 10 p.m. and close the door to the baby's room. Or perhaps they'll ask you to call when the barking starts to bother you, so that they can address the problem right away and you don't spend another sleepless night.

What's more important is that you both recognize that if you are going to continue to live next door, you need to work together to find a solution that satisfies everyone — you, them, and the dog.


## Ask What Standards Should Apply

Generally the best way to manage conflict in a way that safeguards a relationship is to look for standards or fair principles to guide a resolution, rather than trying to haggle with or intimidate the other person. If you can't find a creative way to solve the problem, ask what standards of fairness should apply, and why. In the case of the dog, there may be a local ordinance pertaining to noise, or a method other dog owners in the neighborhood have used to keep their pooches quiet. Industry or local practices, legal precedents, and ethical principles all offer ways to settle the matter without anyone having to back down or lose face.

Not all standards are equally persuasive, of course. Some will seem more directly on point, more widely accepted, or more immediately relevant in terms of time, place, or circumstance. This is one more topic for discussion as you explore the relative fairness of different standards.

**The Principle of Mutual Caretaking.** One dynamic to remember at this stage of a difficult conversation is the tendency we all have to believe that our way of doing things is the "right" way. This can lead us to ascribe the problem to something wrong with "the way they are," and to suggest a "solution" that boils down to doing it our way: "If you would just change, there wouldn't be a problem."

The frustration is understandable, but the argument is not persuasive. Both the challenge and the spice of relationships is in people's differences. Occasional frustration is the price of admission. And as we've noted, no relationship will endure if one party always gives in to the other. A good resolution will usually require each party to accommodate somewhat to the other's differences, or perhaps to reciprocate — going one way on some issues and the other way on others. This is the principle of mutual caretaking.

## If You Still Can't Agree, Consider Your Alternatives

Not every conflict can be resolved by mutual agreement. Sometimes, even after highly skilled communication, you and the other person will simply fail to come up with an option that works for both of you. Then you're faced with a decision: Should you accept less than what you want, or should you accept the consequences of not agreeing?

Let's come back to Henry and Rosario. Rosario's the boss. Henry's a valuable employee. If they can't arrive at a solution to the problem of whether Henry will work the weekend, then they each face some choices. Each needs to think about what they will do if they can't arrive at a solution together.

If you are going to walk away without agreeing, you need two things. First, you need to explain why you are walking away. What interests and concerns are not met by the solutions you've been discussing? Let's imagine Henry decides to take the weekend off despite Rosario's continued insistence that he stay. Rather than just storming out, Henry should be clear about his feelings, interests, and choices. He might say, "Rosario, I really am sorry. I want very much to be a good employee, and to help out when I can. Normally, I'm happy to work weekends and nights — I hope you've seen that in the past. It's simply a matter of notice. I feel badly about leaving you in the lurch;

at the same time, these plans are really important to me, and I gave you plenty of notice and worked hard all week so that I could go away. So I don't like the choice, but given the choice, I'm going to go."

Now Henry needs the second thing: a willingness to accept the consequences. He may return on Monday to find that he no longer has a job. If he can live with that, or indeed prefers that, then going off with his friends makes sense. And as often as not, he may return to find Rosario is both unhappy *and* more respecting of him and his time. Perhaps she will even apologize, or ask to talk about how to avoid such situations in the future.

If Henry can't live with the possibility of losing his job, then his best choice is probably to work the weekend. He'll feel disappointed that he didn't get to spend time with his friends, but he'll know he handled the conversation skillfully and made a wise choice in the end.

## It Takes Time

Most difficult conversations are not, in actuality, a single conversation. They are a series of exchanges and explorations that happen over time. Assuming that Henry and Rosario work things out this time, there will be plenty of other issues that arise between them. Work demands will continue to be high, and they'll have to work together to figure out ways to balance this with Henry's personal commitments. Michael and Jack, the friends arguing over the brochure in Chapter 1, will need to find ways to repair their friendship, and explore whether and how to work together in the future. You and your neighbors will have to try out having your son care for the dog, or letting the dog inside at night, and see how it goes. And however it goes, you should have follow-up conversations to check in and, if necessary, look for new ways to cope.

# 12

# Putting It All
# Together

Jack would like to take another crack at a conversation with Michael.

"I thought that once we got the brochure out of the way, things would settle down between us," he explains. But months later, Michael remains distant and the friendship has become awkward. Jack knows he should talk to Michael, but about what? Jack believes that the bottom line is this: Michael was just being a jerk.

## Step One: Prepare by Walking Through the Three Conversations

In preparation for his conversation Jack sat down and walked himself through the Three Conversations, making notes to himself about how Michael might be seeing things, and what they've each contributed to the problem (an abbreviated version of Jack's notes is included on p. 218). Along the way, Jack made a few discoveries. He realized that Michael probably didn't know Jack had put aside other things and had worked through the night. Jack doesn't really know whether Michael meant to intimidate him. He saw the ways in which he had contributed to the problem by not raising his feelings with Michael at the time, or as soon as the brochure was done.

This reinforced Jack's determination to change this contribution and raise his feelings now. "Rethinking my assumptions about what

218

Create a Learning Conversation

## Jack's Preparation Notes

| What Happened? | | |
| --- | --- | --- |
| **Multiple Stories** | **Impact/Intent** | **Contribution** |
| *What's my story?* I interrupted important work to do a favor for a friend, who then overreacted to an insignificant mistake, and bullied me into redoing the whole job. I got no thank you, and M. took no responsibility for having signed off on it.<br><br>*What's his story?* Michael was counting on me to get it right, and I let him down. Then I argued with him about it instead of making it right.<br><br>*Hmm. This has some truth to it.* | *My intentions:* Help a friend. Do a good job. Persuade M. that the mistake wasn't a big deal(!)<br><br>*Impact on me:* Felt bullied. Unappreciated. Frustrated.<br><br>*M.'s intentions?* Get the brochure fast. Make sure it's right? Intimidate me?<br><br>*Impact on M?* Frustrated? Disappointed? In tight spot with client? | *What did I contribute to the problem?* I didn't tell Michael I was upset at the time, or later. I did make the mistake. I didn't ask M. more questions to understand his predicament.<br><br>*What did he contribute?* Michael also didn't catch the mistake. He didn't call earlier, so it was a rush job. He kept asking, "Are you going to redo it? Yes or no?" which felt like bullying. |

| Feelings | Identity Issues |
|---|---|
| *What feelings underlie my attributions and judgments?* | *How does what happened threaten my identity?* |
| **Angry** | Yikes! This probably does have a lot to do with my identity, mostly because I consider myself such a perfectionist. It's hard to accept that I'd let such a silly mistake slip by me. |
| **Frustrated** | |
| **Disappointed** that this didn't go smoothly, and that Michael has hired someone else. | And more than that, I just wish I'd handled our conversation better. Usually I'm good at these things — managing client problems. |
| **Hurt** | |
| **Guilty**— I wish I'd handled this better. | And now I've got the worst of both worlds. I didn't stick up for myself, and I still lost Michael as a client and as a friend anyway. |
| **Embarrassed/Ashamed**— what a stupid mistake! | |
| **Appreciative** of Michael's support in the past. | |
| **Sad** that our friendship has fallen by the wayside. | |

happened succeeded in shaking my confidence that I was right and that the problem here was Michael," says Jack. "Probably the biggest thing I realized was just that I didn't really understand this thing at all from Michael's perspective. I'm willing to try."

Shaking your confidence may seem like a funny way to prepare for a conversation. But as a result, Jack is more open to hearing what Michael has to say, more curious about learning what he doesn't know (like about Michael's intentions, or what Michael thinks Jack has contributed). And in an important sense, Jack is *more* confident. Accepting his own role in the problem has helped him to feel more grounded rather than less. While he's no longer sure that his story is "right" and that Michael's is "wrong," Jack is absolutely certain that each of their stories matters.

## Step Two: Check Your Purposes and Decide Whether to Raise It

Most important, Jack feels more secure that raising these issues is a good thing to try *regardless* of how Michael reacts. "At first, as I considered whether to raise this issue again, I thought, 'Well, what if Michael thinks it's not important, or just brushes it off? Then I'll feel foolish, or like I failed.' I played with the idea of not raising things, but I would have been running away rather than making a clear-headed choice to let go.

"So I wanted to raise it, but I was nervous. Then I remembered the advice about not trying to control the other person's reaction. I'm raising it because *I* think it's important, and I'm going to do it as well as I can, and if Michael isn't interested in talking, or if he isn't open, well, at least I tried, and I can feel good that I stuck up for myself."

Below, we present parts of the conversation between Jack and Michael as it might realistically go — with one difference: to put what Jack is doing well and less well into higher relief, we're giving him a consultant to coach him when he gets stuck. We're also going to give Jack the chance to start and stop, and to start over if things aren't going quite right.

# Step Three: Start from the Third Story

Below, Jack's first try at getting started, and the result.

> JACK: Listen, Michael, say what you will, but the problem on that financial brochure was that after all the work I did, you treated me badly, and you know it!
>
> MICHAEL: The problem on that project was that I had the poor judgment to use you in the first place. I'll never make that mistake again!

. . . . . . . . . . . . . . . . . . . . . .

> JACK: *Okay, cut. This isn't going right.*
>
> COACH: *What went wrong?*
>
> JACK: *I don't know. He didn't react very well.*
>
> COACH: *Notice that you began the conversation from inside your story.*
>
> JACK: *I should have started from the Third Story. That's right. I'll start over.*

. . . . . . . . . . . . . . . . . . . . . .

> JACK: Michael, I've been thinking a lot about what happened between us on the financial brochure. I found the experience frustrating, and I suspect you did as well. What's most worrisome to me is that it feels like it has affected our friendship. I wonder whether we could talk about that? I'd like to understand better what was happening for you, and how you felt about working together, and I'd also like to share what I found upsetting.
>
> MICHAEL: Well, Jack, the problem is that you're just not careful enough, and then you can't admit it when you make a mistake. It really made me angry when you started making excuses.

. . . . . . . . . . . . . . . . . . . . . .

JACK: *Okay, he's attacking me. I thought if I started from the Third Story he was supposed to be nicer.*

COACH: *Well, Michael's reaction wasn't nearly as confrontational as it was in your first try. You're actually off to a good start. You did a great job of beginning from the Third Story. Remember, persistence. Michael's not immediately going to understand that you're trying to have a learning conversation. You have to be prepared for him to be somewhat defensive.*

JACK: *And say what, if he attacks me?*

COACH: *He's already into his story. The best thing you can do for the conversation is to listen from a stance of real curiosity, to ask questions, and to pay special attention to the feelings behind the words.*

## Step Four: Explore Their Story and Yours

JACK: You felt I was making excuses? Say more about that.

MICHAEL: The truth is, Jack, you shouldn't have argued with me about the chart. You should have just redone the brochure.

JACK: So your thinking was that since the graph was off, it was up to me to correct it and reprint the brochures. And it sounds like when I questioned this, that was frustrating for you.

MICHAEL: *Yeah*, it was frustrating. I had the client breathing down my neck, already less than happy with us.

JACK: Why?

MICHAEL: Because she thought this photograph in one of the other publications was the wrong one. It wasn't, but you just don't argue at times like that. That's what really frustrated me, Jack. You don't seem to understand that the customer is always right.

JACK: So the client was already looking for things to be unhappy about?

MICHAEL: It sure felt that way. And if there was something you
  were going to screw up, the revenue chart was the first thing
  she was going to notice. Her investors are already unhappy
  with some of her recent decisions. Yes, the chart was only off
  by a small amount, and it's not something we'd always rerun,
  but in this case, given the situation, it was something that we
  had to get just right.
JACK: I didn't realize some of this background. It sounds like
  there was a lot going on for you during all of this.

• • • • • • • • • • • • • • • • • • • • • •

  JACK: *Time out.*
  COACH: *You're doing great!*
  JACK: *Yeah, maybe. It's helpful, actually. I'm beginning to get
    a sense for how he's seeing things. But he's not getting a
    sense for how I'm seeing things. When do I get to give my
    side of the story?*
  COACH: *You've done some good listening. Michael may be in
    a better place to start to listen to you.*

• • • • • • • • • • • • • • • • • • • • • •

JACK: From my point of view, Michael, the problem was that I
  did this favor for you, and then you mistreated me. You acted
  badly.

• • • • • • • • • • • • • • • • • • • • • •

  COACH: *Cut! Yes, you want to move into your perspective, but
    first you need a transition sentence, something that ac-
    knowledges that you're beginning to understand his view
    on this, and that you want to share yours. And when you
    do share yours, if you want to share feelings, do so. But
    what you said above is a judgment about Michael, which
    is rarely helpful. Better to say how you feel.*

• • • • • • • • • • • • • • • • • • • • • •

JACK: I'm beginning to get a sense for how you're seeing things, and that's helpful to me. I also want to try to give you a sense for how I was seeing things, and for how I was feeling.

MICHAEL: Okay.

JACK: Hmm. I'm not always good at talking about my feelings, but I'll try. I felt hurt by some of the things you said —

MICHAEL: Jack, I wasn't trying to hurt you, I just needed the brochure done right! Sometimes I think you're too sensitive.

. . . . . . . . . . . . . . . . . . . . . . .

JACK: *Okay, after all the listening I did, now he's gone and interrupted me right off the bat. I didn't even get a chance to get the first sentence out. That's just how Michael is. He always interrupts, and I can never get what I think on the table.*

COACH: *This is where you have to be persistent, a little more assertive in getting your story out there. You can interrupt him to create space for what you're trying to say. You need to be very explicit that you are still explaining your view, and you'd like him to listen.*

. . . . . . . . . . . . . . . . . . . . . . .

JACK: Well, hang on a second. Before we get into how you feel about how I feel, I just want to tell you a little more about how I'm seeing things.

MICHAEL: That's fine, but what I'm saying is that you're taking this question of our business interactions too personally —

. . . . . . . . . . . . . . . . . . . . . . .

JACK: *He did it again. See? That's what he does.*

COACH: *He is good at interrupting. So how are you feeling at this point?*

JACK: *I'm feeling really frustrated.*

COACH: *So you have a few choices here. You could give up, but I think it's way too early for that. You could do some more listening, which is always a good idea. But let's say you don't want to do that at the moment. Instead, you could try two other things. One is, you could simply re-assert that you want to get your view on the table, and I suspect that would eventually work. A second is you could share your frustration at being interrupted.*

JACK: *If I do that he'll interrupt to tell me I shouldn't be frustrated. I think I'll try once more to be assertive.*

· · · · · · · · · · · · · · · · · · · · · · ·

JACK: Michael, I understand you think I'm taking things too personally. We can come to that. Before we do, I want to give you a better sense of where I'm at.

· · · · · · · · · · · · · · · · · · · · · · ·

COACH: *Brilliant! You started with listening, and paraphrasing his sense that you take things too personally. For him, that helps take away the need to keep saying it. And now you're in a good place to continue your story.*

JACK: *I'm getting the hang of it.*

· · · · · · · · · · · · · · · · · · · · · · ·

JACK: So bear with me. Um, here's the thing. When you called, here's what I was thinking to myself: "Oh my God, I'm already overloaded at the moment. I need to get the Anders materials out by tomorrow, and I'm supposed to have dinner with Charlotte tonight." And then I thought, "Well, I'm just going to have to call the Anders folks and let them know their stuff will be a day late, and call Charlotte and cancel dinner." Because, Michael, you sounded like it was an emergency, and I really wanted to help you out.

MICHAEL: And I appreciated that —

JACK: But you never said that. From my point of view, after making these sacrifices, the first feedback I heard was, "Gee, Jack, you really screwed this one up!" Can you see why I would feel upset by that?

MICHAEL: I shouldn't have said that, Jack. I meant to say thank you. I guess I was overloaded with my own frustrations at that point. It's interesting. I wasn't thinking that you were doing me a favor, to be honest, although I can see now that you were. What I was thinking, and what I still think, is that I was also doing *you* a favor. You know, giving you the business. There were other people I could have called, but I thought you'd appreciate the business.

JACK: Which I did. I guess on my end, I was so caught up in just trying to get everything done that it wasn't feeling like a favor from you. But obviously, I do appreciate the business.

⋆ ⋆ ⋆ ⋆ ⋆ ⋆ ⋆ ⋆ ⋆ ⋆ ⋆ ⋆ ⋆ ⋆ ⋆ ⋆ ⋆ ⋆ ⋆

JACK: *This is getting almost fun.*
COACH: *You're doing a great job. Keep going.*

⋆ ⋆ ⋆ ⋆ ⋆ ⋆ ⋆ ⋆ ⋆ ⋆ ⋆ ⋆ ⋆ ⋆ ⋆ ⋆ ⋆ ⋆ ⋆

MICHAEL: Jack, I still want to talk to you about something else. If we're putting all our cards on the table, I get really upset when you try to deny that you've done something wrong. You know, you say that the graph is fine, when it's not.

⋆ ⋆ ⋆ ⋆ ⋆ ⋆ ⋆ ⋆ ⋆ ⋆ ⋆ ⋆ ⋆ ⋆ ⋆ ⋆ ⋆ ⋆ ⋆

JACK: *Okay, it's getting less fun again.*
COACH: *That's how difficult conversations are. They go up and down. You have to keep working at it.*

⋆ ⋆ ⋆ ⋆ ⋆ ⋆ ⋆ ⋆ ⋆ ⋆ ⋆ ⋆ ⋆ ⋆ ⋆ ⋆ ⋆ ⋆ ⋆

JACK: Michael, I wasn't denying anything. I didn't *do* anything wrong!

⋆ ⋆ ⋆ ⋆ ⋆ ⋆ ⋆ ⋆ ⋆ ⋆ ⋆ ⋆ ⋆ ⋆ ⋆ ⋆ ⋆ ⋆ ⋆

COACH: *Okay, let's slow down. You're at a tricky point here, and there's the potential either to get into a big argument or to straighten some things out in a very helpful way.*
JACK: *I believe you, but I'm not seeing it.*
COACH: *Look back at what Michael said. He said he gets*

*really upset when you try to deny that you've done something wrong. He's making one of the big mistakes around impact and intentions, and you're making the other one. In Michael's statement, he's assuming he knows what you were trying to do, what your intentions were.*

JACK: Which he doesn't.

COACH: *Right. So he's making the mistake of assuming he knows what your intentions are when in fact he doesn't. When we do that in conversations, it creates just what happened here. The other person defends himself, and you get into a pointless argument.*

JACK: How can I not defend myself?

COACH: *The best way to handle confusion around impact and intent isn't to defend yourself. First, you have to acknowledge the other person's feelings, and only then should you try to clarify what your intentions were.*

. . . . . . . . . . . . . . . . . . .

JACK: I hear that my response was frustrating for you.

MICHAEL: It was. I'm not trying to be a bad guy. I'm just trying to get it done right.

JACK: Let me try to explain my response. I wasn't trying to pretend nothing was wrong, or trying to put one over on you. I genuinely felt that the graph was fine the way it was. As we've talked about it, I see that my reaction wasn't based on all the information. I'm not sure what I think about the graph at this point. What I do know is that if I thought it should be redone I'd be the first to admit it.

MICHAEL: I don't know about that. I still get a sense that you are sometimes defensive about making mistakes.

JACK: That's not true.

. . . . . . . . . . . . . . . . . . .

COACH: *You did a great job of sorting through the intentions question. It's not easy. Now we're getting into another tricky area. Is it true, in your heart of hearts, that you have* no problem with mistakes?

JACK: Of course not! I hate making mistakes. I can't stand it. It makes me crazy when I make a mistake, especially a stupid one.

COACH: So why did you say you have no problem with them?

JACK: I guess I didn't want to admit that I do have a little bit of trouble around owning up to mistakes.

COACH: Here's the thing. Michael, for one reason or another, senses that you have issues around making mistakes. You might do better by sharing some of your Identity Conversation with him. It's a risk, but in this case, not a very big one since he seems to already know it.

. . . . . . . . . . . . . . . . . . . . .

JACK: Actually, Michael, as I think about it, admitting mistakes is something I do sometimes have trouble with. Even that is hard for me to say.

MICHAEL: Well, I appreciate your saying that. I wish you'd just admit them and then we can get on to the work of correcting them.

JACK: Well, I don't want to confuse two issues. I did make a mistake with the graph, and it was my strong judgment, at least at the time we were talking, that the problem was so inconsequential that it didn't need to be redone.

. . . . . . . . . . . . . . . . . . . . .

COACH: Fabulous. You owned up to a real issue you have, and you also did a great job of using the And Stance to clarify that in this case you felt like you were using good judgment.

JACK: So what's next for me? Are we almost done?

COACH: You're getting there. What else feels important for you to say? What else feels important for you to learn?

JACK: We've talked about what I did wrong on the brochure, but we haven't talked at all about what Michael did wrong. After all, he reviewed it and gave me the go-ahead.

COACH: *That's an important issue. See if you can bring it up as an issue of joint contribution rather than blame.*

• • • • • • • • • • • • • • • • • • • •

JACK: Michael, there's another issue I want to raise. I get the sense that you're thinking the fact that the brochure was off was entirely my doing.

MICHAEL: Jack, we don't need to get into that again. I'm not trying to beat you over the head with it. I understand that you worked hard on the brochure and I appreciate that.

JACK: I know. I just want to offer a different angle on this blame question. You're reaction was that since I did the work, the graph problem was my fault. And my initial reaction was that since you looked it over and gave the go-ahead it was also your fault —

MICHAEL: No, I never said I proofread it. That was your job. What I indicated was that *assuming* there were no mistakes, it was okay for you to print.

JACK: That's just my point. I'm saying that we both had a hand in the problem. We misunderstood each other. I'm not saying there's a right or wrong. If we had each understood the other more clearly, we would have been less likely to have gotten into the mess we did.

MICHAEL: That's certainly true. But so what?

JACK: The point is, we are more likely to avoid this kind of problem in the future if we are more careful to communicate clearly. I should have asked you point-blank whether you had read the brochure carefully, and you might have said more clearly that you had not. Either one of those would have been useful, and would be useful next time.

MICHAEL: I think that makes sense.

• • • • • • • • • • • • • • • • • • •

JACK: *Wow. That was much easier to discuss than blame, and much more helpful.*

COACH: *And notice that talking about contribution focuses*

*you naturally on problem-solving. Let's work a bit more on that. You each have your own view on whether the brochure should have been redone. Do a little problem-solving on that issue.*

## Step Five: Problem-Solving

JACK: Michael, let's think about how we should handle a difference of judgment if it happens again in the future. For example, whether the brochure needs to be redone.

MICHAEL: I think as the client in this situation, we should just do it my way. I don't see it as some sort of joint decision.

JACK: I agree, in terms of the final decision. You should make it in that case. I guess I'm wondering how to give you the benefit of my judgment before the decision is made. I can imagine there will be times when you have a certain view, and then we talk about it, and you change your mind.

MICHAEL: That's true. So maybe if we're more clear about what the purpose of the conversation is, then instead of thinking you're trying to make the final decision, I'll know that you're just giving me your opinion.

JACK: That makes sense.

MICHAEL: But sometimes I don't have time to have a long conversation about it.

JACK: I understand that. It would help me if you would tell me that. Otherwise I don't understand why you're getting so frustrated in the conversation.

MICHAEL: So I can just say, "I don't have time to talk about it"?

JACK: Yes, and also tell me why. That you've got to get something out by noon, or that this revenue issue is a touchy one, or that we can talk about it later. It'll only take five seconds, and it'll save me from getting frustrated with you for not listening.

MICHAEL: I can see why that would be frustrating.

· · · · · · · · · · · · · · · · · ·

COACH: Jack, you and Michael are on your way. Nice job!

JACK: As long as I'm on a roll, I want to bring up with Michael the thing that in some ways is the most difficult, and that's the question of our friendship. I want to make sure that none of this hurts our friendship.

COACH: Check your purposes on that. "Making sure that none of this hurt our friendship" sounds like you're going to put words in his mouth. It's a little controlling. If you're going to ask a question, make sure it's an open question. Just ask him how he's feeling about your friendship. If the problem did hurt your friendship, you want him to be open about saying so.

· · · · · · · · · · · · · · · · · ·

JACK: I'm glad we're working through these issues. I think it's hard to work with friends. I guess I wonder whether you think this has affected our friendship.

MICHAEL: Well, what's your answer to that question?

JACK: Honestly? Now that we've talked it through I feel much better about things. Before we talked I was pretty angry. And probably a little hurt, too. If we hadn't discussed this at some point, it would have been easy for me to figure we were not going to stay friends.

MICHAEL: I'm surprised by that. You and I certainly react differently to this kind of thing. I was not happy with our working relationship, but I thought our friendship was fine. I view them as separate. But since you obviously think about it differently, I'm glad we talked about it.

· · · · · · · · · · · · · · · · · ·

JACK: Looks like we're friends again!

COACH: You handled it skillfully.

JACK: Thanks. I suspect we won't have these sorts of problems in the future.

COACH: *I don't know about that. In fact, I think you are better off assuming that you will. Now, though, you know that it's okay to talk about them, so the misunderstandings may not be as emotionally draining and are less likely to threaten the relationship. But is this the last difficult conversation you'll have with Michael? I doubt it.*

As the saying goes, "Life is just one damn thing after another." It is, of course. And now you have some skills to handle it.

## A Difficult Conversations Checklist

### Step 1: Prepare by Walking Through the Three Conversations

1. Sort out **What Happened**.
   - Where does your story come from (information, past experiences, rules)? Theirs?
   - What impact has this situation had on you? What might their intentions have been?
   - What have you each contributed to the problem?
2. Understand **Emotions**.
   - Explore your emotional footprint, and the bundle of emotions you experience.
3. Ground Your **Identity**.
   - What's at stake for you *about you*? What do you need to accept to be better grounded?

### Step 2: Check Your Purposes and Decide Whether to Raise the Issue

- **Purposes:** What do you hope to accomplish by having this conversation? Shift your stance to support learning, sharing, and problem-solving.
- **Deciding:** Is this the best way to address the issue and achieve your purposes? Is the issue really embedded in your Identity Conversation? Can you affect the problem by changing your contributions? If you don't raise it, what can you do to help yourself let go?

### Step 3: Start from the Third Story

1. Describe the problem as the **difference** between your stories. Include both viewpoints as a legitimate part of the discussion.
2. Share your **purposes**.
3. **Invite** them to join you as a *partner* in sorting out the situation together.

## Step 4: Explore Their Story and Yours

- **Listen to understand** their perspective on what happened. Ask questions. Acknowledge the feelings behind the arguments and accusations. Paraphrase to see if you've got it. Try to unravel how the two of you got to this place.
- **Share your own viewpoint**, your past experiences, intentions, feelings.
- **Reframe, reframe, reframe** to keep on track. From truth to perceptions, blame to contribution, accusations to feelings, and so on.

## Step 5: Problem-Solving

- Invent **options** that meet each side's most important concerns and interests.
- Look to **standards** for what *should* happen. Keep in mind the standard of mutual caretaking; relationships that always go one way rarely last.
- Talk about how to keep **communication** open as you go forward.

# Ten Questions People Ask About *Difficult Conversations*

• • • • •

# Ten Questions People Ask About *Difficult Conversations*

**1.** It sounds like you're saying everything is relative. Aren't some things just true, and can't someone simply be wrong?

**2.** What if the other person really does have bad intentions — lying, bullying, or intentionally derailing the conversation to get what they want?

**3.** What if the other person is genuinely difficult, perhaps even mentally ill?

**4.** How does this work with someone who has all the power — like my boss?

**5.** If I'm the boss/parent, why can't I just tell my subordinates/children what to do?

**6.** Isn't this a very American approach? How does it work in other cultures?

**7.** What about conversations that aren't face-to-face? What should I do differently if I'm on the phone or e-mail?

**8.** Why do you advise people to "bring feelings into the workplace"? I'm not a therapist, and shouldn't business decisions be made on the merits?

**9.** Who has time for all this in the real world?

**10.** My identity conversation keeps getting stuck in either-or: I'm perfect or I'm horrible. I can't seem to get past that. What can I do?

## 1. It sounds like you're saying everything is relative. Aren't some things just true, and can't someone simply be wrong?

Some people who read *Difficult Conversations* wonder if we're arguing that facts are irrelevant or that all views are equally reasonable. This question arises both in practical discussions ("We should close the Newark plant"; "I should be first author"; "Jasper should be grounded for a month") and in more profound ones about values and beliefs ("Health care is a human right"; "Abortion is murder"; "My God is the one true God").

### Facts aren't relative, but they can be hard to pin down

Facts exist, and people can be right or wrong about them. Let's start with a simple everyday example. If the dinner bill is $30, and you conclude that a 15 percent tip is $6.00, you are wrong; 15 percent is $4.50. But if you think 15 percent is too little and that 20 percent is "the correct tip," that's a judgment, not a fact — even if it is based on an actual survey showing that 20 percent is the usual and customary level of tipping for that service in that location. Those are facts, but they don't necessarily make 20 percent the correct amount.

To make conversations productive, especially in a context of strong emotion, high stakes, and complex perceptions, a critical first step is to distinguish clearly between facts on the one hand, and opinions, assumptions, values, interests, predictions, and judgments on the other. That your five-year-old threw his dinner on the floor is a fact; whether and how he should be disciplined is a judgment. The time at which you arrived for work this morning is a fact; your boss's view that arriving late reflects a poor work ethic is an assumption. That hundreds of thousands of people were murdered in the Rwandan genocide is a fact; whether the United States should have intervened is a matter of interests, values, and assumptions.

Facts can be clarified, verified, and measured, though sometimes even facts are hard to pin down. Watch any courtroom drama to see examples. A video that has been entered into evidence appears to reveal that no one was present at the time in question, but is its time stamp accurate? Has the video been edited? There are factual answers to these questions, but we may have difficulty determining what they are.

Moreover, when memory is a factor, the level of uncertainty increases dramatically. Studies show that people are, on the whole, not very reliable witnesses, even when they are paying attention. We often feel certain of memories that are in fact erroneous. We can even transform memories unconsciously, misplacing events in time and location and misremembering who was present, even when the memory itself remains vividly specific. Brain scientists are beginning to understand how this process works neurologically and to confirm that it is not uncommon. Some of the latest research, for example, has found that each time you recollect or retell a memory, you actually rewrite it as you put it back into storage. Even as little as twenty-four hours later, your recollection of what happened may be version 18, depending on how much you've been dwelling on it.

So even when discussing facts, where there is disagreement it is imperative to find out what the other is seeing and how they make sense of it. Is it simple error, a lack of information, misinformation, or selective and revised memories, or are the facts themselves more ambiguous than you had appreciated?

## Not all stories are equal, but it takes a learning conversation to find out

The need to understand the basis of the other person's story intensifies when the disagreement is about interpretations and judgments — about what the facts *mean*. And this is another domain where the question of relativity arises: "Are you saying that his interpretation is just as valid as mine? Because it isn't!" We all feel this sometimes. "I understand where his expectation comes from; I just don't think it's reasonable. I think it's a reflection of his 'issues' and neuroses, not of what's fair."

To be clear, we are not saying that all interpretations and stories are equal. Some interpretations *are* more reasonable than others, or at least are likely to seem so to most people. There are a number of reasons for this. Some stories reflect a more complete understanding of a given situation — that is, they take account of more of the available information. Others rely on fewer or less extreme assumptions, or on assumptions that are more closely tied in time or place to the situation at hand. Still others have fewer logical leaps or internal contradictions.

But again, to be able to compare stories by such standards — and maximize your chances of changing the other person's view — you first have to engage in a learning conversation to explore each story, where it comes from and what it's based on, and how the two stories intersect. This is equally true whether you are trying to persuade an adversary, a teammate, or other observing constituents.

The bottom line? When you think their view is "just plain wrong," take a moment to re-examine your assumptions. There's always a chance that they know something you don't and there's no downside to testing your own view and seeking to understand theirs. Often multiple interpretations of a situation may *all* make sense, as with the famous ambiguous picture that can be seen as either an old woman or a young one. So inquire into their view looking for the *sense* rather than the *nonsense* in it. Paraphrase it back, share where and why you see it differently, and ask them for their reactions. Look for different information, different interpretations of ambiguous information, or different assumptions about missing information that help explain your differing views.

At the end of the day, your counterpart may simply not be persuaded however robust your learning conversation, or may choose not to acknowledge what you or others see, and you will need to assess at what point you are better off moving on to your no-agreement alternative. But most of us give up too soon, before we've really understood and had a fair chance to weigh the integrity of the other's story.

One thing it may help to ask before giving up is what they would have to learn to persuade them to change or reconsider their view.

Even if they say that *nothing* would persuade them, you gain valuable information: you learn that any further attempt to persuade them may be a waste of effort. On the other hand, if their answer is more nuanced, you've identified the challenge and can assess your ability to meet it. (By the way, it's also worth asking *yourself* what you would have to learn to change your view.)

## Whether or not some truths are absolute, as human beings our ability to perceive such truths is limited

Finally we come to the question of dealing with people — ourselves or others — who hold particular beliefs as certain, absolute truth. These may be people with religious views based on a sacred source, such as the Bible, Torah, or Quran. Or they may be people who reject any such faith-based beliefs and insist only on the primacy of observable, measurable facts and evidence.

Our own beliefs notwithstanding, the question for us is how to talk about or across such views productively. While it may seem more difficult in this context, our answer is the same as for any learning conversation: Be respectful, and seek to understand the sense in how others see it. You may have something to learn, and understanding their story helps you know how best to help them learn.

When we ourselves hold beliefs as absolute truth, we tend to think, "surely this should be an exception to that general rule of mutual understanding. If the truth is absolute, isn't it just a question of helping them see it?" In a word, no. We have no power to make other people see something as we do, and our urgent attempts at one-way persuasion usually result in increased resistance rather than greater understanding.

The problem, of course, is that people disagree about what the truth is. However certain we feel, others with different views feel just as sure. Even in a community that believes wholeheartedly in certain absolute truths, there may still be disagreement on the implications and meaning of those truths. Our own experience facilitating a discussion of these issues at a seminary allowed us to witness a deep and complex appreciation of the challenges of being a moral leader and shepherd while maintaining appropriate humility about the ability of any man to perceive the mind of God. "Though we are made in God's image, we all have limited human understanding," one theologian pointed out. "We are all thousand-watt souls with forty-watt bulbs."*

Scientists, too, appreciate the problem. Although scientists assert that there are observable facts and propositions, such as the "laws" of physics, most scientists working on the edges of what we know and understand have a healthy skepticism regarding the current state of knowledge. They know that the next scientific discovery may turn what we assumed to be true on its head, whether that's in space exploration, medical research, or particle physics.

In this sense, the critical question is less whether there *is* absolute truth than whether and how well we can perceive it. Perhaps the only thing a human being can be truly sure of is that one can't be completely sure. That *is* the realm of God, even if you don't believe in God.

This doesn't mean we can't argue with passion and conviction over issues about which we care deeply. But when we do so, we should avoid hubris and maintain some humility and respect. After all, even our own views sometimes change with time. Likewise, those who disagree with us are not necessarily bad or simpleminded, or people who have not thought the issue through.

If finding "truth" is more a journey than a destination, then spirited conversation with those who see things differently is exactly what we need to shed light on our blind spots, recognize and test our assumptions, and expand and deepen our own understanding.

*Father Dominic Holtz, O.P., in conversation with Celeste Mueller, Eric Wagner, C.R., Scott Steinkerchner, O.P., Dominic McManus, O.P., Ann Garrido, D.Min., and Sheila Heen on February 27, 2009, in conjunction with the Truth Symposium Project at the Aquinas Institute, St. Louis, Missouri.

## We can do better

As we write this in the spring of 2010, our corner of the world, and many others, face a challenging set of social, political, religious, and moral divides — including the appropriate size and role of government, health care reform, education reform, abortion, gay marriage, immigration policy, homeland security, climate and energy policy, and, of course, the economy. There is at least a perception that fewer and fewer of us are moderates, and that the gap between people of divergent views is growing. Anger and even outrage are prevalent on both sides of the divide. If we are righteous, we think, it is because there is so much at stake, so much to fear, and because we are so tired of the other side's not listening and not caring. We're sick of the corruption, the lying, the stupidity, the self-interested nonsense that passes for informed opinion and public policy.

Where do the authors of this book come down on all of this? Our various views on the substance of these debates are not relevant. But we have strong views on the process. As divides grow larger and more passionate, good communication becomes more difficult and more important. With a passionate viewpoint comes the responsibility to be informed about the issues involved and to listen to how people with a different point of view see them. Not necessarily with the goal of agreeing or even of finding common ground. But *at least* with the goal of understanding how your neighbor sees it. Not the media, not the Internet or the blogosphere, not bumper stickers and placards, but your *neighbor*, whether across the street or across the country.

Consider this assertion: The more passionate we are about the issues that matter most to us, the more likely we are to have a cartoonish view of those who see things differently. That statement may infuriate you. You may find yourself chafing against such a ridiculous generalization. But flip it around: When others think *your* view is self-interested or shallow, base, and maybe even evil, do you think they see you clearly? Is what they've heard and read an accurate portrayal of what you see and feel? No. They've turned you into a cartoon they can dismiss without having to confront the fact that you care as much as they do, that you are a person of principle and conviction, that you're working hard to do what's right in the face of the very same human limitations and frailties we all confront.

And they are too.[*]

## 2. What if the other person really does have bad intentions — lying, bullying, or intentionally derailing the conversation to get what they want?

We can't know for sure what is motivating another person. What feels deliberate and strategically intentional to us may be a hotheaded emotional reaction in response to a trigger we're unaware of, or an unthinking response by someone at the limits of their ability to stay constructive. Surprisingly often, an "obvious" and self-serving lie turns out to be a person's actual belief.

Nevertheless, people do lie and sometimes have quite bad intentions toward us. And certainly there are situations where people — intentionally or otherwise — manipulate, threaten, delay, obfuscate, bully, or derail in an attempt to get their way.

In these situations we have three initial pieces of advice. First, be careful about rewarding bad behavior. If you give up and hand people what they want simply "to avoid the hassle," you end up teaching them that behaving badly pays off, and you will soon see more of the same.

Second, beware of reacting in kind or "playing their game." Remember that your behavior can affect your reputation far beyond this

---

[*]This is an essential lesson from the work of the Public Conversations Project, which facilitates respectful dialogue among strong proponents of opposing views on issues such as abortion and gay marriage. Time and again, participants in these facilitated learning conversations are surprised to learn how much their deeper values overlap with those of longtime "opponents." Often they have discovered that their profoundly divergent conclusions hinge on the most subtle differences in the weight they attach to the same shared concerns. And always, they come to see the very human face of the "other." For more on this, see the Web site of the Public Conversations Project at www.publicconversations.org.

one interaction. So even if you are being lied to, it will rarely serve you to lie in return and undercut your reputation for integrity.

Note that being trust*worthy* is not the same as being trust*ing*. If they haven't earned your trust, you have no obligation to offer it. If they "dare" you, remember the "And Stance": "Don't you trust me?" "Actually, I don't know you well enough to be sure, and if you are telling the truth I assume you have no problem offering verification or a guaranty." Rather than simply reacting in kind, focus on your objective and how to move toward it.

Third, seek to understand why they think their intentions and actions are justified. We tend to ascribe bad behavior to bad character: They lie because they are bad people. Unfortunately, if we make that assumption, there's not much to be done — they're hopeless. In reality, people are likely to feel that their intentions are somehow justified (for example, by how they believe you have treated them), and that under the circumstances their behavior is necessary to avoid being taken advantage of. While we may not agree with their views, it is helpful to understand their logic. Because there *is* a logic, there is the possibility that you can persuade them that another approach makes sense.

Let's look at an example.

## Colin's Story

Colin and Matt are fifty–fifty co-owners of a Web design firm. Colin explains:

> Matt is usually reasonable enough, but when he really wants something, he uses anger and threats to get it. Recently we were discussing our branding, and suddenly he exploded. "We're redoing everything! I'm sick of you always playing it safe!" I said that I liked our current direction. He responded with a threat: "I'll pull the plug and sell my interest in the partnership if we don't do this my way." At first when he would do something like that, I would just give in. That helped for a while, but of course Matt would fly into a rage the

next time he wanted his way, and I got more and more resentful. So lately, I've been trying to give as good as I get: when he yells, I yell louder. But that just escalates the conflict, and now it feels like things are almost out of control.

Colin has tried to manage this problem both by giving in and, more recently, by reacting in kind. Neither has helped.

**Giving in.** There are times to give in — when you're persuaded the other person is right; when the other person cares a lot about the outcome and you care little; when any solution is better than no solution and you need an answer immediately. But as a long-term strategy for dealing with difficult behavior, it's not going to help. Giving in rewards bad behavior, and what gets rewarded gets repeated.

**Reacting in kind: playing their game.** There are relationships where reciprocal volatility is the norm — an equilibrium that is satisfactory to both sides. Sometimes people say to us, "My husband and I yell and fight all the time, and then we're over it. Are you saying that's not okay?" Our response is that if it's working for both of you, then it's fine. What matters is that both parties be comfortable with whatever level of engagement occurs and that they make the same meaning out of it.

For many people such relationships are *not* comfortable. They reason: "For them to treat me this way is a sign of disrespect. They know how upsetting it is to me." Like Colin, such people can take hours or days to recover from a heated argument or personal attack.

## What Might Help

We can see why Colin feels stuck. If giving in rarely helps, and reacting in kind is no better, then what?

First, of course, it can help to imagine how Matt may see the situation and to look for a possible vicious cycle of act-react contributions. For example, perhaps Matt feels that Colin is bullying *him* by vetoing all change. Matt may even see it as a deliberate — and therefore infuriating — passive-aggressive strategy.

Such insights offer one potentially fruitful new path for discussion. But for our purposes let's suppose that Matt is sticking with his ultimatum approach, in the belief, conscious or unconscious, that it will work. What else can Colin do?

**Name the dynamic: make the trouble explicit.** In Chapter 11, we explain the power of this technique. Naming the dynamic is something to try when persistent good faith efforts at listening and problem solving have failed.

Naming the dynamic requires you to "put on the table as a topic for discussion what you see happening in the conversation." Of particular value is making explicit the other side's implied rule for how to make decisions. In this case the implied rule that Matt seems to want Colin to adopt is: "When I get upset, I get my way." Put that way, it's obvious this would be a lousy way to run a business or maintain a working relationship. The problem becomes even clearer when you apply the test of reciprocity: *What if we were both using this strategy?* A business is not going to succeed by allocating resources or choosing a marketing campaign based on who can cry or shout the loudest.

When Colin names the dynamic, he should avoid the attribution of intent. He shouldn't say, "You try to get your way by being angry." Matt may not recognize or acknowledge that he's angry, and is very likely to take exception to the idea that he's simply trying to get his way by throwing a tantrum. That conversation will likely veer off into a pointless argument over Matt's actual intentions.

Instead, Colin should use the third story to describe the dilemma and invite joint problem solving: "You feel strongly that you want to start over with our branding materials. I like them the way they are. When you and I strongly disagree, how should we decide what to do?" If Matt responds by saying, "Well, if we don't do it my way, I'm quitting," Colin can name *that* dynamic: "So one way we can decide is based on who's more willing to quit. That doesn't seem like a sustainable decision-making process or one likely to produce the best decisions. I think a better approach is for us to step back and look again at our goals for these materials, and then to. . . ."

Naming the dynamic is at once neutral (the third story) and neutralizing (Colin can't force Matt to believe what he does not, but neither can Matt force Colin). Colin's stance is solid and centered: "I'm open to persuasion, but I'm not yet persuaded. And I'm the one who determines when I am. Your anger underscores how strongly you feel, but doesn't affect the legitimate data, reasoning, and principles that would help persuade me."

**Clarify consequences.** Based on his description, it's hard to know for sure how upset Colin is. Is Matt's behavior just an annoyance, or does Colin feel like a punching bag? If the latter, there's a temptation for Colin to want to give the "enough is enough" speech, where Colin demands that Matt reform his mercurial behavior: "I've had it with the yelling and the threats. I'm just not going to put up with it anymore! Enough is enough!"

That sounds good in your head when you're rehearsing just exactly how to let them have it. The problem comes when you examine carefully whether it's going to be an effective strategy. While Colin is giving his speech, consider what might be going on in Matt's internal voice. He may be thinking, "You're crazy, I don't get angry," or "More proof that you're oversensitive," or "Don't tell me what to do," or "I'm more passionate than you — so what?" And notice, from Matt's point of view, *he* was already giving the "enough is enough" speech when he told Colin he was sick of playing it safe. That hasn't had a very good impact on Colin, and there's little reason to believe that Colin would achieve more by trying the same thing on Matt.

So we'd recommend something different. Colin can resolve in his mind that enough is enough — nothing wrong with feeling resolute. But rather than trying to control Matt (by actually *saying* enough is enough), he should focus on what he, Colin, sees, thinks, wants, and will do. Key points might include:

- Here's what I see.

- Here's the impact on me.

- You may disagree with my perceptions or feel that your behavior is justified.

- It doesn't matter which one of us is right about that. Our current way of interacting doesn't work *for me*.

- I am asking you to change this behavior.

- If it continues, here's what I'm going to do.

Colin is not insisting that he is right. He *thinks* he's right, but he can't *know* he's right. What he does know is that things aren't working for him as they are. Colin needs Matt to understand this, not to control Matt, but to give him the information he needs to make informed choices about whether and how to modify his behavior. Of course, to use this approach Colin will have to think carefully about what the real consequences of no change will be and describe them clearly to Matt.

These same strategies are equally helpful with other difficult behaviors. If they are always changing the topic or turning the conversation into an attack on you, work hard to understand their point of view and be open to good faith problem solving. But if they keep making moves that feel like intentional attempts to derail or bully, name the dynamic (there are more examples in Chapter 11), and, if needed, clarify the consequences of no change.

## 3. What if the other person is genuinely difficult, perhaps even mentally ill?

A theme of this book is that human interactions are complex. Trouble arises from the *intersection* of styles, behaviors, assumptions, and interests, not because one person is all good and the other all bad.

Even so, some people really *are* more difficult to deal with than others.

Depression, anxiety, bipolar disorder, addiction, obsessive-compulsive disorder, narcissism, attention deficit disorder, and other underlying pathologies (which can vary in intensity from mild to severe*) can contribute to any number of interpersonal challenges that cause friends and colleagues worry, inefficiency, frustration, and despair. Anyone who lives or works with someone who is mentally ill knows how challenging it can be. Good communication skills can help, especially when you think of the many types of conversations that attend these challenges, but more important will be the support of family, colleagues, and community, as well as mental health professionals.

At least two additional things can help. First, although we often describe the mentally ill person's perspective and behavior as "crazy" or "illogical," in fact, many syndromes actually do have an internal logic. Someone with obsessive-compulsive disorder feels they must follow certain rituals or face potentially extreme (though usually imagined) negative consequences. Though disruptive and in some cases incapacitating, the rituals are a form of self-medication against intense anxiety.

Addiction likewise has an internal logic: The addict is choosing short-term pleasure (or reduction in pain) over short-term pain. Ignoring the fact that this is likely to lead to even greater pain tomorrow makes a certain sense if your goal is just to make it through the day. This doesn't make the logic right or rational or a good choice. But if we can understand the illness from the inside, it can lend insight into why our loved ones or colleagues are behaving as they are, whether and how we can help them, and what we sometimes do that unintentionally makes their symptoms worse.

After all, those struggling with depression, phobias, and mental and emotional disorders are not intentionally being difficult to hurt

---

*We tend to think that people are either mentally ill or not, that they either "have something" or they don't. But it's not either-or. In their book *Shadow Syndromes*, John Ratey and Catherine Johnson argue that people who are not clinically diagnosed with a mental illness or personality disorder can still be suffering from physiologically induced pathologies — "shadow" forms of well-known disorders like obsessive-compulsive disorder, depression, anxiety, addiction, and rage, and that such pathologies are less rare than we assume.

or frustrate those around them. They are often doing what they can to cope with the distorted worldview imposed upon them by the illness. This does not relieve them of responsibility for their actions. But reminding ourselves that it's the disease that is compelling them to behave in upsetting ways can help dampen the impact on us.

And let's remember that aside from clinically diagnosed mental illness, less extreme challenges can also cause serious disconnects in our relationships. Some people are unpredictably emotional, quick to anger, brittle, self-absorbed, or just not very open to seeing things differently. You ask your co-worker how her vacation was, and she fires back that she was "only gone for three days!" Her response seems weirdly defensive until you realize she "heard" your question as an accusation: "Why were you on vacation for *so long*!?" We all on occasion attribute overly negative intentions. That's our point in Chapter 3. But some people do it more often than most and with greater certainty ("I *know* it was an accusation!"). The self-fulfilling loops that result are crazy making and hard to break out of.

In the face of such challenges, it is important to remember that there is no way to guarantee a particular outcome. You can't force another person to change, or to do what you want. Moreover, if you define success by what you can get others to do, you cede to them control of the outcome and set yourself up for aggravation. Your goal should be to do the best you can to fuel a productive interchange and to make sure as best you can that your own actions aren't part of the problem and somehow contributing to the other's reactions.

With that caveat, there often are approaches that can help to change difficult dynamics. The details depend on the specific context, but in each case they flow from first trying to get inside the other's perspective to understand the sense it makes to them, however different or bizarre it may seem to you. To illustrate, let's take a look at three examples.

## Addy's Story

Addy is caught in the middle of a feud between her mother and her mother's sister, Addy's aunt Robin:

Aunt Robin tells me how selfish and horrible my mother is, and tries to get me to agree. For the last five years, I've gently but firmly defended my mother, while trying to help Robin bring some balance to her view. But Robin literally screams into the phone. She'll say almost random things, like, "Your mother says I never remember to send birthday cards to her grandchildren! Well, your mother's a goddamn liar!" I calmly explain my mother's view. Doesn't help. I've also tried sharing impacts: "Robin, when you say things about my mother, I feel upset." Doesn't help. I try empathy, acknowledging that she's going through a tough time. Doesn't help. I point out Robin's contribution to the feud. Doesn't help. And on occasion, I lose my temper: "How dare you talk about my mother like that!" That doesn't help either.

## What Might Help

**Distinguish helping from fixing.** Addy knows that her aunt Robin is lonely as well as difficult, and part of her motivation in interacting with Robin is to help ease those feelings. At least, if asked, this is what Addy would say, and this is what she believes. But when she looks deeper, she finds that her motivation is not *only* to help Robin but to *fix* her, to get her to conform her behavior to Addy's view of how people should talk and interact.

But such change is beyond Addy's control. In her mind, Addy is like Max in *Where the Wild Things Are*, the seagoing boy-king who shipwrecks on an island populated by incorrigible and frightening "wild things." Max waves his wand and utters the words "be still." And they are.

Alas, our world doesn't work that way. While it's hard to give up this illusion of control, doing so is the first step toward finding an approach that helps.

**Think about what might be going on for Robin.** Something important is at stake for Robin in these conversations, or she wouldn't keep pursuing them. The *connection* matters to her. Negative interaction is better than no interaction at all. Robin probably wants to feel loved, that she belongs, and that she has a valued role in the family. In addition, we can assume from her frustration level that Robin feels unheard. She wants to tell someone that she's upset with her sister, but can't get anyone to listen. Addy needs an approach that acknowledges these core interests and at the same time points the conversation in a different direction.

**Consider the Big Reframe.** This approach is intended to knock the conversation off its center. That's usually not a good idea, but if things are stuck or going drastically wrong, sometimes bringing some big energy from a different direction can help.

Here's an example of what Addy might say: "Well, my mother sure can be a pain in the butt! Goodness knows, she's not perfect! Maybe everyone in our family is a pain in the butt. But one thing I know is that my mother loves you, and you love her, and I know that means a lot to both of you."

There are several reasons a statement like this might be useful. First, there's some humor in it, a sense of lightness that serves as a reminder that it isn't the end of the world. Second, there's a strong empathy move at the outset. Agreeing that Addy's mother can be a pain in the butt may seem disloyal, but it's probably true (to the extent that everyone can be sometimes, especially in families). Robin has spent years trying to get *someone* to move beyond defending her sister and to hear her frustration.

Third, it expresses love. By saying "you love each other and it's important to each of you," Addy is reassuring Robin that she is loved and giving her an important role in the family, which should help to assuage her fear of being alone.[*]

[*]The October 13, 2003 issue of the *New Yorker* has an article by Tad Friend about people who jump off the Golden Gate Bridge intending to commit suicide. The article mentions Kevin Briggs, a motorcycle patrolman, who "has a knack for spotting jumpers and talking them back from the edge; he has coaxed in more than two hundred potential jumpers without losing one over the side. . . ." Briggs doesn't talk directly about jumping or not jumping. Instead, he uses the Big Reframe: "What's your plan for tomorrow?" he asks. If they don't have one, he says, "Well, let's make one." (This story first came to our attention in the song "Gatekeeper," by Meg Hutchinson.)

## Peter's Story

Peter is Lucera's boss at a large pharmaceutical firm. As Peter explains:

> Lucera is a brilliant scientist, extremely hardworking, and has great
> instincts in the lab. But she's very difficult to work with. When any-
> one tries to give her feedback, she rejects it almost aggressively, ex-
> plaining why it's wrong, biased, political, whatever. I recently talked
> to her about two of her direct reports who found her to be overcriti-
> cal, and her response in each case was, "Look at the source." She
> then added that she had in fact toned down her criticism of late, and
> had been trying to show more appreciation toward her co-workers,
> which is why she found it particularly obnoxious that they were try-
> ing to sabotage her like this. I asked if there could be any validity to
> their feelings, and she said no, it was obvious that their attack had
> been motivated by professional jealousy.

## What Might Help

**Recognize "Blind Spots."** Peter's story suggests that Lucera may
be hobbled by a lack of awareness. In this dynamic, the very signals
that communicate anger or defensiveness or disgust or vulnerability
lie outside of the communicator's awareness, in what we call a "blind
spot." The big three blind spots are tone of voice, facial expressions,
and body language. The listener is very aware of these, the talker is
not. "Yes, I was disgusted by their failure, but I didn't say anything
about it, so how would they know?" They know because to them it's
obvious; the messages leak out nonverbally, outside the speaker's
awareness.

What this means for Lucera is that she is missing a lot of information about why people are doing what they're doing. From her
point of view, the "new Lucera" is friendly and tolerant, even in the
face of all the incompetence around her. She does not see her more
subtle but equally impactful ongoing contributions to the problem
(for example, how she communicates disgust by eye rolling and tone

of voice). When others then say they are mistreated by her, she is thinking, "But I'm *not* mistreating them." She is then left to wonder why they are claiming to be mistreated when they are not. The answer must be that they have a motivation to give her negative feedback — they are jealous or ambitious or petty or themselves difficult people.

Thus, the reason Lucera has an explanation for why each piece of feedback she is getting is unjust is that she actually believes it to be so. It's the only explanation she can think of.

Two things might help Peter break through Lucera's self-sealing perceptual deficit.

**Give Lucera the missing data.** Lucera may be able to perceive the behaviors she is currently unaware of if she watches herself on videotape. Assuming Lucera is sensitive to such behavior in others when it is directed at her,* she should be able to identify it when watching herself, though it may be a painful realization. Having established that Lucera may be communicating in ways of which she is unaware, it should be easier for her to entertain other explanations for her reports' comments. Peter can then work with her to rethink what's happened with her reports and recraft how she deals with them.

**Address the implications of the alternate view.** Another thing Peter might say is, "Let's put aside for a minute the question of *whether* this complaint is true and instead ask *what if* it were true? What would it mean? What would be the implications for you?"

As we know, one reason people argue about what happened is that the other person's view threatens their identity. This approach addresses that interest directly, perhaps allowing Peter to help Lucera find a way to feel less threatened by the prospect of learning that her behavior has had unintended consequences.

---

*If Lucera is *not* sensitive to such cues in others, it's at least possible that she suffers from a disorder like Asperger's syndrome on the autism spectrum. Since she is generally high functioning, it is likely that with work she could increase her awareness of such cues in herself and others.

Ten Questions People Ask About *Difficult Conversations*

## Matamba's Story

Matamba was working in a group that didn't much like its new boss:

> Our old boss was very collaborative and tried to make all decisions
> on the merits. And if you disagreed, he was pretty easy to confront,
> and at least you'd get a hearing. The new guy is very hierarchical,
> even a little dictatorial. Asking questions is tolerated but hardly
> welcomed. But sometimes he becomes downright rigid, and you get
> the sense that there will be retaliation if you push back. We don't
> want to reward bad behavior, so the group tries to stand up to him in
> these moments, but that always seems to cause a very rapid and de-
> structive escalation in the conflict. "Naming the dynamic" and ask-
> ing to talk about it doesn't seem to work either!

## What Helped

**Recognize that aggression can spring from fear.** In Matamba's
case, a consultant friend suggested the possibility that in these difficult moments the new boss was actually terrified. Matamba knew
that his boss was ambitious and very concerned about always appear-
ing successful, and the consultant's questions highlighted the fact
that these difficult moments with the boss tended to occur when his
subordinates were proposing an untested course of action. The consultant suggested that the boss feared that his subordinates' ideas
might result in loss of face, embarrassment, and public "failure."

**Clarify and validate the concern.** Rather than dig in and oppose
the boss more firmly, as the group had been doing, the consultant
recommended that Matamba and his colleagues ask their boss what
he is worried about: "What are you concerned might happen if we go
in this direction?" When they tried this, they were surprised at how
ready he was with an answer. He laid out a plausible problematic sce-
nario, though not one the group thought likely. Understanding the
fear allowed them to validate and address it: "Wow, that would con-

cern me, too! So let's make sure that doesn't happen. What if we agree to do this, so it *can't* happen?" This in turn led the boss to a response the group didn't expect: "Oh. That would be fine. As long as that's clear, do whatever you want."

## Two Final Thoughts

**Remember joint contribution.** The danger in acknowledging that some people *are* more difficult than others is that we let ourselves off the hook. Even a genuinely challenging personality may become more challenging when you are provocative. As the saying goes, just because he's paranoid doesn't mean they're not out to get him. You should always consider how you may be — wittingly or unwittingly — helping to create or sustain a difficult dynamic. And because seeing your own contribution can be difficult, you may need to enlist the eyes and insights of neutral observers with no stake in the outcome.

**Patience and persistence pay.** Often when someone resists acknowledging their contribution to a situation, it's because to do so would threaten their identity. In these moments, the other person may need your help in finding a way to frame their contribution that preserves their identity or helps them take a more nuanced view of themselves.

For many of us, the concepts of multiple valid perspectives, joint contribution, contribution without blame, and identity without perfection may be novel. It may take them a while to understand these ideas and get comfortable with them. Don't give up too easily or be surprised if change comes haltingly over time. It is an all too common tragedy that, by the time someone starts to show a bit of openness to collaborative dialogue, we have so lost heart that we fail to recognize their subtle overtures.

## 4. How does this work with someone who has all the power — like my boss?

Whether in the context of disagreeing with your boss in a meeting or talking one-on-one to clarify an assignment, using the skills in this book surely feels tougher going up the hierarchy than down. Lots of bosses say they want their employees to challenge them, but far fewer actually mean it. If employees are punished, even subtly, for raising tough issues, then they won't. People align their actions with implicit incentives, not official rhetoric.

We don't encourage you to take risks for the thrill of it or even because it's "the right thing to do." This is not a book about the righteousness of speaking up and getting fired. It's a matter of cost and benefit. There are rare occasions when speaking out really is worth getting fired for, but in most cases it's not. The consequences of speaking up are rarely so extreme, and there are often unseen benefits in doing so. Speaking up (with confidence and skill) may ruffle feathers in the short term but earn you long-term respect among your colleagues, and often even from your boss. And on many occasions, speaking up will not ruffle any feathers at all.

There are some perceptual binds that heighten the challenge. Surveys suggest that a great majority of bosses believe their employees view them as effective, competent, and caring, yet only a minority of employees report that they view their bosses in so positive a light. That's not surprising; getting negative feedback or bad news to move up an organization is like reversing the direction of a waterfall.

What to do?

**Use the power of influence.** Let's distinguish between two kinds of power: control and influence. Control is the unilateral ability to make something happen. Influence is the ability to affect someone else's thinking. Within limits, your boss has the power of control. They could fire or transfer you, or give you projects with little appeal, without having to negotiate. (Of course this is a caricature. Usually there are formal and informal limits on people's ability to implement such unilateral decisions.)

In contrast, you can't fire or transfer your boss. And in fact, explicitly acknowledging that they are the decision maker can actually make them more receptive to listening to your input. So you might say to your boss, "I know there are lots of factors you have to take into consideration, and at the end of the day, I'm onboard with whatever you decide. I just want to make sure that as you think about it, you are aware that. . . ."

Your boss is now more likely to be open to *influence*, because they don't need to push back, defend their turf, or clarify that this is their decision to make. You've given them a clear signal acknowledging their status, which will help them relax and be receptive.

Now tell your boss what matters to you and why. It's surprising how often people will tell us they've "tried everything" to influence their boss, yet when we ask, "Have you told your boss this is important to you?" they respond, "Well, I assume my boss must know." They've never actually said, "This matters to me." Being clear that something matters to you, and why, has an impact on the other person. It may or may not persuade them — that will depend on the strength of your argument and competing considerations — but it will have an impact. The purpose is not to threaten, but to provide your boss the information they need to make an informed decision.

We are often asked how to discuss "joint contribution" when the other person involved is your boss. In most cases it's probably not a good idea to say to your boss, "Sure, I've contributed to the problem, but you've contributed even more!" Yet that doesn't mean you have to drop the subject altogether. Whether your boss admits it or not, they *have* contributed to whatever the problem is, in large ways or small. It may be that they're difficult to approach, or overly confident of their views, expect you to be a mind-reader, or make it clear to you that you aren't supposed to ask questions. Perhaps their "open-door policy" comes with penalties for those who actually drop by to talk.

**Use the language of request.** How to raise these concerns? One way is to use what we call the *language of request* instead of the language of joint contribution. Instead of saying, "Part of the reason I wasn't able to get this in on time was that you waited until Friday afternoon to ask me to work on it," say, "I'm totally committed to ensuring that this doesn't happen again. We've identified three things that I need to do differently: [x, y, and z]. Something else that would be really helpful to me is if I had more lead time on the more complicated projects. If I can get the assignments on Wednesday instead of Friday, that would enable me to balance new projects with my current projects and other hard-to-move commitments. I don't know to what extent that's possible on your end. What are your thoughts on that?"

**Listen!** Paradoxically, there is also considerable persuasion power in inquiry and listening. As we say in Chapter 9, listening is not just about taking in information. Listening well has an impact on the other person — it quiets their internal voice. When they feel heard and acknowledged, it is easier for them to hear you. And it also lets you know what they care about, which lays the foundation for creative problem solving.

**Say what's in it for the boss.** Explain how having a conversation is in your boss's interest: "I want to make this initiative a great success. To do that I need a little more help in making sure I understand the logic well enough to execute effectively." Of course for this approach to work, you have to be open to learning. If your real goal in having a conversation is to show your boss he's wrong, you're on dangerous ground, and you're likely to experience all the usual problems with delivering a message from a stance of certainty.

Being open to learning doesn't mean giving up your view. If you don't see how the new boss's idea will work, then your goal should be to figure out what you might be missing — as well as what you may know that the boss does not. After all, if your boss is the third new manager to come in and recommend a particular approach, there is likely some validity to the view, even if all the department veterans think it's crazy.

If the prospect of "more talk" is frustrating, but likely necessary for collective success, you can acknowledge both of those interests in framing the conversation: "I'm sure we'd all like to move on quickly. At the same time, I imagine it is even more important to all of us that this work. I would very much like this initiative to succeed but don't yet feel confident in my ability to pull it off. Specifically, it would help to spell out how we might answer a couple of the objections I can imagine coming our way. For example. . . ."

## What if my boss simply refuses to talk about my concerns / our relationship?

First, on process, it's crucial when dealing with a difficult boss not to do a hit-and-run conversation. You *must* schedule time on your boss's calendar. You need undivided attention and a defined amount of time.

Once in the meeting, how to start? Say what's on your mind, framing from the third story and why it should be of concern to your boss. For example: "I want to talk about how we raise things, as I think it's affecting morale and productivity." "I want to talk about the best way to disagree with you in a meeting. What's your advice?"

You can't force your boss to talk to you about a particular concern, but you can assertively make the case. This is particularly tough when your boss insists that discussing the matter further is itself a sign of incompetence or weakness on your part. Here, it's crucial to be well prepared. Do the necessary reading or research and try everything you can think of to deal with the issue on your own. This way, when you approach your boss you can say confidently that you've exhausted all other angles and that you're coming to your boss because they are the right person to come to.

## What if my boss is abusive?

In his provocatively titled book *The No Asshole Rule: Building a Civilized Workplace and Surviving One That Isn't*, Stanford Business School professor Robert Sutton shows readers how to deal with "bullies, creeps, jerks, tyrants, tormentors, despots, backstabbers, egomaniacs, and all the other [people]" at work who can make our lives miserable.[*] Citing the emotional, physical, and financial havoc such people wreak, the author's advice is this: *No matter how important such people seem to your business, don't tolerate them.* But of course many businesses do, for reasons ranging from fear of loss of competitiveness to the complexity of sorting through competing claims and perceptions.

There are a variety of reasons people bully. (By the way, bullies are not always bosses, and studies show that the perpetrator is at least as likely to be a woman as a man.) They may suffer from a mental illness or mood disorder. Or they may have "learned" that such behaviors are simply the best way to get what they want, or assume that their particular business culture requires it. For some, this attitude results from the belief that the right to fully indulge their bad moods is a perk of success.

Compounding these problems, often the person with the difficult behavior is blind to it. Consider this example: You inform your boss that your team did not meet its third-quarter targets. Your boss explodes. He verbally attacks you, your teammates, and your customers — anyone who comes to mind as having been responsible for the shortfall. You point out to your boss how angry he seems. He responds by saying, "I wasn't angry; the numbers were bad," as if only one could be true at a time. And that's how he actually experiences it. For him, anger is a self-justifying emotion: It somehow "doesn't count" if there's a "cause." Which makes trying to address the issue even more challenging.

---

[*]Robert I. Sutton, *The No Asshole Rule: Building a Civilized Workplace and Surviving One That Isn't* (Warner Business Books, 2007), back cover.

A big piece of the battle with someone who is abusive relates to your own identity conversation. Their tactics of anger and shaming can undermine your sense of competence, confidence, and worth. You shouldn't take their feedback at face value — nor should you reject it wholesale. Instead, try to find ways to evaluate your work that are independent of the abusive person's assessment. Easier said than done, we know. But working at it helps.

Sometimes the best strategy is a workaround. Deal with the person only when required, cultivate as many other relationships as you can, and try to avoid any obvious triggers. In conjunction with that, recognize that most situations are not all or nothing. You may not get the week off you'd wanted, but you might get a three-day weekend. You might not get the plum assignment you think you deserve, but you might be allowed some input. Accumulating small wins can make a big difference to your peace of mind over time.

Be aware of structural and formal channels within an organization. If your boss is difficult or abusive, you might talk to HR or register a formal complaint with your union. If your boss quashes real communication, several workers (or groups of workers) can band together to raise the issue. If you find your boss's behavior intolerable, you can offer a warning that you will leave your job or take other action if your boss doesn't relent.

At the end of the day, you may find yourself facing these questions: "What are my alternatives?" and "Is this worth it?" We're not arguing that you should leave a job if you see no other prospects on the horizon (especially if you have dependents). But sometimes just knowing there's *some* out gives you the confidence to take a stand against bullying tactics. Nothing builds confidence quicker than the knowledge that you can survive the worst that can happen.

Professor Sutton eloquently sums up the complexity of dealing with these tough questions. If you feel stuck, you can

> . . . protect your body and mind by reframing the abuse as something that isn't your fault and won't magically disappear. . . . You might also . . . seek and fight those little battles that you have a good chance of winning. Those modest victories will help you feel in

control and just might help make things a bit better, and if you keep chipping away and others join your quest, things just might get a lot better for everyone in the long haul. . . . But there is a dark side to these ideas. They might provide just enough protection . . . to stop people from bailing out of . . . relentlessly demeaning situations — even when they have exit options.*

## 5. If I'm the boss / parent, why can't I just tell my subordinates / children what to do?

You can. One of the most frustrating misconceptions we encounter about *Difficult Conversations* is that the authors are against people making and implementing decisions; that talking is more important than doing; that everyone should have an equal say; that unless everyone is onboard, nothing can move forward. That's not our view. Whether you're a CEO or a parent, we encourage you to make decisions as early and efficiently as possible, to explain those decisions clearly, and to take responsibility for their implementation and effectiveness.

It is equally true that whether you are making a decision, implementing it, or problem solving, you can't always, or even usually, succeed merely by "telling." Indeed, it is useful in decision making to distinguish those times when you are:

- *commanding* (I decide, I tell you my decision)

from those situations where you are:

- *consulting* (I ask for your input, then I decide and tell you);

- *collaborating or negotiating* (we decide together); or

- *delegating* (you decide).†

---

*The No Asshole Rule, pp. 152–53.
†These distinctions, or what he calls "buckets," come from Mark Gordon, senior adviser to the Harvard Negotiation Project and a director of Vantage Partners, LLC.

Whatever category you choose, make sure to communicate to others what you expect from them. If you are consulting and they think you're collaborating, they may be surprised to learn that while you *heard* their advice, you didn't *take* their advice. Role clarity upfront is the key. Even if this requires a bit of a difficult conversation when you put someone in a different bucket than they were expecting, it is far easier to have that conversation up front than wait until you get to the point when you are making a decision they don't like.

But let's acknowledge the frustration. We've all felt it: "I'm in charge. I *should* be able to tell you what to do, and you should *do* it." Do this assignment, well and on time. Be home by midnight, sober. Get your team aligned with my vision, heart and soul.

Whether or not these *should* happen, it is simply true that they often don't. It's like a car that doesn't go when you press the gas pedal. The car doesn't care what your rules are about what cars should do. The car doesn't care if you need to get somewhere. The car doesn't care if you're angry. The one thing we know that doesn't help is simply continuing to press the gas pedal. Yet that's often what we do as bosses and parents. We keep "telling," even when we're not getting the results we expect.

If your car were stalled, the first thing you would do is diagnose the cause: Are you out of gas? Is the transmission faulty? Is the battery dead?

That's the step we often skip when we're trying to influence someone else's behavior. Why aren't they doing what we want? An answer we highlight in the main text is joint contribution. When something goes wrong, making it right is rarely in either person's full control. If you *and* your employee have both contributed to the problem, then one-way commands are unlikely to solve it.

But engaging in two-way communication doesn't mean you give up your role, rights, and responsibilities as boss or parent. It all comes back to the And Stance. Consider an example between a parent and child. Should your teenager be allowed to drink and drive? No. This is not a question about which your teenager needs to be consulted. Yet delivering this message clearly and firmly is not the end of the conversation. You need to listen to your teenager's thoughts, feelings, and questions. Not because you're negotiating the rule, but because there are issues that relate to the rule — and especially to having confidence in its implementation — that may require further clarification and perhaps some problem solving. Is getting high the same as drinking? Is going just three blocks considered driving? What's the best way for your son or daughter to contact you? How will discipline be handled if your child engages in underage drinking and calls you for a ride home? What pressures does your child experience around drinking, popularity, and intimacy, and how can they be managed?

Let's take a workplace example. You've decided to put an employee on probation. Beyond informing them of this, what is there to discuss? After all, the decision is final.

Keep the And Stance front and center. As the boss, you've made a decision that is clear, firm, and final. *And*, to understand the various causes of the problem, to build a human connection and improve the working relationship, and to make sure your decision and its consequences are in fact clear, you need to have a two-way conversation. It might sound in part like this: "I understand that you don't think being put on probation is fair. Let's talk about that. I want to hear your view and share mine. Before we do, I want to clarify, though, that I'm not negotiating this or deciding in collaboration with you. I've already made the decision. The purpose of talking is to figure out why we've had a disconnect on this, so that we can try to avoid doing it again as we go forward, and so I can perhaps give you more effective coaching."

That's an example of deciding and still needing to have a two-way conversation. Let's consider the reverse: having a two-way conversation and still needing to decide. Imagine that you've just had an efficient, in-depth learning conversation with an employee about why they consistently take twice as long to finish assignments as their colleagues. You've identified your own contributions to this as well as theirs and examined some institutional and structural drags on their productivity. You've "mapped the contribution system," as described in Chapter 4.

Now it's decision time. Your employee's preferred outcome is to fix these various drags — they'll change their contribution, you'll change yours, and institutional and structural impediments will be addressed. They are certain their productivity will rise dramatically.

You see it differently. After giving the matter serious thought, your conclusion is that while there are important inputs to the problem over which they have no control, your employee is in a role within the organization that does not play to their strengths. Adjusting other contributions will help, but not enough. You think they should be moved into a role that carries less responsibility.

What to do? If you are the decision maker, make the decision. Having a conversation about joint contribution gives you a clearer picture of the underlying inputs into the problem and helps you make a wise decision; it doesn't mandate a particular solution or change who owns the decision.

## Do I always have to start with listening and inquiry?

No. In Chapter 11 we say, "It's always the right time to listen," meaning, it's always a good time, and indeed, all things being equal, it *is* better to listen first. But all things aren't equal, so there are exceptions. Readers who take our plug for listening as a wholesale ban on asserting their views inevitably get all tangled up. A boss, for example, who wants to address his employee's failure to deliver on schedule might end up in a conversation like this:

> BOSS: How do you think you're doing in terms of getting work in on time?
>
> EMPLOYEE: Great.
>
> BOSS: But don't you think there have been a few times when you've been late on important things?
>
> EMPLOYEE: Not really.
>
> BOSS: Well, what about the Vancouver Project?
>
> EMPLOYEE: I thought it went well.
>
> BOSS: But don't you think it was late?

Instead of asking this absurd set of leading questions, the boss needs to assert: "Let's talk about the Vancouver Project. It was three days late. Let's figure out why, assess the impact, and decide how to avoid this going forward." Once you've set the problem on the table, and shared your view if you have one, that's when you switch into inquiry mode, and from there, you'll use a mix of inquiry and assertiveness.

The touchstone, as always, is purpose. One could imagine a conversation where a boss's sole purpose was to learn the employee's point of view, but that's not the boss's purpose in the conversation above. Use questions when you want to learn and statements when you have something to convey. Ultimately it is the combination of assertiveness and inquiry that helps us pool our insights, learn things we didn't know, and lay the foundation for creative and effective problem solving.

We emphasize listening here because the far more common mistake in conversation is failure to listen rather than failure to assert. When we're in a conversation where we feel angry, hurt, fearful, or under pressure, our internal voice roars full blast, and curiosity fades away. That's why, to get yourself to listen well during a difficult conversation, you need to remind yourself again and again (and perhaps enlist others as well to remind you in the moment): "I may feel upset, I may feel like I already know their view, but there's always something I need to learn. In addition to asserting, I'm going to need to inquire, and then inquire some more."

## 6. Isn't this a very American approach? How does it work in other cultures?

People from outside the United States often accuse *Difficult Conversations* of offering a very "American" method of addressing this topic. "We don't talk this way in Korea/Kazakhstan/Colombia/[fill in your region here]," they say.

"Well, most Americans don't talk this way either," we respond. The language we use in our dialogue examples is not how people normally talk in *any* country. We use stylized language for conceptual clarity — for example, to help readers recognize the difference between a true question of curiosity and a "loaded" question that's really an accusation. We assume that once you understand the concepts, you will translate the words into language that feels more comfortable and appropriate given how people really talk in your family, organization, and part of the world.

Still, the question of how these ideas apply across different cultures is important, and, with the impact of globalization, never more so than now.

What we have found is that the *underlying structure* of difficult conversations — the things your internal voice is busy with during a conversation — seems to be the same around the world. People in South Africa and South Carolina are equally focused on who's right and who's to blame. People in India and Iowa all struggle with strong feelings. People in Turkey and Tennessee are reacting to identity quakes (sometimes described as a struggle to "save face").

The phenomenon of an internal voice and the three conversations within it seems to be a universal and fundamental aspect of being human. What does differ across cultures is whether, when, and how the internal voice is *expressed*.

Americans have a reputation for being direct, and for not paying much attention to hierarchy. We feel free to criticize our political leaders and to confess our sins and feelings on reality TV. In contrast, the British have a reputation for being relatively buttoned-up about feelings, and many countries in Asia are thought of as being restrictive about whether it is ever appropriate to disagree or speak up in a hierarchy. So it's easy to view our encouragement to raise things directly, rather than avoiding and letting them fester, as simply part and parcel of our immersion in American culture.

But of course, culture is more complex than these stereotypes. There is a wide variation in directness across regions of the United States, and even between one family and another on the same block. Some American companies are hierarchical; others pride themselves on being flat. Some industries have a "polite" culture; others have direct and aggressive communication norms. Gender equality is the law but not always the reality, and assumptions about appropriate gender roles still vary widely.

To add to the complexity, an outsider's perceptions of the communication norms of another culture are often based on simple misinterpretation. For instance, an American might conclude that in Japan people aren't allowed to speak up to their boss. But many Japanese would argue that, although they don't speak up explicitly, they send clear signals to their boss when they are not onboard with a decision. Sometimes they're conveyed through body language, or word choice, or simply silence. The communication is there — it's just translated into a culturally appropriate language. The American in the room is missing those cues and assumes nothing is being "said." It's all a question of the appropriate time, place, and mode of expression.

The degree of directness or indirectness that people think is appropriate is often tied to assumptions about what is necessary to protect the relationship (or whether that matters). In some places (and families), the norm is vociferous and sometimes heated debate: "Forget the touchy-feely stuff. If I like you, and I respect you, I'm going to tell you what I think. That's the sign of a healthy relationship!" In others, nurturing and protecting the relationship means being indirect about any conflict. It may be hinted at, channeled through third parties, or spoken of in metaphors for fear that anything more direct could risk a disastrous fracture. In some contexts and for some people, relationship is wholly subordinated to outcome: "If you want a relationship, give me what I want." For others, it is the reverse: "Rather than risk the relationship, I'll just give you what you want."

In our view, however, you don't have to choose between protecting the relationship and having a good conversation about the issues between you. It is possible to be respectful and affirming of the relationship even if and as you disagree. It is genuine listening, empathy, and being open to persuasion that preserve and strengthen the relationship, not the degree of agreement. You can make the case for how you see it, explain how and to what extent the other's argument modifies your view and why, and agree only if and as you are persuaded without ever saying — or thinking — "I'm right and you're wrong." Instead you can think, "You may be right, and I may well be missing something (it wouldn't be the first time), and yet so far I don't see it."

To achieve this, no matter what your culture, you must first make the kinds of mental shifts in your internal voice that we talk about in Chapters 2 through 6:

|  | **Difficult Conversation** | **Learning Conversation** |
|---|---|---|
| **The "What Happened?" Conversation** | The question is, whose story is right and whose is wrong. It's either/or. | I wonder why we see things differently? What is each of our data and reasoning? |
|  | They meant to have this impact on me. | I don't like the impact they are having on me; I wonder what they were intending? I know my intent; I wonder whether that was the impact? |
|  | This is their fault. | We have each contributed to this result. Let's identify contributions and figure out how to fix this. |
| **The Feelings Conversation** | My feelings are their fault, and I should either let them have it or keep quiet (since it probably won't do any good). | My feelings say something about me and something about their actions. I can share my feelings without blame, and acknowledge theirs with empathy, without saying their story is right. |

| | Difficult Conversation | Learning Conversation |
|---|---|---|
| **The Identity Conversation** | They're attacking my identity unfairly! I am not. . . ! | Realistically, some part of what they're saying may make painful sense. What am I really afraid of here? How can their story have validity without negating who I am, and vice versa for them? |

Without these shifts, simply being "direct" isn't going to help. There's no way to throw a diplomatic hand grenade, whether you're speaking French, Arabic, or Mayan. Dumping blame and self-righteousness into the conversation unfiltered doesn't go over well anywhere.

On the other hand, once you've made these shifts in your thinking, it's easier in any culture to be more direct, even with those higher in the pecking order. We've worked with people on six continents over the last ten years, listened to their internal voices, and helped them shift their thinking and engage important issues successfully. People do sometimes worry that we are about to put someone's "face" at risk, but then visibly relax as they realize that we have put a joint problem on the table (from the third story, of course) with no hint of the blame frame.

Perhaps even more significant, precisely because of the differences between cultures, these skills have proven critical for successfully navigating cross-cultural communication challenges. As people work in multinational contexts, and especially in virtual teams across geographies by e-mail and conference calls, we find ourselves constantly stepping on each other's toes. Being able to talk about the unintended impacts we're having on one another becomes critical to maintaining good working relationships. Seeing our own contribution to the confusion or frustration, and getting curious about why our colleagues in Uruguay or Uganda feel so strongly about an issue that seems to us of little importance enables us to sort out the differences in our interests, values, assumptions, and implicit rules.

## 7. What about conversations that aren't face-to-face? What should I do differently if I'm on the phone or e-mail?

E-mail and texting have become the primary channels of communication for many of us in both our professional and personal lives. Interestingly, this is true whether we work with colleagues many time zones away or a few steps down the hall. E-mail has benefits and drawbacks: we should learn to use it wisely and avoid its tendency to escalate conflict.

E-mail is a wildly efficient way to keep in touch; it allows reflection and carefully crafted responses, and it maintains an ongoing record of a given conversation. If you're angry, you can take time to cool down before composing a message. If you're tired, you can do it later. If you don't really have time to chat, you can drop an e-mail to at least let your mom know you're thinking about her. Many people use e-mail to initiate hard conversations they don't have the courage to confront in person. For the day-to-day tasks of keeping up with a friend or moving a project forward, it's just about perfect.

But ask e-mail to do anything even slightly more complicated in a relationship, and you can quickly run into trouble. Why? Precisely because of the benefits mentioned above. E-mail isn't dialogue — it's serial monologue. There's no opportunity to interrupt for clarification, to see the other's reaction and correct course, or to test our assumptions about their intentions before locking into interpretations and emotional reactions.

E-mail doesn't convey tone of voice, facial expressions, or body language — all of which help us make sense of the sender's intentions (which as we know from Chapter 3 is difficult even when we're talking face-to-face). When you get an e-mail that reads "I was hoping to have your memo by now" does it mean "I'm excited about reading it" or "You're in trouble"? Is your neighbor writing in all caps because she's enraged, thrilled, clueless, or just a little bit nuts? When your friend writes "You're such a loser! ☺" is it playful intimacy or an actual jab? You write back to ask, and your friend replies: "If I thought you were actually a loser I'd never write that in an e-mail — or would I? ;-)" Hmm. Even with emoticons, intentions can be hard to determine.

It's tempting to think of e-mail as an emotion-free zone; it's just text, after all. But in practice e-mail can be the most emotional channel of communication in an organization. Although rarely stated directly, emotions often suffuse the text, triggering emotional reactions in the recipients, which then get fired back, directly or indirectly. Over time simply seeing certain people's names in your in-box provokes dread or anxiety. By the time we open the e-mail itself, we are reading the sender's words through the lens of our own frustration, resentment, and attributions.

And it's often happening onstage. E-mail is routinely used to communicate to multiple team members, family members, or friends, so the exchange has an audience, upping the stakes and putting everybody's identity more deeply on the line. "Don't make it look like *I'm* the one being difficult about this!" we think to ourselves, before shooting back the "correct" story for the benefit of the boss who is cc'd. Even when the exchange is private, we both know it can be forwarded at any time, with accompanying commentary: *"Can you believe this?"*

Other than that, though, e-mail works great, right? Texting, too, has its challenges. Using half sentences and abbreviations increases the chance of ambiguity and misunderstanding.

So, how to avoid the downward spiral of attributions and misperceptions?

## When reading:

1. **Question your attributions.** Once triggered, your attributions about the sender's intentions and personality flood in. And when

you're tired, stressed, or feeling a bit vulnerable, you're even more likely to see negatives. Remind yourself that you don't actually *know* their intentions. Your initial reading is as likely to be off-target as on. The sender may have mixed or even positive intentions, or, most often, no particular intention about you at all. A week without hearing from them is far more likely to mean they are busy than that they are hoping to make you sweat. And what you experience as an attack might in their mind be meant as a defense against *your* attack. What, you say, you never attacked them? Ah, there's the rub.

**2. Hit pause.** If an e-mail elicits a strong negative emotion, stop. Do nothing. Unless there's an urgent reason why you need to respond instantly — and "because I'm really mad right now" doesn't count — then wait. An hour at least or, ideally, overnight. Come back to the e-mail when you're feeling more balanced. Often you'll have the strange sensation of wondering why you felt so bent out of shape. But if, after taking some time, you're still revved up, move to step three.

**3. Pick up the phone or talk in person.** Bottom line: You can't resolve an e-mail conflict with e-mail. For all practical purposes there are no exceptions to this rule. Once any sort of emotion enters the arena — annoyance, confusion, hurt, anxiety — it's time to switch your mode of communication. "But I'm a good, clear writer," you think. "I'll be extra careful and thoughtful, and I'll even take the high road." Don't get suckered in. *Anything* you write during a conflict can be taken the wrong way. When your colleague gets your generous, well-reasoned, and beautifully crafted e-mail, he might think "How lovely." Or he might think: "Just like her to send that kind of bogus e-mail, with all that 'I'm calm and rational' crap. She makes me sick!" So save yourself a heap of trouble and pick up the phone or talk in person.

## When writing:

1. **Be extra explicit about your intentions, reasoning, and (when they are appropriate to share) your emotions.** Go out of your way to explain yourself. Being clear about your purposes, reasoning, and feelings can help ward off misunderstanding, whether your e-mail is to a close colleague or a contractor from another culture halfway across the world: "I'm asking because my boss will ask, and I want to be sure we're aligned," or "I'm unclear on whether and when I should be doing. . . ," or "My thinking is that there is no significant downside to doing this now, while it will be quite costly if we wait and have to do it later," or "I'm frustrated that this has happened again, so it's really important to me that we spend time diagnosing what happened and coming up with some credible way to reduce the chances of yet another repetition." Even "I get frustrated when this happens" is better than a snippy "FINE! WHATEVER YOU SAY." If you're going to inject your feelings, being explicit invites a conversation, whereas being curt feels like judgment, which they are sure to resent, thus further damaging the relationship.

2. **Let them know if there will be a delay — don't leave them hanging.** One of the most common communication disconnects that occurs with e-mail is the result of delays in responding. One party sends a question. The person receiving it thinks, "Good question. I'm not sure of the answer. I'll have to think about it or ask So-and-so." So they wait to respond until they have a substantive response, which often ends up taking longer than they at first expected. In the meantime the person waiting for the answer is left to interpret the silence, wondering, "Why aren't they answering me?" and answering with their fears: "I must have upset them," or "They obviously don't care," or "They're avoiding me," and perhaps concluding, "I can't work with this person." This pattern is predictable and avoidable. If you're not going to answer right away, send a quick note explaining why and when you expect to get back to them. "Let me check with Dan, and

I'll get back to you in a few days. If you haven't heard from me by Tuesday, please send a reminder. Thanks!"

**3. Take it step-by-step.** If you're wondering about the tone or intent behind their last e-mail, rather than make assumptions, write them a short note to check before you respond. "I can't tell if you're annoyed. Was I supposed to respond earlier?" Clear up the ambiguity before you fire off a shot that further escalates the exchange.

**4. Ask for reactions, thoughts, and what you're missing.** Given the monologue nature of e-mail, work to invite honest dialogue and reactions. Taking seriously the possibility that there's something important you don't know and showing genuine openness to their thinking makes it easier for them to share their internal voice and help correct misunderstandings or missed assumptions earlier rather than later.

## On the Phone:

As a medium for difficult conversations, the phone is less perilous than e-mail, but perilous still. Although the phone conveys tone of voice (a step up from e-mail in that regard), it does not convey facial expressions. That makes understanding subtle emotions and meaning tougher. You hear the other person complaining, but you don't see the vulnerability and sadness in their eyes. If you're talking to your elderly mother about how she's coping with your dad's encroaching dementia, it's easy to flip into problem solving ("You have to get help") or cheerleading ("Everything is going to be fine!"). It requires an extra effort and self-reminder to offer empathy ("Mom, I can't even imagine how stressful this has been for you") and appreciation ("Given all you're going through, you're doing such an amazing job; it's absolutely inspiring to me").

## 8. Why do you advise people to "bring feelings into the workplace"? I'm not a therapist, and shouldn't business decisions be made on the merits?

Every organization has some feelings that are accepted and expressed often and others that are supposed to remain hidden. Stress, frustration, pride, loyalty, and enthusiasm are often an accepted part of organizational culture. Disappointment, self-doubt, jealousy, and hurt are usually less acceptable and less likely to be expressed directly.

But whatever the implicit rules are, the official line in many organizations remains this: stay on task and check your feelings at the door. They distract us from getting things done.

Yet as human beings, we *can't* simply leave feelings behind. They are an integral part of how our brains and bodies work. So we read our e-mail or sit in meetings or listen to people talk about our work — and we have emotional reactions. Surprise, anger, confusion, betrayal, anxiety, dread, indignation . . . the list goes on.

Contrary, then, to the official line, your workplace is already suffused with feelings. In fact, we'd argue that keeping them out of the workplace (if you could) would actually be a bad thing. It is *because* of feelings like determination, pride, satisfaction, commitment, and even anxiety and frustration that people come to work, persist in grappling with seemingly insoluble problems, and find creative solutions. And on the flip side, it is not negative feelings in themselves that distract us from productivity, but the failure to acknowledge them, and to deal with them directly, efficiently, and honestly.

Moreover, a certain amount of emotion is necessary for making decisions. People whose access to feelings is damaged as the result of a brain injury often have trouble making even simple choices, like when to schedule a meeting. They can list the consequences of competing options but not formulate a preference.[*]

Given that feelings are already present in the workplace, the

---

[*] See Antonio R. Damasio, *Descartes' Error: Emotion, Reason, and the Human Brain* (Penguin, 2005), pp. 193–94.

question becomes how to deal with them. Typically we allow them to drive the energy of a conversation — the raised voices, curt e-mail responses, or veiled put-downs — without talking about them explicitly. We often translate feelings into arguments, accusations, or simply silence and withdrawal. When we translate or ignore feelings, we fail to deal directly with what's actually going on (the feelings and their causes). As a result, people feel badly treated, working relationships become strained, morale drops, and feelings start to get *in the way* of work actually getting done.

Why? Because by the time an issue becomes the subject of a difficult conversation, you usually have at least two problems: the substantive business issue or disagreement (what strategy is best, who should handle this issue, or how much should we pay given that mistakes have been made?) *and* the matter of how people have felt treated in the conversations so far (ignored, publicly embarrassed, left out of the loop, or unfairly blamed).

It's hard to solve the business problem and get on with doing the work if you don't understand and address what has gone wrong in the working relationship. This might be as simple as saying, "I'm frustrated. It seems like we're going in circles," or "I was disappointed not to be chosen for that assignment," or "I'm not sure why we're having a hard time getting this done." Or it may take more work, exploring perceptions of what happened and the meaning different stories hold for people, given their past experience.

We're not arguing for a workplace where people sit around idly chatting about every emotion that comes upon them. We're saying that often, dealing more directly with feelings enables you to get to the heart of the matter more quickly — and with a better chance of finding a satisfying resolution.

## Isn't it risky to share your feelings at work?

It can be, depending on what you share, when, and how. If in your corporate culture people don't talk directly about their feelings, then breaking this pattern can feel uncomfortable. Sometimes it's even made explicit that talking about feelings is considered weak, unprofessional, or a waste of time.

In such a culture, it's important to use language that is acceptable and to make clear up front that the point of any discussion involving feelings is to further a business goal. If saying "I feel hurt and taken for granted," will be poorly received, consider something like this: "I'd like to find a way to get this done earlier each quarter. I know I often leave these meetings frustrated, and I imagine you also periodically feel frustrated. Can we talk about why that is and how we might design a better process?"

Timing, location, and context also matter. When you're facing a deadline, it's probably not a good time to initiate a discussion about how you're feeling about your job. Neither is a random meeting in a hallway. But a quarterly coaching session with your boss might be.

Finally, *how* you raise the matter of feelings is critical. Talking about emotions by *being* emotional — crying, screaming, pouting, eye-rolling, or foot stomping — will often make you appear weak, out-of-control, or unprofessional.*

In terms of *what* you share, some feelings are less risky than others. Expressing authentic appreciation for work done by your colleagues or subordinates is rarely rebuffed. Sharing enthusiasm for a new project or pride in a job well done is almost always welcome. Even admitting that you feel confused about your role or the scope of your task, anxious about the potential impact of a decision you've made on your teammates, or curious about others' perspectives are likely to be heard as invitations to engage together in constructive problem solving.

Starting to share these kinds of feelings can be a low-risk way to begin to shift how you and your co-workers deal with each other. Your example may encourage others to do the same, and soon you've

---

*We would assert, however, that in some contexts, crying is not only okay but a good thing. It is not uncommon, for example, for football players to cry when they announce their retirement. It is seen as authentic and human. So too, in the workplace, sorrow or other overwhelming emotion, whether personal or professional, can lead to tears that bring two people together or allow one person to give important support to another. But context does matter. It's less good, for example, to cry because the lawyer on the other side of the table is "being mean."

influenced your team's little corner of the larger corporate culture. After all, a "corporate culture" is actually made up of many individual relationships, and each relationship you change improves the overall culture.

## Shouldn't business decisions be made "rationally," on the merits? How does talking about feelings help with that?

People often fear that talking about feelings will result in lousy decisions. And it can, if you're not careful.

Consider the decision faced by NASA and Morton Thiokol engineers in 1986 about whether, given cold weather conditions, it was safe to launch the Space Shuttle *Challenger*. In a teleconference, Morton Thiokol engineers at first informed NASA that it was their determination that it was not safe. In the ensuing discussion of the safety data, a leading member of NASA's team said he would go along with Morton Thiokol's decision, but that he was "appalled" at their reading of the data and that the information about cold weather was being relayed so late in the process. The word itself — "appalled" — so strong and visceral, seemed to play a significant role in Morton Thiokol's ultimate reversal of their view, even though, as outside observers we know that the description of one person's emotional state has no relationship to whether a launch is safe.*

Yet *not* talking about feelings can also result in poor decisions. Acknowledging that feelings are in play — making them discussable — positions them appropriately as another factor to be weighed on their merits.

A client's preferences on staffing, for example, are worth knowing and understanding before deciding about a change. Identifying people's fears and concerns about how a reorganization might affect

---

*The decision to launch ended in disaster, with the explosion of the shuttle seventy-three seconds after launch. This account is taken from an online article by Roger M. Boisjoly, a Morton Thiokol engineer and key participant in the decision (http://www .onlineethics.org/Topics/ProfPractice/PPEssays/thiokolshuttle/shuttle_telecon.aspx).

their own career may facilitate some creative problem solving or simple clarification that greatly reduces resistance. Or it may illuminate longer-term incentive effects that can help avoid unintended consequences. If, for example, workers feel penalized for taking risks, and such penalties hurt morale and future risk taking, management needs to be able to engage that discussion. If workers are bottled up and not allowed to discuss feeling unfairly treated, management won't know that the current system is discouraging the very behavior they seek.

In such cases, the presence of the feeling itself may not be a reason for making a particular decision, but it may be a clue pointing to a legitimate business reason to consider other approaches. It should be explored and followed up. For example, in the conversation about the *Challenger* launch, Morton Thiokol could have responded to the "appalled" comment not by changing their recommendation, but by validating the concern and inquiring further: "As to the timing of our informing you, it *is* late in the game, and that's putting tremendous pressure on all of us. We just learned of the expected launch temperature, which is lower than ever before, but our concerns have been building over time. We should look at our communication process going forward and make sure this doesn't happen again. As to our interpretation of the data, tell us more about what seems problematic to you or why you read the data differently."

And of course the NASA engineer could do the same: "I hear your concern, and I am aware that you are closest to the data, so it troubles me that the data seems so much less clear to me. I'm wondering what you see that we don't. Why don't you take us through your reasoning again step by step?" The emotion is part of the discussion, but the mere presence of strong emotion shouldn't drive the decision.

Perhaps an even more important reason to make feelings part of a business conversation is precisely so they *don't* overwhelm people's thinking. Listening, understanding, and showing empathy with feelings are the things that help dissipate them, making it easier for the person having those feelings to calm down and open up to other perspectives.

If an employee is not being promoted, for example, they are likely to feel disappointed and hurt no matter what. But if they can't talk with you about their reactions, they may also feel betrayed, unappreciated, frustrated, and ignored. Then they're likely to start making attributions about you — that you're a difficult person to work for, or that you don't like them and are playing favorites, perhaps. If, on the other hand, you elicit their feelings and show that you care about their reaction, they're much more likely to be able to take in your reasoning for not promoting them, and to work with you to improve their performance. Listening to their feelings, and genuinely seeking to understand them, helps relationships and morale, even if it doesn't change your decision. And of course it's possible that you might learn something in listening that would change your view.

Aside from discomfort with the expression of feelings, the main reason we worry about bringing them into business (or personal) conversations is the instinctive fear that the only way to deal with feelings is to give the other person what they want — that, for example, the only way to "fix" the employee's anger is to promote them.

But of course it's not. The key to managing feelings well is to separate acknowledgment from decision making and to give up the responsibility of fixing them. It helps to be explicit about your intentions: "I'd like to talk about how we're each feeling about this situation, and what we each think, so I have as much information as possible in making this decision. Of course, in the end, I'll have to decide based on my assessment of your performance, the criteria for the position, and my sense of what's best for the company." This allows you to listen to and understand how disappointed and angry your employee is *and* nonetheless to decide on the merits whether or not to promote them.

## 9. Who has time for all this in the real world?

Nobody.

No one wants to spend time struggling to understand why

someone else disagrees with your (obviously) brilliant strategic solution. Nobody wants to devote part of their afternoon to dealing with a challenging colleague, or worse, two difficult people who can't get along and are disrupting your team's ability to function effectively or everyone's ability to enjoy the holidays.

After all, you've got data to crunch, presentations to make, experiments to run, e-mail to answer, and kids to pick up from school. These are all pressing tasks, and ones that have tangible outcomes that can be satisfyingly crossed off your to-do list. In contrast, opening up a messy conversation just isn't that inviting. The emotional energy involved makes it exhausting, and there's no guarantee of a good outcome. It's no wonder that in the short term we choose to focus on less disagreeable tasks and to avoid the mishigas of a conversation.

But it's a false choice. We imagine the choice looks like this. Should I:

(a) spend time tackling this difficult conversation? *or*

(b) save myself the time and hassle and have the problem magically disappear?

If that *were* the choice, well, we wouldn't need this book to begin with. Here's a more realistic assessment of the choice.

**We're already spending time and energy dwelling on it.** Unresolved conflict in our work and personal relationships sucks up energy and attention in sneaky ways that we often don't take account of. We should be adding up the time we spend fuming to ourselves, venting to colleagues, complaining to our spouses, designing a workaround, lying awake thinking about what we *should* have said to them, and looking up their personality disorders on the Internet to bolster our case.

**How we're spending our time is actually making it worse.** Triangulating to a colleague gives us a place to vent our frustration but may relieve us of the need we feel to address the problem directly. And now our colleague is pulled into the conflict, either because we've succeeded in passing on our negative view and annoyance or because they're getting it from both sides and are caught in the middle. Complaining to a friend or spouse often reinforces our already one-sided story about why the other person is "impossible" and we're the innocent victim. Even if the friend can see what we're doing to make the situation worse, we rarely give them permission to challenge us — to help us see the other side's perspective and our own contribution. Hence, we walk away convinced our friend is on our side, which is further justification for our righteous indignation. This in turn makes us more likely to spew a skewed set of accusations and assertions, if and when we actually have the conversation.

**Instead, aim energy in useful and efficient directions.** Given that we're already dwelling on the problem, we might as well use that time and energy in ways that will help rather than hurt. Rather than simply venting to third parties and (implicitly) asking them to agree with us, why not enlist their genuine advice and coaching? Friends and colleagues can help us appreciate the other side's perspective, understand our own contribution, and think about the other side's intentions or the identity issues that are making us overreact. They can help us think through what's at the heart of the matter and how we might share our perspective clearly.

As you get accustomed to using the preparation checklist in this book and adapting it to your own particular style and habits, you'll get faster and more efficient at preparing. Pretty soon you will be able to think through the checklist on your commute in to work in the morning or while muting the conference call for a minute or two. Suddenly you're using the time to feel better about a situation, and to formulate a plan for how to tackle it, rather than to wallow in misery.

## Spend seven minutes now and save seven hours later

We fear that readers sometimes get the impression that we're suggesting you tackle every conversation with your name on it, and that each one should be an ongoing, possibly endless endeavor. Let's be clear: Life is too short, and no one has that kind of emotional energy.

In fact, our assumption is that many of these conversations can be quick. The earlier you raise an issue, catch a misunderstanding, or ask a question to clarify intentions, the sooner you clear it up and move on. The longer you let things fester, the bigger the problem becomes. So investing seven minutes now to sort through why you and your client seem to have different expectations about the scope of a project will save you seven hours (or seven months) of confusion, frustration, and cost overruns down the road.

And the more skillful you can be about *how* you raise and discuss something, the more effective and efficient the conversation is likely to be. Asking a supplier a question about why your request poses a problem, rather than simply insisting that it must be honored, will help illuminate why they are resistant and put you on the same side solving the problem. You avoid arguing about it for ten minutes, hanging up frustrated, and then needing to make several more calls to their boss, your boss, or alternate providers.

Finally, as our colleague Stevenson Carlebach says, the time we spend in easy conversations versus difficult conversations is like the difference between human years and dog years. It can feel as if the conversation is lasting seven times as long as it actually is, but that doesn't make it so. In fact, some people we've worked with have started correcting their internal sense of the time spent. After a tough phone call that seems to have lasted forever, they look at the phone display as they are hanging up and note exactly how long the call lasted. Time and again they discover that the "forever" phone call actually took just four minutes — and addressed the real issues.

That's time well spent.

## 10. My identity conversation keeps getting stuck in either-or: I'm perfect or I'm horrible. I can't seem to get past that. What can I do?

Let's start with an example.

### Antonio's Story

When I get criticized, whether at work or at home, I tend to react by criticizing back. Things escalate, or the other person withdraws. The sad part is that this happens even when I know the feedback is right! I keep resolving to respond with a simple, "That's helpful, I'm going to work on that," or, "Thank you, let's talk about it," but when the moment comes, I repeat the pattern as if I'd never even thought this through before. I know it's hurting my relationships, but I can't seem to change it.

Having reflected on this, Antonio has come to see that this behavior is rooted in the belief that a good and valued person doesn't disappoint people or let them down. He worries that if he *does* let someone down, he'll be rejected, or even disowned. And maybe more important, he fears he won't be able to live with himself: "If I know anything about myself, it's that I don't hurt others, I don't let others down." To avoid feeling intolerable guilt or shame, Antonio determines, at least in the moment, that the criticism *must* be wrong or ill-intended. Now angry, he tries to show that the situation was actually the result of mistakes *other* people made, particularly the person raising the concerns.

Later, when his emotions settle down, Antonio can see how provocative and insecure his response appears, but he can't see what's happening *when* it's happening, or think what else to do. Intellectually, he understands that even good, competent, and valued people sometimes have an off day, make an ill-advised or selfish choice, or are just plain mindless. But emotionally, in the moment, he doesn't feel permission to be less than perfect. His heart pounds with fear and desperation, and long-honed instincts take over.

We all know this frustration.

Why is it so hard to change such behaviors and the assumptions about ourselves and our relationships that drive them? And is there anything to be done about it?

## Where identity comes from

Identities develop from the complex interplay of our hard-wiring,[*] life experiences, and what we *choose* to make of those experiences (in other words, the story we tell). We can't change our wiring (although the new science of neuroplasticity is usefully questioning this assumption), and we can't change our past experiences. But we can change our story about those experiences.

As infants and small children, we take for granted that we deserve whatever we get from our parents — good or bad — and construct a story to explain *why* we deserve it. "I got spanked because I am bad." "My parents love me because I am so cute." "I am worthwhile because I am always kind to my sister."

Even before we can talk, we begin to develop images of ourselves in *relationship* with others.[†] As the middle child in a conflict-riddled family, for example, one colleague of ours noticed that she was rewarded for being the peacemaker. She developed an image of herself as "the rational one, who never loses her temper." As an adult, she is much sought after by friends who value her even-handed approach in stressful situations, but she has a hard time sticking up for what she really wants or expressing strong emotion. She sees her

---

[*]See, for example, Jerome Kagan, who asserts that the strength of a baby's "startle response" is a strong predictor of whether a person will become adventurous or withdrawn, outgoing or shy. *The Long Shadow of Temperament,* by Jerome Kagan and Nancy Snidman (Belknap Press, 2004).

[†]See, for example, *Inside the Family,* by David Kantor and William Lehr (Meredith Winter Press, 2003).

identity as the one who makes conflict go away, not as the one who creates it.

These images can develop from our everyday experiences and relationships, but also from traumatic, life-changing events. Antonio, whose parents divorced when he was five, believed that he was the cause of their breakup. The lesson: "My dad left because I was bad. I will never permit myself to be bad again." This helps explain why it is so threatening to Antonio to feel like he is anything less than perfect. Someone else, of course, might learn a different lesson from divorce: "Being good didn't help. People leave, so don't rely on them." This might contribute to an identity as a fiercely independent person, or conversely, as a victim.

As life continues to throw new experiences at Antonio, he will try — as we all do — to interpret these experiences in a way that is consistent with how he sees himself. If he gets feedback that he screwed up, it threatens a key pillar of his identity: "I will never be bad again." If that pillar is destroyed, there's nothing left to hold him up. To protect it, he lashes out: "It wasn't me! It couldn't be!"

Though Antonio now recognizes the downsides of this piece of his self-definition, it remains a struggle to change it. It is familiar, deeply embedded, almost unconscious — and the alternatives seem unclear and scary. Although he's not fully aware of it, Antonio sees two choices: preserve the pillar (denial), or let things collapse (exaggerate).

## What helps?

As we say in Chapter 6, it is helpful to bring this dilemma to light, to recognize unrealistic all-or-nothing assumptions, and to reset our self-expectations to something more realistic. But what if, as with Antonio, that's not enough, because it doesn't "stick"?

The root of the difficulty is that although Antonio recognizes his problematic identity theme and its consequences, he hasn't really found a way to accept himself as someone who could disappoint others. There are several things one can do to help with that kind of challenge.

**Explore the roots of the theme, and re-evaluate them.** It often helps to reflect on where and how we learned to be the way we are. In addition to the divorce, Antonio reflects on two other important memories that likely shaped his identity. One is of a time when his older brother Hector received such bad grades that he was forced to withdraw from the parochial school he attended. Antonio heard his father pronounce his disappointment and label his brother a "failure," and heard his brother crying himself to sleep for days. The other was when Antonio won a school prize for a paper he wrote in fifth grade. Antonio was surprised and hurt when the only reaction he got from his own parents was, "That's nice, Antonio." From these two experiences, Antonio determined that love was contingent upon success, and that even stellar performance might not be enough to win it.

Imagine Antonio's shock years later when he asked his mother about his parents' reaction to his award: "We were so proud of you! No one in our family had ever had such academic success. But we tried not to make a big deal of your achievement, because we were told by the school psychologist that gifted children who are given too much praise can get the message that they are only loved for their achievements." As for his father's reaction to his brother, that was more complex. His father later confessed his regret over being too harsh: "I just didn't want to see Hector make the same mistakes with his life that I made," he confided.

So, love was not as contingent as Antonio thought, it was just being expressed in ways he didn't understand. Antonio had been living within the constraints of narrow rules about how relationships work that he had learned as a small child. Seeing that, and finding different ways to interpret key memories has helped diminish his identity quakes.

Antonio's brother faced a different challenge. Having internalized his father's judgment that he was a "failure," Hector refused to put himself forward for leadership positions at work or in his community and would decline them when offered. In time, he learned that his trouble in school was due in part to dyslexia, and in part to a learning style that needed to grasp the big picture before details would make sense. But at some level Hector still saw himself as the same fifteen-year-old who had "failed" so embarrassingly. As a result, he was both determined not to put himself in that position again and unable to see himself as someone worth trusting with responsibility.

Colleagues, who saw Hector as thoughtful and wise and often sought his advice, had trouble understanding his reticence. Insight came only when Hector opened up to a close friend who wanted him to join a community leadership group. "Hector," the friend said, "what would *you* say to a fifteen-year-old in that situation? Would you say they were doomed to fail forever? Or would you say they should learn from the experience and do better next time? You are nothing like the kid you were then." With this prodding, Hector was able to look at himself afresh as the man that boy had grown into. Then, with some wonder and dawning pride, though not without trepidation, he began to take on leadership roles that were offered. With each success, Hector's confidence rose and the fearful boy retreated.

But none of this is easy. Some of us are physically or emotionally abused by parents, teachers, classmates, or neighbors, and the impacts on identity can run deep. Especially in the case of trauma, there may be physiological changes that inhibit our ability to tell a more empowering or optimistic story about what was going on.

And even in the absence of trauma there is not infinite play in the joints; there are limits to how you can reinterpret experiences. If you had few friends in high school, it's nonsensical to decide years later that you were actually Mr. Popular. If you got lousy grades in school, it's not going to be helpful to "remember" that you were valedictorian.

Coming to grips with your experience is not about making things up; it's about looking under the simplistic identity labels we give ourselves, putting events in context, and, if necessary, grieving the fact that things happened as they did. If you decide that poor grades in high school mean you are "stupid," well, that's a wild and unhelpful generalization. Similarly, and perhaps surprisingly, being labeled "smart" causes some people to be risk-averse and easily frustrated when solving problems. Such people worry that their reputations are on the line with each new challenge. In truth, we are all fast and slow, strong and weak, motivated and lazy in a thousand tiny ways throughout our days that the generalizations simply don't capture.

Nor are the "right" lessons to be drawn from our experience automatically clear. One person might attribute his strong marriage to his early lessons in resilience during an emotionally tumultuous childhood, while another might see his troubled relationships as the inevitable result of such deprivation.

In Antonio's case, his reflections have helped him loosen the grip of an either-or identity, reducing the panic he has traditionally felt at the prospect of disappointing people. In that calmer space he is somewhat better able to remember the alternative responses he would like to try. And with each good experience, each succeeding effort gets easier.

**Create positive experiences.** In addition to reinterpreting past experience, you can also create new experiences that offer positive reinforcement for behaving and seeing yourself in different ways. This may involve acting as if something is true even when you're not sure that it is, just to see what happens. Antonio might *seek out* negative feedback from colleagues, with the mindset of being "someone who is great at learning from feedback." He knows that that's not an accurate description of himself, but as an experiment he can act *as if* it were true. And if he listens and works at it, it will be true, at least this once — at which point he'll have some positive experience to build on, manufactured but real.

**Enlist help to stimulate and reinforce new behaviors.** Under stress, we are likely to fall back on old ways of acting. The neural pathways are simply too well-worn. Without external help, we won't notice, and we won't be able to interrupt these established patterns in a lasting way. To push against this, it is often helpful to enlist the assistance of a friend or colleague. Antonio asked two of his peers to help: "I'm working on taking feedback. I don't find it easy or natural, but you can help me by pointing out when I get defensive. I'm giving you explicit permission to coach me on this, to be direct. At the same time, I'm asking you to be patient. I'll surely mess up, and when I do, please remember that I'm trying hard."

**Give yourself some empathy.** We've all made sense of our experiences as best we could — often with very little guidance — and made choices that did and did not work out.

Life is not easy. What we need is a little empathy for ourselves.

Accepting our *whole* selves — our mistakes, failures, and shortcomings, our moments of weakness, selfishness, and stupidity — and forgiving ourselves these, are essential steps toward finding balance now and growth in the future. For some, this feeling of deep caring toward oneself comes in a flash of insight; for most of us, it's a lifelong project of small adjustments and daily reminders. It's not about making excuses or shifting responsibility toward others. It's the simple intention to accept and care for what *is*.

If we're not satisfied, then we can apologize and grieve, and we can try for better starting right now.

· · ·

## A final thought

We are often approached by readers who share with us just how impossible their teenager/brother/boss/business partner is. They seem eager for help. We ask some questions and make a few suggestions, each of which is quickly dismissed: "tried that," "nope," "won't work."

It was a few years before we recognized that they were not in fact asking for advice; they were asking for permission to give up. "I'm exhausted. I've had it. Is it okay for me to quit?" So we started giving a different answer: "Sounds like you've done your best and tried just about everything."

People *loved* this response; many could scarcely hide their glee. We could almost hear the conversation they were going to have when they got home: "Honey, I went to that talk and I got a professional opinion: Your mother is *officially impossible!*"

Working your way through difficult conversations is hard and often discouraging work — especially when you're not seeing your openness reciprocated or your willingness to be accountable for your contributions appreciated. In many cases you are fighting to break out of deeply embedded patterns and to ease years of friction. If change is coming, it's taking its time.

But then, after months of reaching out and feeling rebuffed, you notice a slight tremor; something is shifting after all. You'll get an appreciative note about the holidays, or at least a less irritable voicemail. You'll see glimpses of warmth, or notice that the usual opening to an argument is passed by.

If you feel that these gestures are making a genuine difference, and can negotiate with yourself to be patient, then these initial small changes may be enough to sustain you.

But we don't mean to suggest that you should beat your head against the wall, or that you should stay indefinitely in a relationship that is doing damage to your self-esteem. You may be making some progress with your paranoid boss, but your family still suffers from your deepening Monday dread. You have empathy for your sister's troubled circumstances, but her addiction continues to wreak havoc with your marriage. You've tried your best. It hasn't helped.

You're allowed to give up.

As we've said, you can't change other people. When you finally give up the idea that you have the power to change others, you are giving up something you never had anyway — control. If someone is unwilling to examine their own contribution to a problem or take responsibility for the impacts of their actions, you can't force them to. All you can do is take a hard look at yourself, be open to seeing things differently, change your own contribution, and be honest about what matters to you.

You can extend an invitation to join you in working to improve things. It's up to them whether to RSVP.

Giving up is hard. You want to be the kind of person who is loyal and supportive, a caring colleague and loving daughter. You are deeply committed to the other person, to the company, neighborhood, and school. Giving up requires you to have a difficult conversation with yourself about making a healthy choice — for yourself and those you love — and to be able to forgive yourself. That may be the toughest conversation of all, but one well worth having.

Good luck.

# A Road Map to
# *Difficult Conversations*

# Notes on Some Relevant Organizations

## The Harvard Negotiation Project

The Harvard Negotiation Project (HNP) is a research project founded in 1979 at Harvard University to develop and disseminate improved methods of dealing with conflict. It stimulated the founding and is part of the Program on Negotiation at Harvard Law School, an inter-university consortium of scholars and activities with a multidisciplinary approach to the theory and practice of negotiation and conflict management. HNP's activities include action research, theory building, education and training, and writing.

**Action Research.** HNP works with people involved in real-world problems to offer help, learn from experience, and develop new theory. For example, the Project has contributed to the resolution of conflicts such as the U.S.-Iranian hostage conflict in 1980, helped to create a substantially improved relationship between the United States and Soviet Union, and helped to structure negotiation and peacemaking processes in Central America and South Africa.

**Theory Building.** Among the ideas developed at HNP are the one-text mediation procedure used by the United States in Middle East peace negotiations since the 1978 Camp David summit, the method of "principled" or "mutual-gains" negotiation, the "core concerns" framework for managing emotions in negotiation, and the approach to productive conversation summarized in this book.

**Education and Training.** HNP developed the seminal Negotiation Workshop taught at Harvard Law School that has influenced educators around the world. Each year in June the Project offers intensive one-week courses on negotiation and difficult conversations to lawyers and the general public as part of the Harvard Negotiation Institute. (For information, contact HNI At 617-495-7703 or on the Web at www.pon.harvard.edu.)

**Publications.** Work at the Project has spawned many publications, including *International Mediation: A Working Guide*, *Getting to YES: Negotiating Agreement Without Giving In*, *Getting Together: Building Relationships as We Negotiate*, *Getting Ready to Negotiate*, *Getting Past No: Dealing with Difficult People and Situations*, *Beyond Machiavelli*, *Coping with International Conflict*, *The Third Side*, *Getting It Done: How to Lead When You're Not in Charge*, *Beyond Reason: Using Emotions as You Negotiate*, *The Power of a Positive No*, and this book, as well as articles, teacher's guides, curricula, and negotiation exercises. (For information on teaching materials, contact the Program on Negotiation Clearinghouse at 800-258-4406 [from within the U.S.] or 1-781-239-1111, by e-mail at chouse@law.harvard.edu, or on the Web at www.pon.org.) For the latest ideas in the field, subscribe to the Program's Negotiation Journal or the Negotiation Newsletter (see www.pon.harvard.edu/publications).

The following two organizations were founded by members of the Harvard Negotiation Project and authors of *Difficult Conversations*. While each has a somewhat different strategic focus, they are the only two licensed suppliers of Difficult Conversations® courses and coaching.

## Vantage Partners, LLC

Bruce Patton is one of five founders of Vantage Partners, a global management consulting firm. It is the recognized leader in helping companies achieve measurable, breakthrough business results by transforming the way they negotiate with, and manage relationships with, key business partners. In addition to offering strategic negotiation advice, Vantage practice areas include strategic alliances strategy and management, sourcing and supplier management, outsourcing governance and relationship management, sales negotiation and key account management, managing internal conflict, and corporate education.

Vantage's partners have worked with Fortune 500/Global 1000 companies for more than twenty-five years to drive billions of dollars in savings and increased profit by taking an integrated approach that addresses how strategy, organization structure, business tools and processes, cultural assumptions, leadership messages, and behavioral skills work together to enable or hinder negotiation success, resilient relationships, cross-matrix efficiency, innovation, and competitive advantage. Meanwhile, customized Vantage corporate education workshops have enabled more than a hundred thousand participants to be more confident and effective in managing internal and external negotiations and relationships and in making difficult conversations productive.

Vantage's partners teach at Harvard Law School, the Tuck School of Business at Dartmouth, and the U.S. Military Academy at West Point; publish regularly in professional and industry journals and in the *Harvard Business Review*, as well as coauthor books such as *Getting to YES, Getting Ready to Negotiate, The Point of the Deal: How to Negotiate When Yes Is Not Enough*, and *Difficult Conversations*; and engage in pro bono peace-building activities through the conflict management arm of Mercy Corps.

. . .

For more information, call 617-354-6090 or visit Vantage Partners on the Web at www.vantagepartners.com.

# Triad Consulting Group

Douglas Stone and Sheila Heen founded Triad Consulting Group, a corporate education and communication consulting firm. The leader in difficult conversations and management communication training worldwide, we believe that key organizational initiatives succeed or fail one conversation at a time — colleague to colleague, inside and across teams and functions. Whether you're making tough strategic choices, creating a culture where honest feedback matters, managing conflict among team members, rolling out a major change initiative, or seeking to improve the day-to-day management skills of senior executives, Triad can help.

Triad's clients span six continents and a dozen industries, and include Boeing, Capital One, Citigroup, Fidelity, General Mills, Honda, Merck, Microsoft, Prudential, PwC, Ropes & Gray, Time-Warner, and Unilever. In the public sector, we have worked with the White House, Justice Department, Singapore Supreme Court, Ethiopian Parliament, UN-AIDS, The Nature Conservancy, The Citadel, and New England Organ Bank. Triad consultants have taught and mediated in South Africa, the Middle East, Kashmir, Iraq, Afghanistan, and Cyprus, and have taught at Harvard Law School, Georgetown, Wisconsin, Dartmouth, and MIT Sloan. Triad consultants have authored dozens of popular and scholarly books and articles in the field.

Triad builds capacity through corporate education, off-site presentations, systems design, executive coaching, consulting, mediation, facilitation, and team interventions. We design our programs to respond to the needs and context of each client, ensuring that the approach is relevant, realistic, and useful.

. . . .

For more information, call us at 617-547-1728 or visit Triad on the Web at www.diffcon.com.